Memory and Mastery

SUNY series in Modern Jewish Literature and Culture
Sarah Blacher Cohen, Editor

Memory and Mastery

Primo Levi as Writer and Witness

EDITED BY

Roberta S. Kremer

State University of New York Press

Published by
State University of New York Press, Albany

Printed in the United States of America

For information, address State University of New York Press,
90 State Street, Suite 700, Albany, NY 12207

Production by Diane Ganeles
Marketing by Michael Campochiaro

Cover photo: Portrait of the Italian writer, witness and Holocaust survivor Primo Levi, by Italian artist Stefano Levi Della Torre. Presented to the Holocaust Education Centre on behalf of the Italian Government by the Italian Cultural Institute of Vancouver.

Library of Congress Cataloging-in-Publication Data

Memory and mastery : Primo Levi as writer and witness / edited by
Roberta S. Kremer.
p. cm.
Includes bibliographical references and index.
ISBN 0-7914-4921-1 (alk. paper) — ISBN 0-7914-4922-X
(pbk. : alk. paper)
1. Levi, Primo—Criticism and interpretation. I. Kremer,
Roberta S., 1946–
PQ4872.E8 Z75 2001
853'.914—dc21 00-034503

10 9 8 7 6 5 4 3 2 1

Contents

Part III: Levi's Poetry

Part IV: Levi and Language

Part V: Levi's Legacy

Acknowledgments

Development of this publication was made possible through the generous support of the Robert England Fund, Department of Continuing Studies at the University of British Columbia and the continuous support and encouragement of the Board of the Vancouver Holocaust Education Centre, Vancouver, British Columbia.

Several people made significant contributions to the development of this manuscript. Many thanks to Leanne Nash, Graham Sharpe, and Jennifer Fillingham. Special thanks to Marcia Crosby, Hayden Kremer, and James Shi Kuan Chen for supporting my tenacious spirit. It was essential in bringing this project to completion.

In memory of Gian Paolo Biasin.

Introduction

Roberta S. Kremer

Some writers, by nature of their subject, are not often given, or escape the luxury of a careful examination of their literary devices. This is especially the case when the writer is a Holocaust survivor: it is as though the "sacredness" of the subject matter imposes a respectful silence when it comes to a critical analysis, as though the Holocaust content defies or takes priority over a serious examination of the writer's means of expression. Holocaust literature, only begun to be studied as a discrete genre since the late 1960s, has therefore made few inroads into mainstream literary criticism.

This volume carefully examines the work of the important Italian writer Primo Levi, with the goal of bringing Levi's writing further into the discourse of literary criticism through an analysis of genre, audience, discourse, canon formation, reader reception, language, and form. It provides Levi's readers with a deeper, more informed, and critical understanding of his work and its role in the social practice of literature, while adding to its greater inclusion in the canon of literary study.

Primo Levi, often referred to as a contemporary Dante and described by Italo Calvino as "one of the most gifted writers of our time," built his reputation of literary renown slowly and steadily over the past fifty years, on diverse landscapes, through many different languages, among a wide range of readers. His books have been published in eighteen different countries and brought Levi during his lifetime all three of Italy's major literary prizes—Bagutta, Strega, and Vlareggio as well as the Antonio Feltrinelli Prize awarded posthumously, seven months after his death. A meticulous translator, Levi's books are read today not only in their original Italian, enriched by the inflections and dialect of the Piedmontese Jews, but also in English, French, German, and fifteen other languages. Two of his earlier works—*If This Is A Man* (1947) and *The Truce* (1963)—as well as a later piece, *The Periodic Table* (1984), are clearly reminiscent of a "classical" literary tradition and are considered "masterpieces." Levi's major works are taught in high schools, as well as graduate studies and in fields as diverse as psychology, philosophy, history, literary criticism, Italian studies, and Holocaust studies. His books continue to be among the most widely read Holocaust memoirs, despite an explosion of new material in this genre. It is Levi that the public and scholars alike return to in their attempt to find meaning and "strenuous clarity" in the events and experiences that have come to be subsumed under the rubric of the "Holocaust," precisely because he is one of the rare survivor-writers whose literary devices assure the greatest "communicability" of his text without compromising the intimate nature of his memoir.

Primo Levi was born in Turin, Italy, the capital city of Piedmont in the Northwest corner of Italy not far from the French border, on July 31, 1919. He was born into a cultivated middle-class Jewish family, the descendants of Diasporic Jews who had settled there after their expulsion from Spain in 1492. Levi grew up in the quiet, centrally-located neighborhood of Crocetta. Both his grandfather and his father were civil engineers. His family, though not religious, observed the major Jewish holidays of Rosh Hashanah and Passover. In 1935, at age eighteen, Primo Levi completed his classical high school program and entered the Chemical Institute to train as a chemist.

On November 17, 1938, Mussolini's Fascist government announced new racial laws which outlawed mixed marriages and prohibited Jews from owning property or holding jobs in government. Jews were now forbidden to study or teach in Italian universities. During the year before these decrees over ten thousand Jews of foreign origin were expelled from their homes in Italy. Fortunately, those like Levi who had already begun their studies were allowed to complete them. This discrimination was a new experience for the majority of acculturated and highly integrated Italian Jews, including Levi who, although always aware of his "Jewishness," now began to feel an increasing sense of social and cultural isolation. Despite these conditions, Levi received his doctorate in Chemistry *summa cum laude* in July 1941, and was presented with a diploma clearly verifying his new status: under his name on the diploma is written "of Jewish race." His father lived long enough to see his only son complete his education but escaped Fascist humiliation by prematurely dying of stomach cancer in 1942.

Levi's first position as a chemist came the following year when he was hired, in spite of the new racial laws, to work in a nickel mine in the mountains near Turin. He was later transferred to a post on the outskirts of Milan. This period marks his first attempts at journal and short story writing. The piece "Lead and Mercury," which later appears in *The Periodic Table*, was drafted at this time.

Levi quit his job as a chemist after the arrival of Nazi forces on Italian soil and joined a small group of Italian partisans fighting German and Italian Fascist forces in the mountains of Levi's youth. Levi describes the group as more passionate than proficient:

> "I went to Val d'Aosta and found assembled in the mountains a number of young men my age. I was twenty-four, for the most part they were disbanded soldiers, I knew some of them because they were from Turin, in a very artful but very incautious manner we tried to launch a partisan band. But these were beginnings, we had no political contacts, we had very little money and almost no weapons, we were a very disorganized group, and besides all that we were so unwary that we took a spy aboard."[1]

The band of inexperienced young partisans were betrayed by an informant and were arrested by Fascist militia on December

13, 1943. Under interrogation, Levi confessed to his Jewishness. On the way to the detention camp of Fossoli, near Modena, he swallowed his false identification papers and buried his notebook containing the list of his fellow partisans. Levi was deported to Auschwitz a month later on a convoy containing 650 men and women. Only three from this group are known to have survived.

As a chemist Levi was immediately drafted to work as a slave laborer in one of the three I.G. Farben laboratories in the Auschwitz 111-Monowitz-Buna complex, thus being spared the gas chamber or a slower death by starvation. In Auschwitz, Levi became number 174517 which formed much of his identity and gave him the subject of his writing. The number was physically imprinted on his left arm a few inches from his wrist and remained a physical reminder of his survivor-status for the rest of his life. Liberated by a Soviet military unit in January 1945 after eleven months in Auschwitz, Levi was forced to endure a long and arduous journey before being able to return to Turin. Levi's immediate family also survived the Nazis—his mother by remaining in hiding nearby, and his sister by using false papers and keeping on the move.

Other than the eleven months he spent in Auschwitz and nine spent on the long circuitous journey back to Turin, Levi was in direct and unbroken contact with the landscape of his birth and his immediate family. Philip Roth wrote: "I don't personally know of another contemporary writer who has voluntarily remained, over so many decades, intimately entangled and in such direct, unbroken contact with his immediate family, his birthplace, his region, the world of his forebearers, and particularly, with the working environment which, in Turin, the home of Fiat, is largely industrial."[2]

His observations of the workings of the concentration camp and the human response to those conditions, as well as his convoluted journey home—which took many months through numerous countries and languages, became the primary content of his autobiographical writings. Levi returned to Turin on October 19, 1945, where he felt an immediate impulse to write and record his experiences and observations. Within two months he had completed a manuscript. "I wrote

Survival in Auschwitz without giving it a second thought: at night, in the lab, on the train, wherever I happened to find myself. But I didn't have much time then—I was also engaged to be married!"[3]

This first memoir, *Survival in Auschwitz*, was turned down by publisher after publisher, and even after it was printed in 1947 by the small press Franco Antonicelli, it was largely ignored. The first edition of 2,500 copies sold poorly with the last 600 remainders being ruined in a Florence warehouse by the flood of 1966. In 1956 it was republished by Einaudi Press to a more receptive Italian audience and soon established Levi as an important writer. *Survival in Auschwitz* has not been out of print since.

Shortly after the war, Levi met and married Lucia Morpurgo and began his work as an industrial chemist and manager of the Turin chemical factory. There he remained for over thirty years before retiring in 1977 to devote himself to writing full time. He claimed to have entered the paint industry by chance. His company, SIVA, specialized in the production of wire enamels, insulating coatings for copper electrical conductors. At the peak of his career he was among an elite group of chemists numbering only about forty in the world working in this area.

Throughout the majority of his career he wrote as an "amateur," stealing time to write outside of his normal full-time workload. Levi wrote after hours at the factory and even during his morning and evening commute, using the metaphors of distillation, paint, varnish, and other chemical processes to describe much of his camp experience. Levi wrote articles for the Turin newspaper, *La Stampa*, for over twenty-five years, the last piece in February 1987 only two months before his death. Bylines of his work most often describe him simply as an "Italian author and chemist."

Levi ended his life on April 11, 1987, when he plunged down the stairwell of the house his family had lived in for generations, the same house where he was born. His death is assumed a suicide. He was 68 years old at the time of his death, suffering from depression and the aftermath of prostate surgery. Those closest to him described him as demoralized and acknowledged how disturbed he was by his inability to write. His last full-length work, *The Drowned and The Saved*, has been interpreted as a pessimistic account of the anguish of the survivor in the aftermath of the Shoah. He was survived by his wife Lucia, his son Renzo, a physicist, a daughter Lucia, a biology teacher, and his invalid mother-in-law and bedridden mother, both in their nineties, who during the last years of Levi's life had become progressively dependent and in need of constant care.

It was the literary world who struggled most to understand Levi's death. His literary reputation had never been more secure. Rumors circulated that he was being considered for the Nobel Prize in literature. His importance as a writer can be seen in the quality and quantity of writers who have felt compelled to comment on his work: Cynthia Ozick, Philip Roth, Italo Calvino, James Atlas, Raul Hillberg, William Styron, and Irving Howe are but a few of the many that have been drawn to comment on Levi's work. Saul Bellow called *The Periodic Table* a masterpiece. Now, with this volume, we can add the distinguished voices of Lawrence Langer, Yaffa Eliach, and Gian Paolo Biasin. *Memory and Mastery: Primo Levi as Writer and Witness* attempts to examine the full range of Levi's work, not only his autobiographical Holocaust memoirs, but his poetry and science fiction work as well.

The first section of this volume, "Levi as Writer," gives the reader an overview of Levi's writing and its relationship to his "status" as a Holocaust survivor. Chapter 1, "The Haunted Journey of Primo Levi," by noted Italian literature scholar Gian Paolo Biasin, traces Levi's development as a writer, from his first published book *Se questo è un uomo* (*If This is a Man*), which marks the beginning of Levi's literary career, to *La tregua* (*The Truce*). Biasin describes the battle Levi waged with the "contagion of the Holocaust" and the "shame that a just man experiences when witnessing another man's crime." Through his observations of Levi's "scientific attitude, humanistic literary tradition, and his lay morality," Biasin examines the influences that constitute Levi's objective, acute, and yet sensitive manner of writing as a witness to the Holocaust.

In chapter 2, "Primo Levi's Concept of Time," historian Yaffa Eliach examines the contingent and relational sense of Holocaust time as expressed throughout Levi's writing. In this chapter, Eliach argues that the "victim's concept of time and his relationship to it during the Holocaust are among the most essential elements in the victim's struggle to survive and to attempt to hold on to his humanity." She notes that survivors often created a hybrid calendar for themselves, constructed from different aspects of their own lives both before and during the Holocaust.

In chapter 3, "The Rhetoric of the *Univers Concentrationnaire*," it is Levi "the literary stylist, the careful lexicographer and the fine crafter of the modern phrase" that Risa Sodi seeks to illuminate. This chapter critically examines Levi's prose, especially the use of specific literary devices used to "construct" the shape and dimension of Levi's literary form. Sodi calls attention to the critical oversight of Levi's accomplished literary techniques in favor of his "captivating views on moral and ethical issues." She provides close readings of Levi's work, carefully attending to each word in her recovery of the possibilities of meaning in his work.

Part II, "Levi and Science," examines the interconnection of Levi's writing with the scientific discourse. Scientific thought and approach, an important theme throughout Levi's work, finds particular expression in a body of science fiction work written under the pseudonym of Damiano Malabila, as well as under Levi's own name in *The Periodic Table*. Chapter 4, Nancy Harrowitz's "Primo Levi's Science as 'Evil Nurse': The Lesson of Inversion," examines "the relationship of Levi's scientific vocation to his philosophy about the Holocaust and his analysis, implicit or explicit, of the role that science played in that event and the role that science plays in a more general way in the construction of culture." Although many critics have examined the "crossover between chemistry and writing" in Levi's texts, Harrowitz carefully underlines Levi's representation of "science" and modern technology as a threatening and morally destabilizing force.

Chapter 5, "Moral Snares and Parables: Between Science Fiction and Midrash," by Mirna Cicioni, examines the short fictional texts Levi wrote after 1940 that describe the possibilities of "future scientific, technological, or biological developments." Many of these stories foreground the processes of dehumanization, which tend also to be the focus of critical analyses. Cicioni questions "whether, or where, they belong in the established parameters of science fiction." Levi himself resisted the use of "science fiction" as a descriptor for his work, and instead preferred to call these pieces "moral snares," which Cicioni connects to the Midrashic tradition of the parable.

Part III, "Levi's Poetry," consists of chapter 6, "At an Uncertain Hour: The Other Side of Primo Levi," by Nicholas Patruno, which identifies Levi's own apprehensions in writing poetry, linking them to a fear of "tarnishing the 'rational' aspect of his persona, which is now his trademark" and his reluctance "to expose his emotional side to the world." Patruno compares Levi's prose to his poetry and reveals significant differences in tone, content, and psychological dimension. Patruno's examination of Levi's poetry reveals that it was integral to his attempt to speak "not only for himself but also for all his brothers and sisters who, having perished, were unable to speak for themselves."

Part IV, "Levi and Language," begins with Brian Cliff's "On Language and Violence" (chapter 7), which explores how violence is done to humanity through the use of language. Cliff focuses specifically upon the dehumanizing elements used in Lager (camp) jargon. By carefully explicating the grammatical, syntactical, and translational aspects of Levi's Lager vocabulary, Cliff reveals the psychological implications upon those who were forced to speak it. He goes on to point out the ways in which Levi resignifies against the jargon, by humanizing language. "In doing so," Cliff argues, "Levi quietly reclaims humanity for himself and for his companions."

Chapter 8, "On Language and Personhood: A Linguistic Odyssey," by Patricia Sayre and Linnea Vacca, explores the disturbing record of the dehumanization of inmates through the systematic destruction of their use of language, as described in Levi's *If This is a Man* and *The Truce*. Sayre and Vacca focus on Levi's own writing and how he demonstrates and describes the corresponding ability of language to reconstruct, recount, and reintegrate oneself into normal life. They focus their attention on "the small miracles of rebirth that unfold on the pages of Levi's story of his journey back—literally to Italy, figuratively to life. The great miracle is that the story could be told at all, and told with such grace."

Part V, "Levi's Legacy," addresses Levi's influence on other writers and artists. In chapter 9, "Bridging the Narrative and Visual: Primo Levi as a Source of Inspiration for Contemporary Artists," Stephen C. Feinstein demonstrates how Levi's writing has served as a springboard for a creative visual investigation of the Holocaust by contemporary artists. Many of these artists have acknowledged that Levi, more than any other writer, has contributed significantly to their understanding of and ability to "visualize" the Holocaust.

Chapter 10, "The Duty and the Risk of Testimony: Primo Levi as Keeper of Memory," by Franca Molino Signorini, reviews Levi's positioning as the "quintessential" witness of the Holocaust experience. She argues that critics' identification of scientific detachment in Levi's writing miss the "much deeper chords linked to reserve rather than to science. The desire to understand, which is at the root of the search for meaning, does in fact require an unbiased outlook and therefore necessarily distances the observer from the object of his research." Signorini points out that Levi makes no attempt to evade suffering, but records the events while leaving judgment up to the reader.

In chapter 11, "Legacy in Gray," Lawrence Langer reviews and critically examines the reception of Levi's work in North America and describes significant differences in the English and Italian versions of Levi's work. He argues that "American publishers have tried to twist his intentions as a writer into an affirmative direction by altering the titles of his books." Langer carefully refutes the claim that Levi's writing is a vehicle of hope: "Such revised titles might easily deceive readers into believing that Levi's main interest was to mine gleaming nuggets of human fellowship from the barren landscape of Auschwitz. It was not."

The volume concludes with a comprehensive bibliography of work on and by Primo Levi. This bibliography contains the works cited within essays and publications on or by Levi in both Italian and English. This bibliography complements and increases the utility of this volume for scholars and students of Levi's work.

Notes

1. Caracciolo, Nicola, *Uncertain Refuge: Italy and the Jews During the Holocaust* (Chicago: University of Illinois Press, 1995), pp. 76–77.
2. Philip Roth, "A Man Saved By His Skills," *New York Times Book Review* October 12, 1986, p. 40.
3. Risa B. Sodi, "An Interview with Primo Levi," *Partisan Review* MA 54.3 (1987), p. 366.

Part I

Levi as Writer, Levi as Witness

1

The Haunted Journey of Primo Levi

Gian Paolo Biasin

The first chapter of *Se questo è un uomo*, Primo Levi's account of his survival in Auschwitz, bears the title "The Journey," a title that appropriately describes the beginning of the author's ordeal when, with 649 other Italian Jews, he was transferred from the concentration camp of Fossoli in northern Italy to the infamous Lager in the desolate Polish plain in the winter of 1944.[1]

But "The Journey" is also the beginning of Levi's work as a writer. It should be emphasized that he was not a writer to start with. In 1943 he was a young chemist, and his writing was the direct and unexpected result of his experience in the Lager and the urgency he felt to give testimony about the unspeakable atrocities he had witnessed and survived. In doing so, he discovered himself as a writer, and what a writer he was.[2]

His scientific competence was accompanied, as was often the case for young people of the affluent Italian bourgeoisie, by the classical education that during the secondary school years of the Liceo classico familiarized him with the great authors of the Italian canon, from Dante to Tasso, from Galileo to Manzoni, as well as non-Italians of the western tradition, from Homer and Vergil to Rabelais and Descartes, from Balzac to Tolstoy.[3] Furthermore, he came from a Piedmontese lay family, whose beliefs and morality were in sharp contrast not only with the predominant Catholic society, but even with part of the Jewish community. Thus, when he started writing his testimony, Levi possessed three characteristics—a scientific attitude, a humanistic formation, and a lay morality—that remain at the basis of his work and contribute decisively to its achievement—the terse precision of the prose, the sharp observation of human and social reality, the soft-voiced tone of an inflexible moral judgment.

"The Journey" describes the travel from a still normal human life to the gates of Auschwitz with its truly inhuman conditions, and right from the beginning Levi is able to convey the bewilderment and the enormity of his experience through the intensity, the simplicity, and the immediacy of the words he chooses and the episodes he relates. Suffice it to recall just one example, the eve of the departure:

> All took leave from life in the manner which most suited them. Some praying, some deliberately drunk, others lustfully intoxicated for the last time. But the mothers stayed up to prepare the food for the journey with tender care, and washed their children and packed the luggage; and at dawn the barbed wire was full of children's washing hung out in the wind to dry. Nor did they forget the diapers, the toys, the cushions and the hundred other small things which mothers remember and which children always need. Would you not do the same? If you and your child were going to be killed tomorrow, would you not give him [something] to eat today? (11)

The image of the barbed wire full of children's washing hung out to dry in the wind is truly unforgettable, brimming with humanity and compassion as it is; and so are the two impassioned rhetorical questions which follow it like a cry of the heart, obliging us, each one of us, to reply: yes, I would do the same, yes, I would be a victim. The whole of *Se questo è un uomo* is filled with such moving details and intense participation.

But "The Journey" is also a literary topos that for Levi goes back to the origins of Italian literature, to the journey of Dante Alighieri to Hell, Purgatory and Paradise—in fact, one of the Germans who escorts the prisoners into the infernal city of Auschwitz is called by the Dantean epithet of Charon, "our Charon" the one who ferries the dead souls into the otherworld; this German Charon does not shout threats of eternal damnation (Dante's "Guai a voi, anime prave"); he simply asks the prisoners "courteously" (and ominously) if they have "any money or watches to give him, seeing that they will not be useful . . . anymore" (17). But I shall resist the temptation to call Levi "a Dante of our time," as Risa Sodi has intriguingly suggested, despite their obvious differences.[4] What can be said is that, after surviving the Nazi hell, Levi went through a sort of unlikely purgatory, which he chronicles in his second book of memories, *La tregua* (*The Reawakening*), written in Turin in 1961–62; and when he finally reaches his paradise, when he returns to his motherland and goes home again, he realizes that his long journey is not over, because even this paradise is haunted by the enormity and the irrevocability of the Lager.[5] Or, to put it more bluntly, he realizes that the Lager has permanently undermined the very notion of paradise, that paradise is no longer a stable possibility after the Lager, but has become a fragile condition to be defended at all costs.

In many ways, then, *La tregua* is a fundamental work that continues the quiet testimony of *Se questo è un uomo*: for example, the frequent comparisons of human beings with a variety of animals are a telling sign, an echo or a prolongation of a habit that was formed in the Lager in the course of the dehumanizing treatment to which the prisoners were subjected. As just one among the many possible specimens there are the following comparisons: Jadzia moves around a man "with the blind, mute, tremulous, slow, but sure movements which amoebae show under the microscope"; "Noah was a young Pantagruel, as strong as a horse"; "while the feeble Jadzia limited herself to throwing out her tenuous threads, like a rock-mollusc, Noah, a high-flying bird, cruised along all the roads of the camp" (28).

Even more importantly, hunger and the search for food constitute a fundamental theme of both books, although it is less obsessive in *La tregua* than it was in *Se questo è un uomo*, and understandably so, since after the liberation hunger is no longer a matter of life and death, and the search for food can acquire adventurous, picaresque, even colorful tones; the importance of this theme is underscored from the very first by a line in the introductory poem about the prisoners' dreams "[o]f going home, of eating, of telling our story," in which eating is at least as cogent as returning and telling. The theme is concluded at the end of the book, after more than thirty episodes concerning food, when the train with the former prisoners arrives near the Italian border and fills up with "Italian smugglers, who brought us the greetings of our homeland, in the absence of official authorities, and generously distributed chocolate, grappa and tobacco" (220).

But beside continuing the testimony of his first book, in writing *La tregua* Levi seems to discover and reveal the roots of much of his literary production, including his poetry (part of which was written soon after the return and, expressing his innermost urges as a victim, frames his prose) and his science fiction (where at least some of the stories are the nightmarish evocation of the monsters generated by the sleep of reason—I am thinking in particular of the terrifying short story "Angelica farfalla" in *Storie naturali*). Some of the episodes narrated in *La tregua* appear to prepare the ground, so to speak, for both Levi's later fiction (his encounter with the group of enthusiastic, young Zionists headed for Palestine, the first settlers of modern Israel, is perhaps a first inspiration for Levi's novel *Se non ora, quando?*, which gives voice to his desire for his own and his people's redemption) and his inexhaustible essayistic and moral engagement culminating in *I sommersi e i salvati* (*The Drowned and the Saved*). As for example in his reaction at the sight of the vanquished Germans:

> We had felt no joy in seeing Vienna undone and the Germans broken, but rather anguish: not compassion, but a larger anguish, which was mixed up with our own misery, with the heavy, threatening sensation of an irreparable and definitive evil which was present everywhere, nestling like gangrene in the guts of Europe and the world, the seed of future harm. (215)

Or in the streets of Munich full of ruins:

> We felt we had something to say, enormous things to say, to every single German, and we felt that every German should have something to say to us . . . Did 'they' know about Auschwitz, about the silent daily massacre, a step away from their doors? If they did, how could they walk about, return home and look at their children, cross the threshold of a church? If they did not, they ought, as a sacred duty, to listen, to learn everything, immediately, from us, from me; I felt the tattooed number on my arm burning like a sore. (218)

In fact in *La tregua*, Levi for the first time addresses not the Holocaust as such, but the consequences of the Holocaust, in a sustained and not occasional manner, and begins to fathom the depths of the evil that the Nazis have caused in the Lagers. To address these consequences and to fathom these depths, Levi has recourse to narrative techniques that combine different genres (autobiography, historical memoir, travelogue, picaresque story, moral reflection). And since the actual circumstances of his liberation took Levi through Poland, Belarus, Ukraine, Romania, Hungary, Austria, and Germany, from January to October 1945, when he finally returned to Italy, *La tregua* has the preeminent feature of a book of travel, in which the marvel of the narrator at seeing strange lands, peoples and customs is heightened by his recent escape from death in the Lager and by his sudden, extreme freedom—a vacation (albeit an involuntary one) that at first allows him to savor life again in all its aspects and unpredictability.

And another model, or prototype, is immediately relevant for the book of travel—not Dante but Homer, the singer of the wanderings of Ulysses after the fall of Troy (a different hell). Dante had of course picked up the theme in the famous Canto of Inferno that plays such a prominent role in Levi's account of the Lager, in his sustained presentation (an entire chapter of *Se questo è un uomo*) of the importance of spiritual nourishment (Dante's text), along with material food (the cabbage and turnip soup) for his salvation.[6] So it seems natural that Levi should pick up the Homeric model of the Odyssey when he describes his own wanderings through strange lands before returning home in *La tregua*, a book that becomes a sort of modern, collective odyssey indeed. Levi is quite conscious of this, and shows his self-awareness as writer in intertextual references that are quite explicit. For instance, when he sees Russian troops returning home from the front, he describes them with the following words: "They were cheerful, sad and tired, and took pleasure in food and wine, like Ulysses' companions after the ships had been pulled ashore" (59).[7]

No wonder, then, that *La tregua* takes on a "Homeric," solemn and yet vivacious tone. And like its model it is a colorful gallery of extraordinary places and characters:

> In those days and in those parts, soon after the front had passed by, a high wind was blowing over the face of the earth; the world around us seemed to have returned to primeval Chaos, and was swarming with scalene, defective, abnormal human specimens; each of them bestirred himself, with blind or deliberate movements, in anxious search of his own place, of his own sphere, as the particles of the four elements are described as doing in the verse-cosmogonies of the Ancients. (33)

The language Levi uses is both that of a scientist (scalene, human specimens, sphere, particles, four elements) and that of a humanist (the verse-cosmogonies of the Ancients: not just Homer, but also his beloved Lucretius), and the examples of such a rich layering of his style could be multiplied.

But let me simply emphasize how Levi's portraits of the persons he encounters are based on both physical features and moral traits, and how some of the characters he portrays remain etched sharply as the ones who in different ways teach Levi types of life he had never known before, adding novelty to his own rediscovery of life after the Lager. For example, Mordo Nahum, the great Greek Jew from Salonica, "had large pale watery eyes and a great curved nose, which gave his whole body a rapacious yet halting appearance, like a nightbird surprised by light, or a shark outside its natural environment" (35). He is immediately distinguished by his shoes, "of leather, almost new, of elegant design: a real portent, given the time and the place" (35), and these shoes are indeed the mark and the tool of his power, because with them Mordo can go places, barter, exchange, buy and sell all sorts of things: to the amazed Levi who remarks that in a time of truce bread should be more important, he memorably replies, "War is always" (51):

> The Lager had happened to both of us; I had felt it as a monstrous upheaval, a loathsome anomaly in my history and in the history of the world; he, as a sad confirmation of things well known. "War is always," man is wolf to man: an old story. He never spoke to me of his two years of Auschwitz. (51)

Or consider Cesare, the *simpatico* charlatan from Rome, full of life, pleasure-seeking, "as lively as a grasshopper" (72), "a child of the sun, everybody's friend; he knew no hatred or contempt, was as changeable as the sky, joyous, cunning and ingenuous, bold and cautious, very ignorant, very innocent and very civilized" (81); he is enterprising and charming, whether he is able to buy a hen from Russian peasants without knowing a word of Russian, or to sell fish, previously injected with water to increase the weight, to Russian soldiers; Levi says, "to watch Cesare's enterprises, even the most modest and trivial ones, constituted a unique experience, a live and fortifying spectacle, which reconciled me to the world and once more lit in me that joy of living which Auschwitz had extinguished" (81).

Galina, the Russian country girl who sings "like a thrush," is "alert, ingenuous, a bit of a flirt, very vivacious, not particularly well educated, or particularly serious; yet one felt in her the same force, the same dignity as in her comrades and in her boyfriends, the dignity of a man who works and knows why, of a man who fights and knows that he is in the right, of a man who has his life ahead of him" (66). She represents a tacit, unconfessed possibility of love for Levi, and when she goes home, "sucked up into the emptiness of Russian space," she leaves behind "a sharp scent of earth, of youth and of joy" (67).[8]

The extraordinary characters Levi encounters during his peregrination are so many and varied that it is simply impossible to do them justice. The three mentioned above should suffice as "specimens," as Levi would say, of his sharp observation of human nature. And they, and the many others that appear in Levi's account, live in extraordinary places like the Katowice market, lively amid "ruins everywhere" (79), the Red House at Starye Dorogi, "full of mystery and pitfalls like a fairy castle" (152), the Russian forests and plains, "solemn, austere and untouched like no other scenery known to us" (152). While for his part Levi, an unobtrusive and self-effacing Ulysses, sees equally extraordinary sights, like a camel in Romania, "a worn-out, grey, woolly camel, laden with sacks, exhaling haughtiness and stupid solemnity from his prehistoric leporine muzzle" (200), or the first jeep he had ever seen, "a squat, graceless, military vehicle, as flat as a tin can with a white, and not a red, star painted on its side" (215); and he witnesses extraordinary events, such as Victory Day, the first unequivocal signs of the sudden build-up of the cold war, the disinfection of the former prisoners with DDT, the first news about the marvel of penicillin and the horror of the atom bomb.

But the brilliant surface of the book of travel does not mislead the attentive reader: the prevalent tone is one of melancholy or even sadness, which no outburst of joy can really overcome. The long journey home becomes a haunted journey, haunted by the memories of horrors past, memories which seem marginal or even episodic, but which project their long shadow over the entire narration, encircling it from beginning to end in an anguished contemplation of the human condition after the Lager. I am not suggesting, with Theodor Adorno and the early Lawrence Langer, that the experience of the Lager has radically changed the condition of artistic expression, causing an unbridgeable rupture within the western, classic tradition.[9] On the contrary, Levi clings to this tradition with all his strength precisely in order to prevail against the onslaught of Nazi evil, of the irrational forces that have so profoundly shaken the human values on which civilization is supposed to be based. And his use of traditional models and paradigms—from Dante to Homer—contributes powerfully to making the Holocaust and its survivors' experience writable for him and understandable for us.[10]

At the beginning of *La tregua*, Levi states his position in sober, solemn terms, when he describes the arrival of the four young Russian soldiers at the gates of Auschwitz and the emotions that their sight stirs in the prisoners:

> They did not greet us, nor did they smile; they seemed oppressed not only by compassion but by a confused restraint, which sealed their lips and bound their eyes to the funereal scene. It was that shame we knew so well, the shame that drowned us after the selections, and every time we had to watch, or submit to, some outrage: the shame the Germans did not know, that the just man experiences at another man's crime; the feeling of guilt that such a crime should exist, that it should have been introduced irrevocably into the world of things that exist, and that his will for good should have proved too weak or null, and should not have availed in defense. (12)

Levi's language is astonishingly effective in conveying not just shame, which was so torturous for the victims with its components of sense of guilt, impotence, and outrage, but also their other, mixed, strong emotions:

> So for us even the hour of liberty rang out grave and muffled, and filled our souls with joy and yet with a painful sense of prudency, so that we should have liked to wash our consciences and our memories clean from the foulness that lay upon them; and also with anguish, because we felt that this should never happen, that now nothing could ever happen good and pure enough to rub out our past, and that the scars of the outrage would remain within us forever . . . and in the stories that we should tell of it. (13)

Levi poignantly underscores the mixed emotions of the liberated prisoners—the joy of liberation, the pain of not being able to cleanse oneself of the horrible experience, the dawning awareness that the violence they suffered will remain forever within them and in their stories. But what is fundamental for him is not simply the exact recollection of these emotions, it is a meditation on the nature of evil:

> Because, and this is the awful privilege of our generation and of my people, no one better than us has ever been able to grasp the incurable nature of the offense, that spreads like a contagion. It is foolish to think that human justice can eradicate it. It is an inexhaustible fount of evil; it breaks the body and the spirit of the submerged, it stifles them and renders them abject; it returns as ignominy upon the oppressors, it perpetuates itself as hatred among the survivors, and swarms around in a thousand ways, against the very will of all, as a thirst for revenge, as a moral capitulation, as denial, as weariness, as renunciation. (13)

Such is the awful privilege of Levi's generation and of his people—please note: for the first time in Levi, not the Italian, but the Jewish people. And yet his words singularly echo and expand those of the Italian novelist and moralist Alessandro Manzoni in *I promessi sposi* (*The Betrothed*) more than a century ago:

> Those who provoke or oppress, all those who do any wrong to others, are guilty not only of the harm they do, but also of the perversion they cause in the minds of those they have injured. Renzo was a peaceable young man and averse to bloodshed—an open youth who hated deceits of any kind; but at that moment his heart only beat to kill, and his mind turned only on thoughts of treachery.[11]

I wish to offer only two comments: in comparison with Manzoni, Levi's words enlarge the scope of the moral meditation from one person (the novelistic character Renzo Tramaglino, who suffers violence by Don Abbondio, the cowardly priest who refuses to marry him for fear of Don Rodrigo) to an entire generation; and the nature of the "perversion" caused by the offense is more subtle and more dangerous than an outburst of contemplated violence. It pullulates in a thousand different ways, from abjectness to infamy, from hatred to desperation, from vengeance to renunciation. Both Manzoni and Levi are adamant and categorical in their condemnation of the offenders. But in the passage I have quoted Levi shows an uncanny, prophetic awareness of the large-scale and long-lasting consequences of evil, even the "weariness" and "renunciation" that might have contributed to his own death—I do remember the profound tiredness of his voice on the phone, three months before he died—and in so doing, Levi also prepares the ground for his own ongoing investigation and denunciation of these evil consequences in his relentless examination of the post-Holocaust era.

In *La tregua*, Levi only begins his task, because he is mainly focused on a faithful account of the events of the liberation and the return home. But it is already clear that these events in themselves are only a "lull" (as the Italian title suggests) inside the souls of the survivors, just as they are a lull in contemporary history between the second world war and the cold war: "The months just past, although hard, of wandering on the margins of civilization now seemed to us like a pause, a parenthesis of unlimited availability, a providential but unrepeatable gift of fate" (220).[12]

In his account, then, exile and nostalgia are dealt with as normal, human emotions worth dwelling upon, not as impossible and dangerous dreams that inside the Lager would have undermined the will to resist and to survive. Only after the liberation, only after the immediate threat of annihilation and dehumanization is over, can Levi and the other prisoners feel again normal, human feelings, and thus return from the dead:

> I was overcome—as if a dyke had crumbled—by a new and greater pain, previously buried and relegated to the margins of my consciousness by other more immediate pains: the pain of exile, of my distant home, of loneliness, of friends lost, of youth lost, and of the host of corpses all around. (15)

This new pain recurs at intervals throughout the many months that still separate Levi from his "distant home" and the many miles of journey in foreign lands that still keep him far from his motherland. Exile and nostalgia are indeed what their etymological roots tell: the pain and the longing to return (Greek *nostos* + *algia*) felt by one who has been forced out of his soil, his native country (Latin *ex* + *solum*). Many examples recur in Levi's pages, explicitly, when the words exile and nostalgia appear. For example:

> Nostalgia is a fragile and tender anguish, basically different, more intimate, more human than the other pains we had endured till then—beatings, cold, hunger, terror, destitution, disease. Nostalgia is a limpid and clean pain, but demanding; it permeates every minute of the day, permits no other thoughts, and induces a need for escape. (152)

Or consider the episode of the theatre at Starye Dorogi, with the number of the song, "The Three-Cornered Hat," famous among Italians because its words are progressively substituted for by gestures, which was performed by the improvised actors in a macabre and lugubrious rather than joyous and festive key:

> The "Three-Cornered Hat" number took away one's breath, and every evening was greeted with a silence more eloquent than applause. Why? Perhaps because, under the grotesque appearance, one perceived the heavy breath of a collective dream, of the dream emanating from exile and idleness, when work and trouble have ceased, and nothing acts as a screen between a man and himself; perhaps because we saw the impotence and nullity of our life and of life itself, and the hunch-backed crooked profiles of the monsters generated by the sleep of reason. (184)

Or the much-awaited arrival at the Italian frontier:

> Late at night we crossed the Brenner, which we had passed in our exile twenty months before; our less tired

> companions celebrated with a cheerful uproar; Leonardo and I remained lost in a silence crowded with memories. Of 650, our number when we had left, three of us were returning. (220)

Notice that in "The Journey," the initial chapter of *Se questo è un uomo*, when describing the crossing of the Brenner pass in the opposite direction, towards Auschwitz, Levi had not used the term exile, because it was a journey towards death, and only the return, a return that was achieved by just a handful of survivors, allows normal human feelings.

Exile and nostalgia are also present implicitly in *La tregua*, when comparisons with domestic habits or landscapes spring up spontaneously in front of strange occurrences or different lands. For example: "The immense, heroic spaces of Russia gave a sense of giddiness to us Italians, accustomed as we were to a landscape of mountains and hills and a plain alive with the presence of man, and weighed down our hearts with painful memories" (133). Or, closer to home, at the Rumanian border:

> A surprisingly domestic scene opened up before our eyes; no longer a deserted, geological steppe, but the green hills of Moldavia, with farms, haystacks and rows of vines; no longer enigmatic Cyrillic signs, but, right in front of our truck, a decrepit hovel, blue-green with verdigris, with clear writing on it, curiously similar to the Italian words: "Paine, Lapte, Vin, Carnaciuri de Purcel." (200)

But finally the return is not joyful, the peregrinations throughout eastern Europe are not concluded by a happy ending, the reality of the home becomes haunted—perverted—by the memory of the offense. This is excruciatingly clear at the conclusion of *La tregua*, a subdued yet ominous conclusion that takes up a poem which Levi had written soon after his return, on January 11, 1946 and which he uses many years later, significantly, to introduce the book with its obsessive dream—so that the poem-epigraph and the last page of the book constitute the frame within which the story (the "lull" of the title) is told. The poem reads in part:

> Dreams used to come in the brutal nights, . . .
> Of going home, of eating, of telling our story. . . .
> Now we have found our home again,
> Our hunger is quenched,
> All the stories have been told.
> It is time. Soon we shall hear again
> The alien command:
> *Wstawàch.*

And here is the concluding page:

> A dream full of horror has still not ceased to visit me, at sometimes frequent, sometimes longer, intervals.
>
> It is a dream within a dream, varied in detail, one in substance. I am sitting at a table with my family, or with friends, or at work, or in the green countryside . . . ; yet I feel a deep and subtle anguish, the definite sensation of an impending threat. And in fact, as the dream proceeds, slowly or brutally, each time in a different way, everything collapses and disintegrates around me, the scenery, the walls, the people. . . . Now everything has changed to chaos; I am alone in the centre of a grey and turbid nothing, and now, I know what this thing means, and I also know that I have always known it; I am in the Lager once more, and nothing is true outside the Lager. All the rest was a brief pause, a deception of the senses, a dream; my family, nature in flower, my home. Now this inner dream, this dream of peace, is over, and in the outer dream, which continues, gelid, a well-known voice resounds: a single word, not imperious, but brief and subdued. It is the dawn command of Auschwitz, a foreign word, feared and expected: get up, '*Wstawàch.*' (221–22)

The frightful power of this dream derives from its structure as much as from its substance: a dream within a dream is a nightmare, it signifies that an escape is doubly impossible. And in fact, Levi's dream turns the very notion of exile upside down—as if Levi felt paradoxically exiled from the Lager rather than from his home, as if the only reality were the grim world of the offense, and the everyday reality of normal and peaceful life were only a dream. Such is the contagion of the Lager, such is the awful perversion caused by the offense. Levi's terrifying dream is the perfect and disquieting illustration of what Italo Calvino asserted about modern literature: its strength lies in giving words to what has remained unsaid in the individual or social unconscious, because (as Shakespeare showed in the middle of the Renaissance and Sade did during the Enlightenment) "the more our houses are well-lit and prosperous, the more their walls are haunted by ghosts; the dreams of progress and rationality are visited by nightmares."[13]

But if normal human life is only a dream, what can the person who still lives it do? Primo Levi, acting perhaps like Prince Sigismund in Calderòn's *La vida es sueño*, lives his life after the return from the Lager normally and honestly. But he does more. He fights against the contagion of the offense for the rest of his life, and he fights with the only weapons that his native culture has given him: reason, humanness, moral courage, and, yes, writing, literature. If it is true, as George Steiner maintains in *Language and Silence*, that humanistic culture did not stop the Nazis from committing their crime against humanity, it is equally true that this same culture has not only helped some victims, like Levi, to survive (as the Canto of Ulysses episode amply demonstrates), but it has also empowered them to build a barrier of awareness against the offense and its consequences, as Levi's entire literary oeuvre testifies.[14]

We should all remember what might well be his final message in *I sommersi e i salvati*, pointedly delivered with an impeccable, and implacable, Cartesian logic: we should always be awake, we should always be alert, because the Holocaust "happened, therefore it can happen again."[15]

Notes

1. All references will be to the English translation by Stuart Woolf, *Survival in Auschwitz* (New York: Collier Books, 1961).

2. Actually he had written a few pages during his stay in Milan (1942–43), but without giving them undue importance: see Fiora Vincenti, *Invito alla lettura di Primo Levi* (Milan: Mursia, 1973–87), p. 43.
3. A "personal anthology" of the authors that were most important for Primo Levi can be found in his *La ricerca delle radici* (Turin: Einaudi, 1981).
4. Risa B. Sodi, *A Dante of Our Time: Primo Levi and Auschwitz* (New York: Peter Lang, 1990). Dante went to Hell figuratively, as an interested and sympathetic observer who was on his way to Paradise, always guided by a divine presence and transcendence that gave meaning to his experience. Levi actually went to hell in person, with little hope to survive, no superior guidance, no hope to reach a paradise, no transcendence. Dante's hell is predicated on the religious presupposition of a divine as well as poetic contrapasso, articulated in a series of "appropriate" punishments meted out for specific sins; no idea of justice or punishment underlies the philosophy of the Lager, where the only "sin" to be punished is that of being a Jew. And while in Dante's hell the sinners retain their individuality and even their human dignity, in Auschwitz the prisoners were deprived first of all of their personal identity and treated literally like beasts, dehumanized before annihilation. But, notwithstanding all the differences, Sodi succeeds in comparing the respective attitudes of Dante and Levi towards the problems of retributive justice, the neutral zone between good and evil, and the different functions of memory (both remembering and memorizing) for the victims and the oppressors.
5. All references will be to the English translation by Stuart Woolf (Boston: Little, Brown, 1965).
6. On the importance and meaning of the *Canto* of Ulysses for Levi see my *The Flavors of Modernity. Food and the Novel* (Princeton: Princeton University Press, 1993), pp. 140–41; and Piero Boitani, *L'ombra di Ulisse. Figure di un mito* (Bologna: Il Mulino, 1992), pp. 183–86.
7. Another, less pervasive and more generic reference, in this context, is the Bible, as for example "the extraordinary spectacle of the Red Army returning home: a spectacle as dramatic and solemn as a biblical migration, and at the same time as rambling and colorful as the passage of a circus," p. 82.
8. It is worth noting that Levi is extremely sensitive, delicate, and felicitous in his portrayals of women: not only Galina, but

Hanka, Jadzia, Frau Vita, Olga, Marja Fjodorovna Prima, Sore and her silent sister, Flora the prostitute, the sad Ukrainian women returning home from Germany.

9. See Theodor Adorno, *Minima Moralia: Reflection from Damaged Life*, trans. E. F. N. Jephcott (London: Verso, 1978) and Lawrence Langer, *The Holocaust and the Literary Imagination* (New Haven: Yale University Press, 1975).
10. I have partly dealt with this problem (especially the intertextuality that is such a prominent feature in Levi's writing) in the last chapter of *The Flavors of Modernity,* p. 135 and note 12.
11. Alessandro Manzoni, *The Betrothed*, trans. Archibald Colquhoun (New York: Dutton, 1961), p. 27.
12. The text offers many other explicit explanations: see especially pp. 51, 59 , 125.
13. Italo Calvino, *The Uses of Literature: Essays*, trans. Patrick Creagh (San Diego: Harcourt Brace Jovanovich, 1986), p. 19.
14. George Steiner, *Language and Silence* (Harmondsworth: Penguin, 1979), p. 83.
15. Primo Levi, *The Drowned and the Saved*, trans. Raymond Rosenthal (New York: Summit, 1988), p. 199.

2

Primo Levi and His Concept of Time: Time of the Gun, Time of the Spirit

Yaffa Eliach

In Memory of Primo Levi on the Tenth Anniversary of His Death (1987–1997)

Primo Levi is among the greatest humanists and intellectual authors of the Holocaust. Among the most fascinating philosophical, historical, and literary elements in his writings is his preoccupation, as a Holocaust victim, with the concept of time and, to some degree, with space as well.

The victim's concept of time and his relationship to it during the period of the Holocaust were among the most essential elements in the victim's struggle to survive and to attempt to retain his humanity.

Unlike in previous tragedies for the Jew, the ultimate victim during the Holocaust, there were no legal options for survival due to the crude biological definition, rather than ideological one, as to who is a Jew. Expulsion and conversion, historical survival options, belonged to a vanished past. Only the hearts and minds of the "Righteous Among the Nations" provided shelter and assistance. Even major neutral and major allied countries kept their doors closed during the tragic years. In Switzerland, a common slogan was "the boat is full" preventing the entrance to the country of a significant number of refugees. In the United States and Canada, the ill fated ship, St. Louis, was turned back to Europe. Others, seeking refuge in Palestine, found its shores blockaded by British gunboats. The ultimate victims had to create their own options which basically depended on their inner physical and spiritual strength, creativity, and imagination. Central to this option was their concept of time. Clinging to their own time in a debased Holocaust universe was often their only inner reality when humanity betrayed them. Time is central to Judaism and is responsible for the survival of Jews in the Diaspora, away from their homeland for thousands of years.

Paul Tillich writes that: "Judaism is more related to time and history than to space and nature." Jewish tradition, by its very nature, is time oriented. Time is classified into two major units: sacred and profane. Those two fundamental dimensions of time dominate Jewish law (*Halakha*) and life. Its most obvious manifestation is the Jewish lunisolar calendar with its division of the days of the year into sacred and secular days, into holidays and regular days. Many precepts (*mitzvot*) can be fulfilled only at very specific times of the day and night. The Sabbath and holidays begin and end at a precise minute. The holidays are governed by the clock, by the sun and the moon. The cycle of the week, the phases of the moon (the new moon coinciding with the new month and the full moon with the fifteenth of the month), the seasons and their prescribed holidays, dominate the life of the individual Jew.

> Even in the skies above Auschwitz, the full moon always appeared on the fifteenth of the Jewish month. A person brought up in this tradition, where time plays such a major role, has a constant awareness of time. The many interesting Jewish calendars compiled in camps and hiding places confirm this time-consciousness.[1]

Bertha Saltz attributed her survival to a "camp calendar." In a moment of despair, she was about to touch the electrified fence when suddenly she heard a weak female voice chanting "God of Abraham," a prayer recited by women on Saturday night. Bertha followed the voice. She found herself facing an elderly, emaciated women. "How did you know that today was

Saturday?" Bertha asked her. The woman stood up and pointed to her dress. On it were seven knots. "This is my calendar, for each passing day I tie a knot. When I have seven knots, I know that it is the Sabbath." Bertha then tied her first knot on her stripped concentration camp dress. When she had seven knots, she returned to the hut in search of the elderly woman, but she was no longer among the living. Bertha survived.

Like Bertha, many survivors of various backgrounds, traditional or secular, found moments of strength and hope in dates on their calendars, whether personal, religious, or national. For the majority, the issue was not to observe the special days according to traditions such as Yom Kippur, Hanukkah, or Passover, but simply to impose their own concept of family and personal time, like recalling a birthday[2] or anniversary or dates of national holidays and historical events; time endowed the victims with brief moments of humanity.[3] It plucked them out from a dehumanized, debased life where they functioned as walking skeletons, faceless, nameless slaves. Joseph B. Soloveichik writes about the concept of time with regard to freedom and slavery: "The basic criterion which distinguishes free man from slave is the kind of relationship each has with time and its experience. Freedom is identical with a rich, colorful, creative time-consciousness. Bondage is identical with passive intuition and reception of an empty, formal time-stream."[4] These few moments of reprieve, of holding on to spiritual freedom helped the victims to retain their humanity, sanity and possible survival.

Primo Levi (1919–1987) was obsessed with the concept of time. This obsession is reflected in the titles of his books *If Not Now, When?* and *Moments of Reprieve*. It dominates much of his writing, and his concept of time was among the factors which led to his survival in Auschwitz and ultimately to his suicide in Turin.

Primo Levi's interpretation of time was more grounded in Italian, European, and universal-humanistic perceptions, rather than Jewish culture. His family came to Italy after the Expulsion from Spain in 1492 and settled in Turin. Like many of the fifty thousand Italian Jews in the closing decades of the nineteenth century and the four decades of the twentieth century prior to the Holocaust, they were an assimilated group. In his mother's family were prosperous merchants; both his paternal grandfather and father were civil engineers. Levi's father was a lover of books and always instructed his tailor to make the pockets of his suits large enough to hold them.

Primo Levi studied Latin, Greek, Italian history and literature (Dante in particular), but his major was chemistry. In 1941, he received his degree in chemistry, *summa cum laude*. In contrast to the family's sophisticated European education, their knowledge of Judaism was minimal. Primo Levi's definition of a Jew reflects his upbringing: "A Jew is a person who does not have a Christmas tree in his house, is not permitted to eat salami, but eats it anyway, is learning a bit of Hebrew when he is thirteen years old and forgets it soon afterwards."[5] The family did observe some Jewish holidays like Rosh Hashanah, Purim, and Passover; these were the Jewish times in the Levi household. Unlike other European countries, anti-Semitism scarcely existed in Italy. Primo Levi was utterly at home in Italy. He saw himself as a universal man living without any particular attachment to Judaism.

In the autobiographical notes he was preparing for his Italian publisher, he wrote that his purpose as an author was "[t]o find the key to the universe, to understand the why of things."[6] Levi said that Judaism never had an imprint on his ideology, especially after his experiences in the camps.[7] When he joined the partisan movement, it was in order to fight Fascism in an active manner with a gun in hand, and not in order to save himself, his family, or other Jews. As a matter of fact, he refused to go into hiding with his own family. His cousin, Segara, who was fourteen at the time Primo Levi was arrested, wanted to leave the family hiding place with a kitchen knife to rescue Primo. It did not happen. Primo Levi considered himself a poor partisan, but in his view, "anyone able to walk and shoot must consider himself a partisan."[8] The essence of the partisan's role was not based on intellectual or spiritual ability or achievements, but rather the time of the gun.

According to Primo Levi, since the Russian Revolution and the rise of Fascism, spiritual time was replaced by the time of the gun. In his book, *If Not Now, When?* dealing with Jewish and non-Jewish partisans in Eastern Europe, the time of the gun is the central issue.

> "In my village there weren't many clocks. One on the church steeple, but it had stopped years and years ago, maybe during the Revolution. I never saw it working, and my father said he hadn't either. Not even the bell ringer had a clock."
>
> "So how was he able to ring the bells at the right time?"
>
> "He would listen to the time on the radio, and he would judge by the sun and the moon. For that matter, he didn't ring every hour, only the important ones. Two years before the war began, the bell rope broke. It snapped near the top; the stairs were rotten; the bell ringer was an old man, and he was afraid to climb up there and put in a new rope. So after that he announced the time by shooting a hunting rifle into the air; one shot, or two or three or four. That went on till the Germans came. They took his gun away from him, and the village was left without any time."
>
> "Did he shoot the gun at night, too, this bell ringer of yours?"
>
> "No, but he hadn't rung the bells at night, either. Everybody slept at night, so there was no need to listen to the hours."
>
> The only one in the village who really cared for time was the Rabbi. He had to know the correct time so that he could tell when the Sabbath begins and ends. He had two clocks, a grandfather clock and an alarm clock. When they agreed, he would be in good humor; when they didn't, he turned quarrelsome and hit the children's fingers with his ruler.[9]

But later the Rabbi and all the Jews ended up in a pit; they were shot. The Jewish watchmaker, Mendel, survived but became an artillery man during the war, mending guns, not clocks. The name of the village was Strelka, (meaning firing with a rifle, pistol, etc.).

Spiritual time disappeared into oblivion during the Holocaust. Only Mendel the watchmaker, who dealt with the technical aspect of time, survived the massacre of the Jews in his shtetl of Strelka. He joined the partisan movement. Time of the gun dominated his life. He never discussed his pre-Holocaust profession, yet clocks were his criterion in fantasy and reality for evaluating every aspect of the Holocaust. In one of his rare dreams, clocks played a central role:

> Mendel hadn't dreamed for a long time: he could no longer remember when it happened last, before the war had broken out, he thought. That night, perhaps because he was exhausted by the tension and the march, he had a strange dream. He was at Strelka, in his little watch-mender's shop, which he himself had set up in a cubby-hole of his house: it was cramped. Mendel couldn't even stretch his elbows to work. Still he was working, he had dozens of clocks in front of him, all stopped and broken, and he was mending one, with his loup in his eye, and with a tiny screwdriver in his hand. Two men had come looking for him, and they ordered him to come with them; Rivke didn't want him to go, she was angry and afraid, but he went with them anyway. They led him down a stairway, or perhaps it was the pit of a mine, and then down a long tunnel: the ceiling was painted black, and there were many clocks hung on the walls. These were running: their tick could be heard, but each of them marked a different time, and some were actually running backwards; for this Mendel felt vaguely responsible. Along the tunnel, towards him, came a man dressed in civilian clothes, with a necktie and a contemptuous manner; he asked Mendel who he was, and Mendel couldn't answer, he didn't remember his name anymore, or where he was born, nothing.[10]

Even in his dream, the clocks in the black tunnel, although they were ticking, did not function properly and some were actually running backwards. Correct time disappeared during the Holocaust, not only in reality but even in one's dreams. Mendel was not able to impose his concept of time, even from a technical aspect. He forgot even his own personal pre-Holocaust time, past and identity. He lived in and for the present.

Occasionally, Mendel measured time by the moment, without connection to anything else. When he assessed his relationship with a Polish Catholic partisan, although they came from totally different backgrounds, Mendel felt that both of them functioned well together. "Mendel thought: two good clocks mark the same hour, even if they are of different make. They only have to start together."[11] What he and the partisan shared were the gun-killing Germans.

The lives of Mendel the watchmaker turned gun mender and his other fellow partisans were not based on Primo Levi's personal memories, though his writing was inspired by the brief period in his life when he was an Italian partisan. To write *If Not Now, When?* Primo Levi spoke to East European partisans, learned about their lives and even studied Yiddish. The title of the book was not attributed to traditional historic time, but rather on a partisan song, written by a partisan named Gedaleh.[12] In all of his books, with the exception of *If Not Now, When?*, Primo Levi is the main protagonist as a concentration camp inmate and a camp survivor.

In Auschwitz, unlike it was among the partisans, the time of the gun was gone. It was not in the hands of the victim, but rather in the hands of the executioner. Death dominated every moment and time was measured heartbeat by heartbeat. Primo Levi did not impose any traditional, secular, or philosophical elements of time on his struggle for survival. In Auschwitz, Levi was preoccupied only with time as it applied to physical existence, to save the body and not to impose any spiritual time-related elements in the struggle for life. Since the day was dense, one had to think about satisfying hunger, about how to elude fatigue and cold, and how to avoid the blows. Primo was busy looking for bread, patching his shoes, stealing a broom, or interpreting the signs and faces around him.[13] Yet, these moments of reprieve were mixed with moments of humanity which gave Primo Levi and other inmates the strength to survive, like writing a letter for a gypsy to his beloved girlfriend for the price of a piece of bread.

Auschwitz was the largest ingathering of souls. Jews with a multitude of backgrounds from the extreme political Right to the extreme political Left, and totally assimilated individuals, met people of other nationalities, religions, cultures, and political views. Primo Levi, like other inmates, was exposed to them and learned much in Auschwitz-Monowitz about his own culture as well as others'.

During a storm, on an important day in his personal calendar, his twenty-fifth birthday, he entered a pipe with another inmate named Tischler. It was also Tischler's twenty-fifth birthday. Tischler told Levi that this made them twins and it called for a special observance since most likely they would not celebrate their next birthday. He shared with him an apple. In the pipe opposite them a woman took refuge, a Ukrainian belonging to the Todt Organization. Tischler saw Lilith, the she-devil, in the woman's posture and body language. Primo Levi never heard about Adam and Lilith and received a lesson in the Bible and mysticism. In Auschwitz, Tischler died while Primo Levi survived.

> It is inexplicable that fate has chosen an unbeliever to repeat this pious and impious tale, woven of poetry, ignorance, daring acumen, and the unassaugeable sadness that grows on the ruins of lost civilizations.[14]

Although Primo Levi learned much in Auschwitz about spiritual time, it did not alter his concept of time. Once, in a difficult moment of life and death, he almost succumbed to spiritual time, but intellectually was able to overcome it.

> Like Amery, I too entered the Lager as a nonbeliever, and as a nonbeliever I was liberated and have lived to this day. Actually, the experience of the Lager with its frightful iniquity confirmed me in my non-belief. It prevented, and still prevents me from conceiving of any form of providence of transcendent justice: Why were the moribund packed in cattle cars? Why were the children sent to the gas? I must nevertheless admit that I experienced (and again only once) the temptation to yield, to seek refuge in prayer. This happened in October 1944, in the one mo-

> ment in which I lucidly perceived the imminence of death: when, naked and compressed among my naked companions with my personal index card in hand, I was waiting to file past the "commission" that with one glance would decide whether I should go immediately into the gas chamber or was instead strong enough to go on working. For one instant I felt the need to ask for help and asylum; then, despite my anguish, equanimity prevailed: one does not change the rules of the game at the end of the match, not when you are losing. A prayer under these conditions would have been not only absurd (what rights could I claim? and from whom?) but blasphemous, obscene, laden with the greatest impiety of which a nonbeliever is capable. I rejected that temptation: I knew that otherwise, were I to survive, I would have to be ashamed of it.
>
> Not only during the crucial moments of the selection or aerial bombings but also in the grind of everyday life, the believers lived better: both Amery and I observed this. It was completely unimportant what their religious or political faith might be. Catholic or Reformed priests, rabbis of various orthodoxies, militant Zionists, naive or sophisticated Marxists, and Jehovah's Witnesses—all held in common the saving force of their faith. Their universe was vaster than ours, more extended in space and time, above all more comprehensible: they had a key and a point of leverage, a millennial tomorrow so that there might be a sense to sacrificing themselves, a place in heaven or on earth where justice and compassion had won, or would win in a perhaps remote but certain future: Moscow, or the celestial or terrestrial Jerusalem.[15]

Levi attributes even his own survival to small causes, where spiritual time was meaningless.[16] They were the type of small causes which always had an impact on history. He survived due to being infected with scarlet fever. He remained in the infirmary while sixty thousand inmates went into the night on a deadly march. His best friend, Alberto, perished. Elie Wiesel survived this same deadly march.

After liberation, space, time, and language played a central role in the life and death of Primo Levi. Most Holocaust survivors who became Holocaust authors in the post-Holocaust era moved to new countries, built new lives, dramatically changed their pre-Holocaust social, religious, and political status, learned a new language in which their books are written, retained some of their traditional time and adopted new ones like Yom HaShoah, as well as the special national time of their new homelands. Space, language, and time were positive essential factors in building their new lives.

In sharp contrast to most survivors, in October 1945, Primo Levi returned to his house in Turin which he loved very much. He said, "I live in my house as I live in my skin."[17] The war spared much of his Italy and he picked up where he left off. He was reunited with his mother and sister and resumed his work as a chemist.

He married, had two children, a son and a daughter, and only when they reached the age of fifteen did he tell them about his Holocaust experiences; they cried bitterly.[18] He wrote in Italian about the Holocaust, unlike many Holocaust authors who had to learn a new language not only for daily life, but also for their literary work as well. He faced no major challenges in his post-Holocaust life.

In an interview with Philip Roth, while discussing family, home, and factories as good things in themselves, Primo Levi replied that "they deprived me of something that I still miss: adventure."[19] Indeed, the lives of other Holocaust authors were more difficult, but definitely more challenging and adventurous as they rebuilt lives in new countries, and learned new languages and new cultures. Primo Levi, since his return to Turin, was always struck by an eerie sameness between pre and post Holocaust Italy, including his family and his work as a chemist. The only adventurous element in his life was the indelible time he spent in Auschwitz. Levi himself was amazed at how decades later he could still remember every smell, every feeling, every conversation verbatim, even in languages he had never heard before. He said that after his return, he felt almost an incessant compulsion to grab whoever was in Auschwitz, listen to him and recount his story.[20] He was always anxious to hear a new story, to bear witness and to write it in "four hands," with the individual who told the testimony to him.[21] All these were for the sake of the future, to assure that the lessons of the Holocaust will have a positive impact on universal time.

However, when he was asked to be a witness at the Eichmann Trial and to testify about the Holocaust from an ethical and moral perspective, he declined the request and never discussed the issue.[22] Primo Levi saw Israel as his second homeland, so his refusal to testify probably was not a political one, but rather one associated with time.[23] Primo Levi wanted total control of time regarding his Holocaust experience. He travelled with students to Auschwitz, gave talks to local schools, answered all of his mail about his experiences during the Holocaust, made himself available to scholars and journalists, and discussed his experiences with photographers. One such photographer was Jerry Bauer, whom both of us have met. Levi always hoped to bring a universal humanistic message to all. When he visited America in 1985 to receive the Kenneth B. Smilen award, he gave a series of informal talks. He expected to have a wide audience representing American intellectuals and the literary community. He was greatly puzzled and disappointed that the audiences attending his lectures were entirely Jewish. He remarked that "I began to wonder if any goyim lived in America. I did not come across a single one of them."[24]

Like most former concentration camp and prison inmates, Primo Levi wanted total control of time, but he began to fear that he was losing control of it.[25] In February 1987, he entered a hospital for a prostate operation, sensing that this was the beginning of his end. He could not relinquish power over time to anyone or anything, not even surgery. Prior to the operation, all that he could see was his Auschwitz number tattooed on his arm. Unlike survivors with traditional backgrounds who see in their numbers a promise to survive and other positive time related elements, Primo Levi saw nothing except perhaps the Auschwitz identity from where he came, and where he was to return, i.e., death.[26]

On April 11, 1987, a Saturday, Primo Levi hurled himself down the central stairway of his house he was born in and loved. He followed in the footsteps of Paul Celan,

Hans Mayer, alias Jean Améry, and other European Holocaust authors. There was no buffer between them and the Holocaust, no buffer of language, space, or time. They wrote about the Holocaust in the same language in which they experienced it, lived in the same spaces in Europe (Primo Levi even in the same house!) and had no control of the universal—humanistic time element to which they aspired. Finally, they had no relationship to their historical Jewish, national, or personal time.

Primo Levi chose a brutal death as if in Auschwitz, where and when the only control the inmates could have was the time of their death, the end to their miserable lives. Primo Levi made sure that he completed his cycle of life in the Auschwitz tradition. As a prominent chemist, who even knew how to use chicken manure to enhance lipstick, he could have chosen a peaceful, more respectable death. But he probably felt that this would not fit the Auschwitz time and style of death. Primo Levi wrote about the death of his Christian friend, Lorenzo, who worked in Auschwitz and helped him to survive:

> He [Lorenzo] fell ill, and thanks to some physician friends of mine I was able to get him into a hospital, but they gave him no wine and he ran away. He was assured and coherent in his rejection of life. He was found nearly dead a few days later, and died in the hospital alone. He, who was not a survivor, had died of the survivor's disease.[27]

According to Primo Levi the disease was rejection of life and total control of one's own time of death.

Baudelaire tells the story of a man who stopped his carriage, declaring that he wanted to fire a few shots into space merely to kill time. "To kill that particular monster," the poet writes, "is the most ordinary and legitimate occupation of each person."

Primo Levi succumbed to the power of Auschwitz time, for an Auschwitz inmate is not an ordinary man who could defend and kill the monster of time. Levi made his life and death decision. He controlled the time of the gun.

Notes

1. Yaffa Eliach, *Hasidic Tales of the Holocaust* (New York: Oxford University Press, 1982), p. xxix.
2. Viktor Frankl, recalling his wife's twenty-fourth birthday in Auschwitz, illustrates this point. Viktor Frankl, *Man's Search for Meaning* (New York, 1972), p. 67.
3. Yaffa Eliach, *Hasidic Tales of the Holocaust*, pp. 13–15, 16–19, 42, 43, 155–159, and Yaffa Eliach, "Jewish Tradition in the Life of the Concentration Camp Inmate" in *The Nazi Concentration Camps* Jerusalem: Yad Vashem, 1984, pp. 195–206.
4. Joseph B. Soloveichik, "Kodesh and Chol," *Gesher*, Vol. III, No. 1 (New York: June 1966) p. 16.
5. Primo Levi's statement at a BBC interview, quoted in Avi Lan, "Ulai Pashut Nafal," *Shavuon 7 Yamin*, Yediot Ahronot, November 27, 1987.
6. James Atlas, "The Survivor's Suicide," *Vanity Fair*, January 1988, p. 78.
7. Avi Lan, "Ulai Pashut Nafal" p. 34 op. cit.
8. Primo Levi, *If Not Now, When?*, p. 79.
9. Primo Levi, *If Not Now, When?* (New York: Summit Books, 1985), pp. 19–20.
10. Primo Levi, *If Not Now, When?* pp. 227–228.
11. Ibid., p. 225.
12. Ibid., pp. 168–169.
13. Primo Levi, *The Drowned and the Saved* (New York: Vintage International, 1989), p. 148.
14. Primo Levi, *Moments of Reprieve* (New York: Penguin Books, 1995), p. 25.
15. Primo Levi, *The Drowned and the Saved*, pp. 145–146.
16. Primo Levi, *Moments of Reprieve,* pp. 75–80.
17. James Atlas, "The Survivors Suicide," p. 79 op. cit.
18. Avi Lan, "Ulai Pashut Nafal", p. 34 op. cit.
19. James Atlas, "The Survivors Suicide, p. 79 op. cit.
20. An Introduction, Primo Levi, "Shame," *Esquire*, January 1988, p. 99.
21. Avi Lan, "Ulai Pashut Nafal," p. 34 op.cit.
22. The letter of invitation to testify at the Eichmann Trial was found in his archive. Afi Lan, "Ulai Pashut Nafal," p. 34 op. cit.
23. Ibid., p. 34.
24. James Atlas, "The Survivors Suicide," p. 82 op. cit.

25. On the place of time in the life of a prisoner see Roger Cohen, "Ways of Doing Time." *The New York Times Book Review*, May 4, 1997.
26. Yaffa Eliach, *Hasidic Tales of the Holocaust*, pp. 68–69.
27. Primo Levi, *Moments of Reprieve*, p. 118.

3

The Rhetoric of the *Univers Concentrationnaire*

Risa Sodi

> *there is in my heart as it were a burning fire*
> *shut up in my bones,*
> *and I am weary with holding it in,*
> *and I cannot.*
>
> —Jeremiah 20:9

Over time, Primo Levi has come to represent the entirety of Italian Holocaust writing—and more. Much as Elie Wiesel is recognized today as both a superlative writer and an actor on the world stage, so Primo Levi has assumed a role that goes well beyond the realm of literature. He, like Wiesel, has come to assume the antonomastic mantle of "survivor" and is increasingly invoked as a "watchman" of Holocaust memory. Such is the international esteem for him that his works are excerpted in virtually every recent anthology of Holocaust writing, and his extraordinary success in America is, according to Alexander Stille, "one of the most interesting American cultural phenomena in recent memory" (203). Today, his fame is meta-literary, springing from the solid foundation of his works but equally tied to an increased interest in the Holocaust and, perhaps, to the mysterious circumstances of his death in 1987.

Nonetheless, for all the serious attention surrounding Levi's belated entry into the mainstream of Italian letters and the fanfare surrounding his North American debut, only a handful of scholars have looked beyond Levi's commanding and captivating views on moral and ethical issues to focus on the ways in which Levi communicated these views. Foremost among them is Pier Vincenzo Mengaldo. His exhaustive eighty-page introduction to the third volume of Levi's *Opere* is a masterful compendium of the rhetorical, literary and stylistic devices used by Levi, and confirms many of the claims of this study. Other critics who have looked carefully at linguistic structures in Levi are Gian Paolo Biasin, Cesare Cases, Adam Epstein, Sander Gilman, Fabio Girelli-Carasi, and Gabriele Motola.[1] Though of superior quality, these studies pale beside the dozens, if not hundreds, of articles, essays and commentaries on thematic issues published until now. One consequence is that Levi has been denied the sort of bare bones literary and linguistic analysis he merits as an author—the sort of analysis routinely accorded his distinguished contemporaries or even fledgling writers whose bookshelves are but a fraction of his.

There are several possible reasons for such puzzling neglect by literary critics, starting with the perception that Levi was an amateur writer and therefore not subject to rigorous literary analysis—a perception that was encouraged by the author himself. Indeed, many critics took their clue from Levi's own words and disregarded the literary underpinnings of his work, focusing primarily on his message, his testimony and, in large measure, his biography. They seemed willing to overlook the causal relationship between the framing of the message and the reader's reception of the same. In an age when literary theory often privileges the critic's discernment over the author's original intent, it is baffling that so few sought to challenge what amounts to Levi's disingenuous demurral. Other reasons for this neglect, as JoAnn Cannon notes, stem from both the slow maturing of the field of Holocaust studies and from a greater critical fascination with the neo-avant-garde and "Gruppo 63" writers, (31–2).

By means of partial remedy, this study will focus on Levi's Holocaust writing and, in particular, *Se questo è un uomo*. It will consider three key devices in Levi's stylistic armamentarium: the use of apologies and disclaimers; the incorporation of the languages of the Holocaust into Italian; and the emergence of an incursive present tense (what Lawrence Langer calls "durational time").[2] Lastly, in the interests of critical rigor and as an antidote to current impulses toward hagiography, it will also explore some of the flaws in his Holocaust writing.

When Levi penned his Auschwitz memoir in 1946, one of his first acts was to apologize to his readers for the flaws in his account: "Mi rendo conto e chiedo venia dei difetti strutturali del libro," (3) ("I recognize, and ask indulgence for, the structural defects of the book," [9]). In fact, this type of initial apology became a fixture of Levi's non-fiction: it resurfaced in *La ricerca delle radici*:

> Poiché dispongo di input ibridi, ho accettato volentieri e con curiosità la proposta di comporre anch'io un "antologia personale." . . . Volentieri, dunque, ma con qualche riserva e qualche tristezza . . . Forse, leggendo, mi sono inconsapevolmente preparato a scrivere, così come il feto di otto mesi sta nell'acqua ma si prepara a respirare (vii–viii);
>
> Since I have hybrid inputs at my disposal, I gladly, and with some curiosity, accepted the proposal that I, too, compose a "personal anthology." This gladly, but with some reservations and some sadness . . . Perhaps, by reading, I was unconsciously preparing myself to write, just as an eight-month-old fetus is suspended in water but is preparing himself to breathe;

in *L' altrui mestiere* ("Il mio destino, aiutato dalle mie scelte, mi ha tenuto lontano dagli assembramenti: troppo chimico, e chimico per troppo tempo, per sentirmi un autentico uomo di lettere," v ["My destiny, helped along by my choices, has kept me far from the throng: too much a chemist, and a chemist for too long, for me to feel like I was an authentic man of letters," 9]); and in *I sommersi e i salvati* ("Un'apologia è d'obbligo," 23 ["an apology is in order," 34]). Remarkably, Levi was taken at his word and his gambit was indeed successful—in fact, perhaps too successful for his reputation as a writer.

In *Se questo è un uomo*, this initial apology is followed by a singularly arresting phrase. Levi states in his famously understated prose, "Mi pare superfluo aggiungere che nessuno dei fatti è inventato," ("It seems to me unnecessary to add that none of the facts were invented," 10). Similar disclaimers are scattered throughout Holocaust fiction (for example, in Jean François Steiner's *Treblinka* or Thomas Keneally's *Schindler's List*, both of which try to adhere closely to the facts of the Holocaust). But they are far more frequent in works of documentary literature, like Levi's. Indeed, disclaimers recur throughout *Se questo è un uomo.*[3] If on the one hand they represent an awkward attempt at *captatio benevolentiae*, on the other they tellingly capture the Holocaust survivor's very real fear of not being believed.[4]

This first disclaimer, embedded in the author's preface and, therefore, part of the "extraliterary" apparatus of the book, is terse, direct, but also vaguely belligerent. Why "superfluo"? Why such an offhand tone to drill home a crucial point: namely, that what follows are facts, incontrovertible, undeniable, and indisputable? Is it, indeed, necessary to underscore the facticity of *Se questo è un uomo*? And why does Levi, an eyewitness to events occurring just a short time earlier, seek to anticipate the objections—and potential denials—of his readers?

An answer to the question of tone can be found in the preface itself, when Levi categorizes the Holocaust phenomenon as "the disturbing question" ("l'inquietante argomento") about which *Se questo è un uomo* will "furnish documents for a quiet study of certain aspects of the human mind" rather than "formulate new accusations" (9), ("Esso non è stato scritto allo scopo di formulare nuovi capi di accusa; potrà piuttosto fornire documenti per uno studio pacato di alcuni aspetti dell'animo umano," 3). This is not to say that accusations are absent from *Se questo è un uomo* or his other works. On the contrary, they abound, especially in *I sommersi e i salvati* and in certain poems (one thinks in particular of "Buna," "Un altro lunedì" and "La bambina di Pompei"). Moreover, his accusations take both the form of "quiet study" (as in "A giudizio") or strident outrage (as in "Per Adolf Eichmann"). A resolute accusation was also slipped into *Se questo è un uomo* despite Levi's words to the contrary. It bursts off the page in Levi's marvelous, contorted, and brutal paraphrase of Deuteronomy, the 1946 poem "Shemà" ("listen!" in Hebrew), the only lyric in this prose work and the recipient and repository of his burning wrath.

As to why Levi felt a need to anticipate possible objections, the answer can be found both in the historical record (historians Yehuda Bauer and John Conway attest to the disbelief that met the first reports of mass exterminations in the Nazi Lagers), and in Levi's own assertions that for weeks after their arrival, even the prisoners in Auschwitz themselves, Levi included, were often unaware of and loath to believe the reason for the giant smokestacks that dominated the camp skyline (22–3; 48–9). Indeed, the same initial ignorance followed by grim resignation is registered in the superlative Italian Holocaust memoirs by Liana Millu, Bruno Piazza and Giuliana Tedeschi.

Thus, if by their silence, many critics seem to have taken Levi's recurrent disclaimers as an opening ploy strategically inserted to absolve the author of literary responsibility, they were led astray by the author himself and by prevalent popular views. Now, however, with the full weight of Levi's opus on our side and informed by current critical studies of Holocaust literature, this regularly repeated device should be read as an indication of Levi's full, albeit still inchoate, awareness that the very act of writing inevitably infuses even the most sincere documentary testimony with components of the imaginative enterprise. This is a problem that Holocaust theorists like Lawrence Langer, Geoffrey Hartman and Sidra Ezrahi have grappled with, and one that has also dogged other survivor-authors. Levi's friend, Giuliana Tedeschi, for example, author of *C'è un punto sulla terra . . . Una donna nel lager di Birkenau*, cautions, "È meglio . . . non mescolare la letteratura con la realtà di testimonianza." In fact, she insists: "si dovrebbe completamente dividere l'esperienza letteraria e l'esperienza [dei sopravvissuti], che è un'altra. Secondo me, sono assolutamente diverse, talmente da non studiare insieme" ("It is better . . . not to mix literature with the reality of testimony. The literary experience must be separated completely from the [survivors'] experience, which is different altogether. In my opinion, they are so absolutely dissimilar as to not be studied together.").[5]

Tedeschi's trepidation over acknowledging a literary "gray zone"—a perilous morass spanning and blurring the boundaries between fact and fiction—springs from a psychological phenomenon common to Holocaust survivors: the terrible and ineradicable schism in their world, the powerful division between "inside" and "outside."[6] Levi and his fellow prisoners felt they had been let into a world that was beyond the ken of their fellow man. The very incogitability of the Auschwitz experience led Levi, the quiet investigator, to gainsay his own experience as an inmate. In perhaps the strongest disclaimer in his memoir, he writes, "Oggi, questo vero oggi in cui io sto seduto a un tavolo e scrivo, io stesso non sono convinto che queste cose sono realmente accadute," (106) ("Today, at this very moment as I sit writing at a table, I myself am not convinced that these things really happened," [103]). Not only could the Holocaust experience not be imagined or explained, it could hardly be believed, sometimes even by the survivors themselves. This presents a special problem for writers of Holocaust memoirs. Not only must they contend with the issue of credibility, but also with the problem of how to make their tales understood. This task is further complicated by postmodern interpretations of literature, what Paul Ricoeur calls the "hermeneutics of suspicion." The use of disclaimers—a hallmark of Levi's Holocaust non-fiction—then fulfills two important functions. First, it allows Levi to check his own disbelief, thereby establishing a compact of trust with his readers. Second, by admitting his own incredulity, he is able to overcome his readers' potential doubt.

Part and parcel of this authorial stratagem is Levi's disavowal of metaphor, either a metaphor that would "explain" Auschwitz, or the deployment of Auschwitz itself as a metaphor to explain human nature. He comes closest to the first stance in his many references to Dante's *Inferno*,[7] but this must be seen as a heuristic device intended to initiate the reader into the *univers concentrationnaire*[8] and not an overarching metaphor intended to define Levi's Holocaust experience. By contrast, the second approach is eschewed entirely. Wiesel says, "If it is a novel, it is not about Auschwitz, and if it is about Auschwitz, it is not a novel" (paraphrased in Hilberg [23]). Auschwitz, in Levi's non-fiction, is never anything but a *Vernichtungslager*.

How, then, to appease the critics, appeal to the reader and maintain the integrity of the discourse? Throughout time, tale-tellers have made recourse to myth and fable to circumvent the strictures of fact while seeking a truth with even more human resonance than realism. Yet the testimonial imperative of the Holocaust survivor often precludes the creation of a myth or metaphor. Their primary concern is veracity, not universality. Documentary writers like Levi and Piazza repudiate the mythical through their use of disclaimers and their efforts to hew to the objective. Likewise, they betray a degree of apprehensiveness that turning to the imagination might cast doubts on the facts or "reality" of their experience. Survivor-authors, especially those who emerged directly from the concentration camps (like Levi, Millu, Wiesel or Charlotte Delbo) often eschew any but the thinnest veneer of fictionality in their documentary works. And interestingly, these documentary works are invariably the first books written upon liberation—indeed in the cases of the four authors just mentioned, all of whom later went on to write fiction.

Nonetheless, throughout his memoir Levi veers inescapably toward the side of simile, metaphor, apostrophe and embellishment: in other words, toward all the accouterments of the literary enterprise. One could argue persuasively that, in spite of Levi's apprehension, it is the very literary underpinning of his book, combined with its probing meditations, and Levi's privileged position as witness, that over the years have made *Se questo è un uomo* the classic it is today. Levi possessed the uncommon ability to express atrocity in exquisite prose. When he writes of a "vortice di truci nubi sanguigne," "nembi di polvere fetida," "una fretta animalesca di perfonderci le viscere con l'intruglio caldo," "dolci cose ferocemente lontane," "una marea di bislacche parole magiare," or "la turba di nudi spaventati," he is penetrating the reader's psyche at two levels: the music and rhythm of unexpected expression spur us to keep reading, while the meaning of his phrases penetrate and sear our consciousness.

Levi rails at the inadequacy of language to express such simple concepts as "hunger," "tiredness," "fear," "pain," and "winter."[9] "Sono parole libere," he says, "create e usate da uomini liberi che vivevano, godendo e soffrendo, nelle loro case. Se i Lager fossero durati più a lungo, un nuovo aspro linguaggio sarebbe nato," (127) ("They are free words, created and used by free men who lived in comfort and suffering in their homes. If the Lagers had lasted longer a new, harsh language would have been born," 123). (He later expanded on these reflections in the "Comunicare" chapter of *I sommersi e i salvati*.) The paramount example of this "new, harsh language" is the hybrid Latin-Polish word, *selekcja* (to be "selected" was to be marked for death, "selections" being overseen by the infamous Dr. Mengele). *Selekcja* was a word, Levi says, "che si impone all'attenzione, infine ci perseguita," (127) ("forces itself on [the inmates'] attention, and in the end persecutes [us]," [124]). The dominant Holocaust lexemes of Yiddish, Hungarian, Czech, Polish and Slovak surrounded the Italian inmates; the German of Goethe and Gatterman, so dear to Levi in his youth, had been replaced by the *Lagerdeutsch* of the camps. *Zugang, Muselmann, Häftling, Stücke, Krankenbau, Kapo, Blockältester, Schmutzstück* and *Ka-Zet*; the unpronounceable names of the Nazi camps where Italians were imprisoned; the legion of acrostics of the Third Reich; the branches of the German police state: many of these terms work their way into his memoir. Levi's unusual openness to these mongrel locutions in his writing, combined with his adherence to the classical mechanisms of Italian expression, give *Se questo è un uomo* much of its impact. It proved an effective device for translating the brutality of the camp into Italian—a language better known for its *dolce stil nuovo* than its *rime aspre*. At the same time, it can also be argued, as Gilman seems to suggest, that Levi's rich exogenous vocabulary was an attempt to wick away linguistic culpability from

Italian to the "foreign" languages of Auschwitz (German, Polish, etc.).[10]

Consonance is one of the most effective devices Levi uses in this regard. As the phrases quoted above show, he peppers his account with the long "u"s of German, the multiple consonants of the Slavic languages and the hard consonants so typical of the languages of the East. Thus Levi tries to make Italian reflect the linguistic phenomenon of camp life. Auschwitz, he seems to say, was spoken as well as endured.

By way of contrast, Levi uses the opposite device, incorporating soft assonances and rhythms to express pity or approval. When describing the meticulous mourning ritual of a family of Libyan Jews on the eve of deportation, Levi says, "Allora si scalzarono, si sciolsero i capelli, e disposero al suolo le candele funebri, e le accesero secondo il costume dei padri, e sedettero a terra a cerchio per la lamentazione, e tutta notte pregarono e piansero," (8) ("they unloosened their hair, took off their shoes, placed the Yahrzeit candles on the ground and lit them according to the customs of their ancestors and sat on the bare soil in a circle for the lamentations, praying and weeping all the night," (16). Not only does he make repeated use of the soft sibilant tones of the "s," especially in the first part of the sentence, but he insists on the lulling rhythm of proparoxytone nouns and adjectives ("cerchio" and "funebri") and *passato remoto* verb forms ("si scalzarono," "si sciolsero," "disposero," accesero," "sedettero," "pregarono," and "piansero").

The brutality of the camps is underlined in Levi's prose by liberal use of juxtapositions contrasting expressions of human compassion and the harsh language of the camps. Again, the touching episode of the Libyan Jews can serve as an example. Levi writes with Dantesque *reticientia*, "Molte cose furono allora fra noi dette e fatte; ma di queste è bene che non resti memoria," (9) ("Many things were then said and done among us; but of these it is better that there remain no memory," 16). One can just imagine the tender and mournful words exchanged that night, or the acts committed out of love and desperation. In this mood, the fierce and scornful words which in the morning greet the inmates ring out equally as an indictment of the Nazis' inhumanity and as an example of the inhumanity they tried to foist on their captives: "Wieviel Stück?," a Nazi marshal asks his aide. Six hundred and fifty, comes the reply: six hundred and fifty "pieces."

Another stylistic ploy of Levi's, and the third I will look at here, is to conflate and confuse verb tenses, consciously shifting between present and past and thus inexorably ushering the reader into the interminate present of the barbed-wire kingdom. *Se questo è un uomo* opens with the words, "Ero stato catturato dalla Milizia fascista il 13 dicembre 1943": "I had been captured by the Fascist militia on December 13, 1943."[11] This use of the past perfect brings the reader back to a time before the schism, an impossibly distant time—just three years earlier. Levi continues, abruptly switching from the past perfect to the *passato remoto*: "Tre centurie della Milizia . . . irruppero in una spettrale alba di neve nel nostro rifugio, e mi condussero a valle come persona sospetta," (5–6). This is the beginning of his voyage "to the bottom" (recounted in the homonymic chapter "Sul fondo"), his initiation into the Nazi maelstrom that culminated with his imprisonment in Auschwitz. "Sul fondo" further illustrates the nexus between form and content—or, more appropriately, between form and purpose. In Levi's grammatology, the present tense conveys the interminate past events of Auschwitz, and the past tenses refer merely to the mechanical, habitual actions of everyday life.[12] Levi calls this "la voluta confusione dei tempi verbali" ("the deliberate confusion of verb tenses") in the annotated edition of his memoir (Levi 1986, 30) and, according to Mengaldo, it is the "most characteristic stylistic phenomenon of *Se questo è un uomo*" (xli).[13] The following passage upends the standard temporal *consecutio* and presents us with the inmates' voyage "all'ingiù" ("downward"). Thus, the succession of verb tenses—*passato remoto*, present perfect, present—takes us on a reverse Orphic voyage, from the free man's finite past to the pervasive Holocaust present:

> Il viaggio non *durò* che una ventina di minuti. Poi l'autocarro *si è fermato, e si è visto* una grande porta, e sopra una scritta vivamente illuminata (il suo ricordo ancora *mi*

> *percuote* nei sogni): ARBEIT MACHT FREI, il lavoro *rende* liberi . . . Questo è l'inferno (emphasis added). (15)
>
> (The journey [from Auschwitz I to Buna] did not last more than twenty minutes. Then the lorry stopped, and we saw a large door, and above it a sign, brightly illuminated (its memory still strikes me in my dreams): Arbeit Macht Frei, work gives freedom. . . . This is hell. (22).

Indeed, for the rest of the book, Levi turns to the *passato remoto* to describe the ordinary workings of the *univers concentrationnaire*, the interrogations, transports, leave-takings, work details, food service, sicknesses, and burials.[13] They are all part of a ritual, Levi seems to say, an indecipherable *danse macabre* wherein the inmates followed a scenario without understanding it or internalizing it.

What did endure and was internalized, however, was a strange awareness born of the Lager and loath to die off at liberation. As French survivor Charlotte Delbo replied to a interviewer's question, "Do you live with Auschwitz?" "No," she said, "I live beside it" (qtd. in Langer, *Holocaust Testimonies*, 5). Levi brilliantly conveys this unrelentingly incursive past through the use of an iterative present tense—his own special grammar of the Holocaust. Thus, the nagging question posed in the title of his book—*Is this a man?*—can only be asked and answered in the present because it strikes at the heart of man at Auschwitz yet does not shrink from extending its reach to all humankind. This concept was succinctly encapsulated in the title of a 1988 Turin conference on Levi: "Il presente del passato" (The Present of the Past). It is reflected in Millu's recent comments about her presentations on the Holocaust to Italian school children: "Inizio sempre nello stesso modo. Io mi presento dicendo, 'Sono il numero A5384,' e dico, 'Sono . . .' e sbaglio perché parlando di cinquant'anni fa dovrei dire, 'Sono stata . . .' Invece dico, 'Sono . . .' perché chi è stato cinquant'anni fa rimane così anche oggi" ("I always begin the same way. I introduce myself by saying, 'I am number A5384.' I say, 'I am . . .' and I am wrong because if I am talking about fifty years ago I should say, 'I was . . .' Instead, I say, 'I am . . .' because we who 'were' fifty years ago remain the same even today"). And it also has echoes throughout Holocaust literature, most notably in Jorge Semprun's 1963 novel, *The Long Voyage*, written exclusively in the present tense though set in a Nazi Lager.

A corollary question must be, what, then, of Levi's use of the future tense? Or, to put it another way, what was the inmate's outlook on the future? One can begin to answer by noting that, if anything, Levi's *Häftlinge* see at best a *futuro remoto*, a future so implausible as to take Levi's breath away when he contemplates returning to his beloved mountains outside Turin (in "Il Canto di Ulisse"). But more often, the "future" merely meant the promise of the next meal, the chance to survive the next work detail, the next blow from the Kapo, the next visit to the Ka-Be, the next selection. The lives of the Jewish inmates were measured in terms of the amount of work they could perform before being murdered, from exhaustion or by gas; the inmates themselves measured their lives in minutes, for death could come that quickly. When the morning transport trucks with the day's soup rumble by, Levi knows it must be nearly ten o'clock. Ten o'clock means that noon cannot be far away. Noon means he will eat. Yet Levi tells us that even that handful of minutes are hidden by "la nebbia del futuro remoto," (67) ("the fog of the remote future," 69). In Auschwitz, a glance to the future rarely penetrated all the way to liberation; only the *Zugänge*—the new arrivals—talked of returning home or gave credence to reports that the war would soon end. Most—the *anziani*, like Levi—instead gave credence to retorts like that of the Ka-Be nurse who cynically told Levi, "Du Jude kaputt. Du schnell Krematorium fertig," (45). Would they ever return home? In a cruel play on the deeply moving words of the Passover liturgy, one Jewish inmate blackly calls out to Levi, "L'anneé prochaine à la maison! . . . à la maison par le Cheminée!," (71).

Present and past were all that were available to the inmates: memories of their past lives, "velati e lontani, e perciò profondamente dolci e tristi," (146) ("veiled and distant, and therefore profoundly sweet and sad," 116), and the present, "il nostro mondo di fango," (147) ("our world of mud," 116). The future meant hope, and hope was inaccessible, even dangerous, to them. No one, Levi states elsewhere, can seriously think of the future. "Sapete come si dice 'mai' nel gergo del campo? Morgen früh, domani mattina," (138) ("Do you know how one says 'never' in camp slang? 'Morgen früh,' tomorrow morning," 133).[15]

Until now, this study has looked at three main hallmarks of Levi's Holocaust writing: his use of apologies and disclaimers; his incorporation of the languages of the Holocaust; and the emergence of an incursive present tense. Two additional narrative strategies must be mentioned, if only in passing. A striking one was noted by Biasin in the title of his paper, "Our Daily Bread-Brot-Broid-Chleb-Pain-Lechem-Keynér": that is, Levi's proclivity for lists—a technique which, in the *volgare*, is at least as old as Petrarch's "Non Tesin, Po, Varo, Arno, Adige e Tebro." Sometimes, these lists take the form of long, symmetrical passages where the entire construction is dependent on a single word, as in the following example (controlled by "bisogna," one has to):

> Bisogna risalire la corrente; dare battaglia ogni giorno e ogni ora alla fatica, alla fame, al freddo, e alla inerzia che ne deriva; resistere ai nemici e non aver pietà per i rivali; aguzzare l'ingegno, indurare la pazienza, tendere la volontà. O anche, strozzare ogni dignità e spegnere ogni lume di coscienza, scendere in campo da bruti contro gli altri bruti, lasciarsi guidare dalle insospettate forze sotterranee che sorreggono le stirpi e gli individui nei tempo crudeli. (94).
>
> One has to fight against the current; to battle every day and every hour against exhaustion, hunger, cold and the resulting inertia; to resist enemies and have no pity for rivals; to sharpen one's wits, build up one's patience, strengthen one's will-power. Or else, to throttle all dignity and kill all conscience, to climb down into the arena as a beast against other beasts, to let oneself be guided by those unsuspected subterranean forces which sustain families and individuals in cruel times. (92)

or the three sentences in "Il viaggio" governed by "Vi si oppone," (9–10) ("The certainty of death opposes it," etc., 17).

Other times, lists appear in shorter forms, like "Ausrücken e Einrücken, uscire e rientrare; lavorare, dormire e mangiare; ammalarsi, guarire o morire," (30) (Ausrücken and Einrücken, go out and come in; work, sleep and eat; fall ill, get better or die," 36) or "questi ammirevoli, terribili ebrei Saloniki, tenaci, ladri, saggi, feroci e solidali," (70-1) ("those admirable and terrible Jews of Salonica, tenacious, thieving, wise, ferocious and united," 71). Other times still, they take the form of synonym series, used to best effect in the closing lines of "Il canto di Ulisse" ("Kraut und Rüben . . . Choux et navets. Kaposzta és répak") but also evident throughout, as in "I suoi mattoni sono stati chiamati Ziegel, briques, tegula, cegli, kamenny, mattoni, téglak . . ," (72) ("Its bricks were called Ziegel, briques, tegula, cegli, kamenny, mattoni, téglak . . ," 72–3), or the line quoted by Biasin from the chapter "Iniziazione."[16]

Second, there is a wellspring of Jewish and Old Testament references peeking out from behind the even more numerous (and oft-studied) nods to Dante and the Christian tradition. Appropriately enough, the initial biblical reference in *Se questo è un uomo* is to the opening lines of Genesis. The first book of the Pentateuch states (in Italian),

> Elohim allora ordinò: "Vi sia luce." E vi fu luce. Quindi Elohim vide che era buona quella luce. Perciò Elohim separò la luce dalla tenebra. Ed Elohim diede nome alla luce "giorno" ed all tenebra diede nome "notte." Poi *venne sera*, poi venne mattina: un giorno (emphasis added).

Levi describes the obverse process: not the explosion of light into the world, nor the separation of light from darkness, nor the first day of creation, but the last night before the long trip to Auschwitz, the descent into lightlessness, the day before annihilation. To underscore this retelling of what he calls elsewhere "una nuova Bibbia," (64) ("a new Bible," 66), Levi adopts the finality and solemnity of a biblical *passato remoto*: "E *venne la notte*, e fu una notte tale, che si conobbe che occhi umani non avrebbero dovuto assistervi e sopravvivere," (7) (emphasis added) ("And night came, and it was such a night that one knew that human eyes would not witness it and survive," 15).

Many are the other Jewish and Old Testament references, ranging from allusions to the five books of Moses ("ci discese nell'anima, nuovo per noi, il dolore antico del popolo che non ha terra, il dolore senza speranza dell'esodo ogni secolo rinnovato," [8] ["and we experienced within ourselves a grief that was new for us, the ancient grief of the people that has no land, the grief without hope of the exodus which is renewed every century," 16], or the "Torre del Carburo" ("Carbide Tower") renamed "Torre di Babele" ("Tower of Babel") (72; 72–3), to acknowledgements of anti-Semitism ("una rabbia vecchia di secoli," [12] ["a millennial anger, 19]), and an awareness of the multiform culture of non-Italian Jewry: Hasidism, kabbalah, Ashkenazim and haskalah (42–3, 66–7, 94–5 [47–8, 68, 92–3]). This sampling of embedded Judaica reflects a fascination with ancient Jewish texts which also found expression in *L'altrui mestiere* (with its excerpts from the Book of Job), *Lilít e altri racconti* (its title and, especially, the section "Passato prossimo"), and was to reach its apex in Levi's homage to East European *Yiddishkeit, Se non ora, quando*?[17]

These points of interest notwithstanding, it should also be mentioned that there are notable stylistic shortcomings to *Se questo è un uomo*. Cases, for example, notes a certain stilted "schoolboyishness" ("un residuo scolastico") in Levi's early writing, exemplified by his frequent use of the adverb "quivi" (Cases further posits "quivi" as a "hidden reference to Dante," especially to the Ulysses Canto [ix; xvii–xix]). Or one might note the haphazard shifts in person from "we" to "you," even at times including a sort of "royal we" ("Questa, di cui abbiamo detto e diremo . . ." or "Noi siamo infatti persuasi . . ." or "Noi non crediamo alla più ovvia e facile deduzione . . ."). The book also contains occasional repetitions and omissions, and the grossly disappointing contrast between the ringing Nietzschean title of "Al di qua del bene e del male" and that chapter's often petty concerns.[18]

Its biggest flaw, however, lies in its ending. An unfortunate consequence of Levi's plan to write in order of urgency is that the last chapter of the book, "Storia di dieci giorni," is nearly devoid of any sense of narrative drive. In today's movie-influenced jargon, one could almost call it a "prequel." It does little more than describe the circumstances of Levi's liberation and introduce us briefly to characters and personal situations that will play prominent roles in the "sequel," *La Tregua*.[19] The chapter is written in the form of a diary, with date headings setting apart the separate entries. Were it not for these headings, much of what happens therein would be a timeless blur, the action hardly being advanced by anything other than the annotation of the passing days.

Lillian Hellman, who, according to Paul Fussell in *The Great War and Modern Memory*, kept "copious and detailed diaries" during World War II in the hopes of registering important experiences, found upon reading them later that they did not include, in Hellman's words, "what had been most important to me, or what the passing years have made important," (311). Fussell concludes on the basis of Hellman's diaries and many other World War I diaries he examined that "the further personal written materials move from the form of the daily diary, the closer they approach the figurative and the fictional" (i.e., the more diffuse and universal their interest), (310). By contrast, it is this close hewing to the daily diary format that robs Levi's last chapter of the impact it could and should have. Indeed, in Levi's case, one could say that the closer *Se questo è un uomo* stays to the form of the daily diary, the farther it moves from consequential and compelling narrative.

The final paragraph of the book informs us of the fate of some of the inmates encountered in the chapter—characters who, with the exception of Charles, hardly compare in description and vividness to others encountered previously (one thinks, for example, of Alberto, Elias, Null Achtzehn Pikolo, or Steinlauf). In lieu of any sort of denouement, summation, insight, reflection or closure, *Se questo è un uomo* ends with a laconic round-up of the cast of characters. The memoir merely ceases its narrative when the author's pencil slips off the page and returns to his shirt pocket (and here my comments deliberately recall and contrast the conclusion of *Se questo è un uomo* with the masterful resolution of one of Levi's finest short stories, "Carbone," in *Il sistema periodico*).

Thus said, these shortcomings hardly mar the lustre of Levi's by-now sterling reputation. By advancing some objections, this study seeks to avoid hagiography and refocus attention on the literary artisan who began his career writing hurried notes on scraps of Buna lab paper and rose to become a writer of international prominence. Taken together, both his stylistic flaws and his stylistic virtues are the catalysts that make his writing a model of linguistic chemistry: measured, deliberate, yet not entirely predictable. After many years as the preeminent Italian Jewish writer, the premier Italian Holocaust writer, the embodiment of the Italian Holocaust survivor, it is time to make room for one more "Primo Levi": the literary stylist, the careful lexicographer, and the fine crafter of the modern phrase.

Notes

1. See Biasin, "Our Daily Bread-Pane-Brot-Broid-Chleb-Pain-Lechem-Kenyér"; Cases, "L'ordine delle cose e l'ordine delle parole"; Epstein, "Primo Levi and the Language of Atrocity"; Gilman, "The Special Language of the Camps and After"; Girelli-Carasi, "The Anti-Linguistic Nature of the Lager in the Language of Primo Levi's *Se questo è un uomo*"; and Motola, "Primo Levi: The Language of the Scientist." These papers, however, are more concerned with how Levi's concepts are revealed by language than with the language itself. Several recent books on Levi also contribute to the analysis of Levi the writer, including Nicholas Patruno's *Understanding Primo Levi* (Columbia, SC: University of South Carolina Press, 1995), Mirna Cicioni's *Primo Levi: Bridges of Knowledge* (Oxford-Washington, D.C.: Berg, 1995), and other recent studies by Belpoliti, Carasso, Ioli and Santagostino.
2. In Langer, "Legacy in Gray." *Primo Levi: Writer, Witness, and Holocaust Educator.* University of British Columbia and the Vancouver Holocaust Education Centre. 4 November 1995.
3. For example, when he is asked for his academic credentials during his examination for placement in the "Kommando Chimico," Levi replies, "Mi sono laureato a Torino nel 1941, summa cum laude—e, memtre lo dico, ho la precisa sensazione di non esser creduto, e a dire il vero non ci dredo io stesso . . ." p. 110. ("I took my degree at Turin in 1941, *summa cum laude*—and while I say

it I have the definite sensation of not being believed, of not even believing it myself," p. 106).

4. Levi himself was undoubtedly familiar with *captatio benevolentine* both as a rhetorical term and as a concept; in fact, he used it in *La tregua* in relation to one of that book's most colorful characters, Mordo Nathum, "un maestro, un'autorità, un super-greco." Levi comments, "Percepivo che la sua eloquenza, il suo fortunato sforzo di 'captatio benevolentiae' non muovevano soltanto da considerazioni di opportunità . . . ," *Opere* I: 248–49 ("a master, an authority, a super-Greek [. . .] I realized that his eloquence, his successful attempt at captatio benevolentiae, did not derive solely from opportunistic considerations . . . ," pp 211–12). For more on the credibility of the witness, see Giorgio Agamben, *Remnants of Auschwitz*, trans. Daniel Heller-Roazen (New York: Zone Books, 1999), especially 11–39.
5. Tedeschi, letter to the author, 29 April 1994, and personal interview, 26 February 1995.
6. See also Shoshana Felman and Dori Laub, *Testimony: Crises of Witnessing in Literature, Psychoanalysis and History* (New York and London: Routledge, 1992), especially 232ff.
7. See Sodi, *A Dante of Our Time: Primo Levi and Auschwitz.* See also Gunzberg, "Down Among the Dead Men: Levi and Dante in Hell" and "Nuotando altrimenti che nel Serchio': Dante as Vademecum for Primo Levi."
8. The phrase comes from the title of David Rousset's 1946 book, *L'univers concentrationnaire* (Paris: Editions du Pavois) and has become a commonplace in Holocaust studies. In *All Rivers Run to the Sea* (New York: Knopf, 1995), Wiesel adopts an alternative phrase, "the barbed-wire kingdom."
9. See also Charlotte Delbo, *Auschwitz and After*, trans. Rosette C. Lamont (New Haven, CT: Yale University Press, 1995).
10. In "The Special Language of the Camps and After," (in *Reason and Light: Essays on Primo Levi*, edited by Susan R. Tarrow, Cornell University, 1990) Gilman points to Levi's ambiguous relation to his native Italian, suggesting that Levi felt a need for it to be cleansed of culpability. Giovanni Tesio discusses the linguistic confusion in the Lagers in "Ritratti critici di contemporanei. Primo Levi" (*Belfagor* 34, 1979). Another explanation comes from Mengaldo, who holds that the use of foreign languages—part of what he calls Levi's "marmoreità linguistica" ("linguistic marbling")—derives from "a need to distance himself from a topic searingly close to his memories and feelings," *Opere*

III: ix. See also Cases xv, especially note 2, and Marco Coslovich, *I percorsi della sopravvivenza* (Milan: Mursia, 1994), 226–245.

11. Stuart Woolf translates "I *was* captured . . ." There are instances (some also cited by Girelli-Carasi in "The Anti-Linguistic Nature of the Lager in the Language of Primo Levi's Se questo e un uomo" in Tarrow, pp. 58–9) where Woolf's translation fails to capture the full or exact meaning of the Italian. A prime example comes in the concluding line of "Ottobre 1944," where Woolf translates Levi's "Se fossi Dio, sputerei a terra la preghiera di Kuhn" with "If I was God, I would spit at Kuhn's prayer."
12. Motola finds that Levi uses the present tense to describe the "actual reliving of a particular experience" and turns to the past tense in describing "a more general though no less terrifying communal experience" involving "objectification" and "historicity" ("Primo Levi: The Language of the Scientist," *The Literary Review*, Winter 1991). See also Biasin, p. 10.
13. Mengaldo offers two other possible explanations for Levi's iterative use of the present: 1) the book's origins in oral discourse (Levi repeatedly affirmed that it was preceded by many prior narrations of the book's events), and 2) the possibility of "subtly articulating the layers of the story," *Opere* III: xlii–xliii. Mengaldo also emphasizes 3) the effect created by repeated use of the present tense in "bringing into the present and dramatizing the events narrated," as if to suggest that "Auschwitz is not an experience that the author, or anyone, can assume to be exhausted, circumscribed by its own past tense . . . that present imperceptibility slips from historical to a chronological, to the eternal," xlii. Had Mengaldo expanded his theoretical research beyond philological-linguistic studies (such as Bertinetto's *Tempo, aspetto e azione nel verbo italiano: Il sistema dell'indicativo*, cited by Mengaldo in this regard) and also examined the role of the "historical present" and memory in Holocaust writings, as described by such theorists as Ezrahi or Young, he might not merely have placed this third explanation as one of a triad of possibilities but have emphasized its undoubtedly primary role in shaping the narrative and temporal structure of *Se questo è un uomo*.
14. Elsewhere, in his non-Holocaust works, Levi makes light of linguistic conventions, including use of the passato remoto. For example, in "Breve sogno" he writes that Riccardo, the protagonist, "si sarebbe fatto scuoiare prima, come del resto qualsiasi piemontese o lombardo si farebbe scuoiare vivo prima di usare

un passato remoto" (*Lilit e altri racconti*, pp. 244–5) ("he would rather have been skinned alive, like any Piedmontese or Lombard would rather have been skinned alive than use a passato remoto").

15. Levi later contrasts the Lager-bound conception of an unreachable future expressed in *Se questo è un uomo* with the "approximate value" of "tomorrow" in the Soviet Union, the site of many of the adventures recounted in *La tregua*: "in armonia con le abitudini russe, ["domani"] vale piuttosto 'un giorno fra i prossimi,' 'una volta o l'altra,' 'in un tempo non lontano': insomma, il rigore dell adeterminazione temporale vi è dolcemente sfumato," *Opere* I: 393 ("in harmony with Russian habits, ["tomorrow"] meant rather 'one of the following days,' 'sometime or other,' 'in the near future'; in short, the rigorous temporal determinant is softly blurred," p. 346). Mengaldo notes the underlying contrast between the "rigid and mortuary" Teutonic-Nazi order in the Lagers and the lively, anarchic disorder in the Russian DP camps, *Opere* III: lxxii. In a remarkably resonant passage which expands the context of abjection and hopelessness, Carlo Levi reports that southern Italian peasants use a variant of the Latin *cras*, "tomorrow"—"crai"—to mean "never" (*Christ Stopped at Eboli*, trans. Frances Frenaye. New York: Farrar, Straus and Giroux, 1974; 186, 209). Indeed, after "niente" ("nothing"), it is their most common word.
16. Lists are also evident in Levi's essays, as in the following example taken from an untranslated chapter of *L'altrui mestiere*, "Tradurre ed essere tradotti": "L'autore [di un'opera tradotta] che trova davanti a sé una sua pagina tradotta in una lingua che conosce si sente volta a volta, o a un tempo, lusingato, tradito, nobilitato, radiografato, castrato, piaillato, stuprato, adornato, uccisos," *Opere* I: 696 ("The author [of a translated work] who finds himself face-to-face with a page translated into a language he knows feels by turns, or all at once, flattered, betrayed, ennobled, x-rayed, castrated, flattened, raped, adorned, killed." Mengaldo offers additional examples from *Se questo è un uomo* and other works of Levi's (*Opere* III: xxxviii), noting that synonymy is common throughout Levi's opus.
17. In his introduction to the second volume of Levi's collected works, Cesare Segre points out other biblical, and specifically Old Testament, references: for example, the poem "Pasqua," set against the Big Bang; and the title of *Se non ora, quando?*, part of Hillel's famous question from the Talmudic *Pirké Avoth*

(*Opere* II: xxiv). To these references, one could also add the title and introduction to an excerpt from Ludwig Gatterman's 1939 chemistry text, *Die Praxis des Organiscen Chemikers*, in *La ricerca delle radici*, "Le parole del Padre" ("the sayings of the Father"), a paraphrase of the title *Pirké Avoth*.

18. See also Sodi, *The Holocaust in Italian Literature*. Diss. Yale University, 1995. Ann Arbor: University of Michigan, 1996, pp. 138–40.
19. It should be pointed out that at the time Levi wrote *Se questo è uomo*, he had no plans to write a subsequent memoir. *La tregua* was not written until 1962, and most likely would never have been written if *Se questo è un uomo* had not been reprinted by Einuadi in 1956 to critical acclaim. In addition, Levi himself considered those ten days his "finest hour," a judgment repeated by Jean Samuel, aka "Pikolo" ("Germaine Greer Talks to Primo Levi, *The Literary Review*, November 1985, 18; "The Memory of the Offense," BBC, 1992.)

Part II

Levi and Science

4

Primo Levi's Science as 'Evil Nurse': The Lesson of Inversion

Nancy Harrowitz

Primo Levi was not only a Holocaust survivor and writer whose book of memoirs, *Survival in Auschwitz*, is critically recognized as among the most powerful, moving and philosophical works treating the subject of the *univers concentrationnaire*. Levi was a scientist as well, trained as a chemist in Fascist Italy. He spent most of his professional life in this vocation, although he continued to write books of poetry, testimony and fiction. At a certain point, however, the exigencies of writing upstaged his long scientific career, and Levi retired from the practice of chemistry in order to devote himself full-time to the practice of writing.

In some of his essays, Levi has articulated the crossover between chemistry and writing, and it is a topic to which critical attention has been paid as well.[1] What has not been carefully examined is the relationship of Levi's scientific vocation to his philosophy about the Holocaust and his analysis, implicit or explicit, of the role that science played in that event and the role that science plays in a more general way in the construction of culture. An examination of the way in which he treats science as a topic in his writings, especially his fiction, will help articulate that philosophy and demonstrate the complex and difficult relationship that Levi had to his own discipline.[2]

Levi evokes the name, the theory and the practice of science in three distinct moments in his works. The first moment is to be found in *Survival in Auschwitz*, in which he recounts his experience as part of the chemical kommando in the concentration camp and credits his knowledge of chemistry and his knowledge of German as two crucial factors that helped him survive. The second, and perhaps most obvious, is to be found in *The Periodic Table*, which tells the story of his vocation as a chemist, set against the backdrop of Fascism in Italy, the anti-Semitic racial laws, and the period immediately following the Holocaust, in which he re-established his professional and personal life. The text can well be described as an autobiography of his life as a chemist, yet we also learn of his reactions to Fascist persecution of the Jews, to the early years of the war, and to his own identity as a Jew in Italy. Levi describes his text in the following way: "the book goes beyond simple autobiography. Rather, it contains the story of a generation [. . .] the chapters entitled Argon, Zinc and Gold [. . .] refer to the situations and events preceding my deportation, and reflect my condition as a Jew in Mussolini's Italy: assimilated and integrated, but not Fascist. Argon is a gas which does not interact with other gases."[3]

In *The Periodic Table*, elements of this table function as catalysts for recalling historical moments in the author's life, often serving as metaphors for specific experiences. Science is thus both an organizing principle, and a way to experience history. Ruth Angress has said about *The Periodic Table* that there are chapters which are "Holocaust-related."[4] The episodes are historically linked to the Holocaust because of events in Levi's life. Only in a peripheral fashion does the text take on the larger questions of what science meant to the Holocaust, and what the Holocaust has meant to science. The space which fiction allows gives Levi more play when it comes to a harder look at science and scientific ethics. Levi's own words on fiction writing substantiates this point:

> Writing about things seen is easier than inventing, and less joyful. It is writing-describing: you have a trail, you dig into your close or distant memories, put the speci-

> mens in order (if you have a talent for it), catalog them [. . .] you can ennoble the things you portray, or report them in an impersonal, modest and honest manner, or on the contrary give them a distorted, flat, unfocused, off-center, under or overexposed image, but in every case you are guided, held by the hand by the facts, you have ground under your feet. Writing a novel is different, it is superwriting: you are no longer on the ground, you fly [. . .] the first sensation, destined to be reduced later on to smaller dimensions, is one of unlimited, almost licentious freedom.[5]

These remarks, which Levi wrote after publishing his novel *If Not Now, When?* in 1982 are clearly applicable as well to the fiction writing Levi had already done, evidenced by the publication of his science fiction collection, *Storie naturali* (*Natural Stories*) in 1966. The forum that Levi chose to engage some very difficult issues involving scientific practice is this lesser-known collection of stories whose English translation is found in a collection entitled *The Sixth Day and Other Tales*, and which constitute the third moment of science found in Levi's works. In *Storie naturali*, science in the future tense is a strategy employed to experience and explore the limits of science as a discipline, testing its moral fiber along the way. The specter of a future world is evoked through science fiction, and the role that science could play in determining the ethics of that future world is scrutinized through imaginative scenarios.[6]

Levi first published *Storie naturali* under the pseudonym of Damiano Malabaila, which he said could mean "evil nurse" in Piedmontese dialect: nature as "evil nurse," in other words, that which should nurture can also destroy.[7] The topic of these stories ranges from machines that can copy life forms and write poetry to chemical substances that effect sensory metamorphoses. One of these stories, entitled "Versamina," is particularly useful in exploring dual but related questions: first, how Levi viewed science as a political and moral arena, beyond the parameters of his own chemical science, and second, how he uses a moment in high culture, Shakespeare's *Macbeth*, in order to gloss the notion of what science is, what it can be and what it should be.

The title "Versamina" refers to a chemical substance which converts the sensations of pain into perceptions of pleasure. Levi begins the story with the following affirmation:

> There are trades that destroy and trades that preserve. Among those that preserve, the better ones, by their very nature, are precisely those that consist in preserving something: documents, books, works of art, institutions, traditions. It is common knowledge that librarians, museum guards, sacristans, beadles and archivists not only are long-lived but are preserved for decades without visible alteration. (45)[8]

Both trades that destroy and trades that preserve are theorized, yet the only examples given are of those that preserve. The rest of the story, primarily about medical experimentation, demonstrates a practical application to the theory about trades, and fills in the missing example of a trade that destroys. A scientist named Dessauer, after a twelve year absence, returns to the institute he used to work in before the war. The year and geographical specifics are not given: but there is no doubt that this is postwar Germany. Dessauer looks around for his former colleagues and discovers only one, Dybowski, who recounts to him some experimentation done by a scientist in the Institute named Kleber after Dessauer had left. The meaning of the beginning of the story, about trades that destroy and those that preserve, thus becomes understandable only after we comprehend what is at stake in another kind of trade, that of drug experimentation.

Kleber, in his experiments with benzoyl derivatives, had accidentally discovered that one of them was capable of effecting the most profound sensory changes in the animals to whom he administered the substance. Naming it "versamina," he noted its ability to convert pain to pleasure, in other words to make what are normally painful sensations almost unbearably pleasurable. But the end result was always the same: the animal would destroy itself, through a drive to find more pleasure through pain. Kleber, nonetheless, continued to experiment with versamina, hoping to create a new analgesic medicine for a drug company. We learn of the effects of versamina through the story of a mongrel dog to whom Kleber gave the substance:

> [H]e was no longer a dog. There was no longer anything canine about him—he no longer liked meat, he would scratch up dirt and pebbles with his claws and swallow them. He ate salad greens, straw, hay, newspaper . . . the hotter the weather, the more trouble I had getting him to drink: when I stood there he pretended to drink, but you could see very well that water repelled him; one time, however, he slipped into the laboratory on the sly, found a basin of isotonic solution and drank it all . . . he howled at the sun, yapped at the moon, wagged his tail for hours on end before the sterilizer and the hammer mill, and when I took him for a walk he snarled at every corner and every tree. In short, he was a counterdog . . . In my opinion he had understood like a human being, he knew that when you're thirsty you must drink, and that a dog must eat meat and not hay, but error, perversion were stronger than he. In my presence he made an effort to do the right thing, not only to please me and so that I should not get angry, but also, I believe, because he knew, continued to know, what was right. (50)

The dog's life ends when, in a desperate search for more pain, he kills himself by running under a streetcar. Versamina effects an inversion in its ability to render this change of sensory perception from pain to pleasure, from bad to good. Levi's use of the word "perversion" to describe the dog's behavior signals a larger agenda here, one that goes beyond the parameters of the ethics of a single medical experiment; as he says: "the error, the perversion were stronger than he." Perversion, and the very name of the substance, versamina, share the Latin root *vertere*, to turn. The OED informs us that the Latin *pervertere*, from whence "perversion," means "to turn round or about, turn the wrong way, overturn, turn to error or ruin." Thus the difference between turning, as in turning pain to pleasure, and perversion, or turning the wrong way, is but an etymological hair's breadth. In his human-like awareness of the difference between right and wrong, a difference that the human scientist seemed not to understand, the dog shows himself to be morally superior to the scientist administering the drug to him. Kleber himself finally succumbs to the temptation of versamina and tries it out on himself. Dybowski recounts Kleber's fate under the power of the drug:

> He lost weight, pined away like someone afflicted by cancer. You could see that he tried to resist, to keep for himself only the good, that avalanche of agreeable, perhaps even delicious sensations that the versamine procured so easily and gratuitously . . . he forced himself to eat, although he had lost all liking for food; he could no longer sleep . . . he also made mistakes in speaking—sometimes he said 'bitter' instead of 'sweet', 'cold' instead of 'hot'; generally he corrected himself quickly, but his hesitation before certain choices didn't escape me, and also a certain at once irritated and guilty glance when he saw that I had noticed. A glance that hurt me: it brought back to mind that other one, his predecessor, the mongrel dog who cowered with flattened ears when I caught him doing things the wrong way around. [Kleber] died because of a traffic accident here in town, in his car, on a summer night . . . Kleber did one thing right: shortly before dying he destroyed the entire versamine dossier, and all the preparations he was able to get his hands on. (52–3)

Only after taking the drug himself does Kleber understand the right and wrong of it, evidenced by the guilty glances he gives Dybowski when caught doing things inversely. Kleber's own self-experimentation has thus succeeded in raising him to the level of moral understanding of the dog.

Versamina proves to be very tempting indeed: Dessauer himself, by the end of the story, even after he has heard of the end of the animals who were given versamina and what has happened to the principal investigator, becomes nonetheless seduced by its possibilities:

> He thought that if versamines could convert into joy also the most burdensome and longest of pains, the pain of an

> absence, of a void around you, the pain of an irreparable failure, the pain of feeling you are finished—well, in that case why not? (53)

At this crucial moment in the text, when it looks as if the temptations of evil will certainly prevail despite the hard lessons already learned, another text is suddenly, dramatically evoked. Dessauer remembers Shakespeare's *Macbeth*, in a moment that can only be described as corrective, and which ends the story:

> But by one of those associations with which memory is so generous, he also thought about a heath in Scotland, never seen but better than seen, a heath filled with rain, lightning bolts and wind, and about the gay-malicious chant of three bearded witches, experts in pains and pleasure and in corrupting the human will:
>
> > 'Fair is foul, and foul is fair:
> > Hover through the fog and filthy air' (54)

Levi first evokes Macbeth's witches, and then ends his tale with their actual words. At first reading, it appears that the principal interest in *Macbeth* lies in the idea of inversion found in the line "fair is foul and foul is fair." In other words, the two do not lie very far apart, they can be, and are, in the world of Macbeth, easily confused: just as pain and pleasure are confused in the world of this scientific experiment.

Levi's reading of *Macbeth*, however, goes much farther than this. His analysis of the role of the witches is that they are "expert in pains and pleasure and in corrupting the human will." Reviewing the events of the play, however, casts this statement in a rather dubious light. The witches, by giving Macbeth the prophecy that he will become King, set off a bloody chain reaction in which Macbeth kills Duncan the current king, Banquo, Macduff's entire family and a score of others before he himself is vanquished. Have the witches corrupted his human will, as Levi asserts, perhaps through the temptation of the prophecy? Does this purported corruption of his will suggest that Macbeth is somehow not responsible for his crimes? A look at the facts suggests otherwise. Macbeth is clearly the agent of his own demise, and that of many others. He quite literally sets out to fulfill the prophecy that he has heard. After he has become king, he begins to worry about the last part of the witches' prophecy in which they state that it is Banquo's children who will be kings—not Macbeth's own. He summons the witches again and demands more information, which they give him through a series of bloody and frightful ghostly apparitions, including those of children. To achieve the conjuring of the apparitions, they prepare a cauldron (of "double double toil and trouble, fire burn and cauldron bubble" fame) to which they add all sorts of organic materials: eye of newt, toe of frog, wool of bat and so on. The cauldron serves as the medium through which the apparitions present themselves. Macbeth learns from them that he must beware Macduff, and that his conqueror is not of woman born. This turns out to mean that Macduff, his eventual killer, was born prematurely via cesaerean section—but no matter, by the time Macbeth finds this out, it is too late and he is killed.

What precisely is at stake in Levi's citation of *Macbeth*? There are thematic links in the play to the unrestrained, murderous world of the Holocaust that go beyond the power of the witches upon which Levi concentrates. For his unleashed killings, for example, Macbeth is figured as an irrational monster. He murders Macduff's family even though according to the prophecy it is Banquo's son who will generate a line of kings, not Macduff's. Not only is Macbeth a murderer, he is a child killer as well. Infanticide is a central topos in the play, evoked repeatedly at key moments. It is referred to early on by Lady Macbeth, who, in order to spur Macbeth's ambition towards killing Duncan, says to him: "I have given suck, and know/ How tender 'tis to love the babe that milks me;/I would, while it was smiling in my face,/Have plucked my nipple from his boneless gums /And dashed the brains out, had I so sworn/ As you have done to this"[9] (1:7, 56–9). In her dream of infanticide, Lady Macbeth is theorizing an invertive passage from love to murderous ambition. One of the ingredients for the witches' cauldron used to conjure up prophetic apparitions is "finger of birth-strangled babe" and one of the apparitions thus conjured is that of a bloody child (4:1, 30).

The infanticidal images so central to the play are acted upon by Macbeth, who has Macduff's children killed along with their mother, as he directs his murderers: "give to th' edge o' th' sword/His wife, his babes, and all unfortunate souls/That trace him in his line" (4:1, 166–8). The homicidal familial theory of infant killing espoused by Lady Macbeth at the beginning of the play has now turned to practice, and the killing of Macbeth's rivals has grown to a genealogical massacre, as he desires to wipe out not only Macduff, but his entire family. Infanticide, and familial slaughter, evokes a world without any moral or ethical restraint.

In *Macbeth*, infanticide is naturalized through the ideology of ambition, just as the Nazis naturalized the killing of Jews, Gypsies, and the mentally and physically handicapped among others, through the ideology of eugenics. The Nazis deliberately focused on the murder of children since children and women of childbearing age posed the biggest threat to the notion of race hygiene.[8] Levi is not merely evoking *inversion*, fair to foul and back again, but by quoting from *Macbeth*, Levi conjures up another time and place, never far from his own memory, where moral order has been subverted, in fact perverted, turned to error or ruin.

The very process through which murder in the name of eugenics was actualized provides another link between Levi's story, *Macbeth*, and the Holocaust. The central issue at stake in both scenarios is the use, or abuse, of knowledge: scientific knowledge during the Holocaust, those dangerous prophecies for Macbeth.

The responsibility of scientists and academics working during the Third Reich has been explored by the German geneticist Benno Muller-Hill, who, in his book *Murderous Science*, describes the willing participation of psychiatrists and anthropologists first in the forced sterilizations performed on psychiatric patients, and the mentally and physically impaired, and then in the euthanasia program begun in 1939 to murder this same population. Muller-Hill begins his study of the role of anthropology, psychiatry and genetics in the Holocaust with the following statement:

> But when I think today of the story of how genetics was once put to use in anthropology and psychiatry, I see a wasteland of desolation and destruction. The blood of human beings, spilt millions of times over, is completely and resolutely forgotten. The recent history of these genetically orientated human sciences is as full of chaos and crime as a nightmare. Yet many geneticists, anthropologists and psychiatrists have slipped from this dream into the deep sleep of forgetfulness.[11]

Scientific knowledge was used not only to prop up the racist ideology that led to genocide, but to actively engage with its accomplishment as well. Medical doctors were present at the gassing of prisoners both in institutions and at the concentration camps, and were involved in inhumane medical experiments performed on prisoners. Muller-Hill outlines other medical abuses common at the time: for example, psychiatrists who routinely performed sadistically extreme electric shock treatments on patients, mental patients who were starved to death in institutions. The misuse of knowledge was crucial both in the ideological framework of race hygiene and genocide, and in its undertaking. Levi refers to the responsibility of science and technology for mass murder when he discusses the role of the German firms that built the crematoria and supplied the gas:

> The crematoria ovens themselves were designed, built, assembled and tested by a German company, Topf of Wiesbaden (it was still in operation in 1975, building crematoria for civilian use and had not considered the advisability of changing its name). It is hard to believe that the personnel of these companies did not realize the significance of the quality or quantity of the merchandise and installations being commissioned by the SS command units. The same can be, and has been, said with regard to the supplies of the poison employed in the gas chambers at Auschwitz: the product, substantially hydrocyanic acid,

> had already been used for many years for pest control in the holds of boats, but the abrupt increase in orders beginning with 1942 could scarcely go unnoticed. It must have aroused doubts, and certainly did, but they were stifled by fear, the desire for profit, the blindness and willed stupidity that we have mentioned, and in some cases (probably few) by fanatical Nazi obedience.[12]

Levi's analysis turns from the industries that produced supplies used for genocide to the individuals involved, those petty bureaucrats who took the orders and unquestioningly filled them. He stops, however, just short of looking at the technology itself as a principle target for his ethical retrobation. What he concentrates on, instead, is the question of complicity involved. Complicity is a major issue in the study of the Holocaust which cuts across categories of perpetrators and bystanders. It is an issue that Levi has raised repeatedly in his work. What bystander complicity signifies is the denial of knowledge. Both the denial and the abuse of knowledge are for Levi crucial issues in his thinking about the collaboration of science and scientific institutions in the Holocaust.

If we wish to draw more parallels between Levi's citing of *Macbeth* and the evoked but never named backdrop of the Holocaust for his story of versamina, we could name Macbeth as a figure for Hitler and the Reich, who use murder as a modus operandi, and those witches as Reich scientists irresponsibly and immorally using their knowledge to aid and abet in these crimes. Chemistry, whose historical antecedent was after all alchemy, itself closely related to magic, is figurally represented in *Macbeth* through the witches' cauldron. Their science, if you will, has a supernatural power achieved through combining organic materials to produce otherworldly figures who speak in riddled prophecies that leave Macbeth confused, but willing to take the bait: mesmerized by the temptations that knowledge affords.

Levi's autobiographical writings about his relation to chemistry underscore the magical element and the fascination that the discipline held for him. In an interview with Ferdinando Camon, he says that "I was excited by the parallel between the formula written on paper and that which took place in the beaker: already it seemed to me something magical, and chemistry seemed to be the principal key to open up the secrets of the earth and sky. I had read that a specterscope allowed one to understand the chemical composition of a star. This seemed to me to be one of man's maximum powers."[13] It is not the organic materials that chemists use that pose the threat. As Levi says in "Nitrogen," "matter is matter, neither noble nor vile"—it is rather the knowledge applied to handle the materials that cannot be neutral.[14] Inversion is thus always a moral inversion that employs matter as its instrument, just as the cauldron in Macbeth is a medium used to conjure darker powers.

Another, even more critical look at Levi's interpretation of *Macbeth*'s witches is now in order, after looking at the context in which they appear, both in *Macbeth* and in Levi's story. Are the witches, as he asserts, expert in pains and pleasure and in corrupting the human will? It is, after all, the witches' job to prophecize, as Shakespeare's witches are closely connected to the Parcae, mythological figures of prophecy. And what about their purported expertise in pain and in pleasure? Pain, yes, if one extrapolates that as a result of their prophecy Macbeth has caused himself and others great pain. Pleasure is, however, conspicuously absent in this play. Yet in the world of versamines, the two are inextricably entwined. At this point we could ask ourselves: Has Levi misread Macbeth? Is he casting those witches as scapegoats, thereby exonerating Macbeth? Why exactly does he quote from this particular play as a way of answering his narrator's temptations regarding versamina? Levi's assertion that the witches have corrupted Macbeth's will suggests that he is saying more about the danger of scientific knowledge than he is about Macbeth: the logic of inversion has thus become not only the theme of "Versamina," but the reigning interpretative principle of the story as well. Seeing the witches as an analogy for irresponsible science and the corrupting power of knowledge allows a deeper understanding of what lies behind Levi's use of them: a displacement of pressing concerns regarding the role and responsibility of science during the Third Reich.

In "Versamina," it is only the lesson of *Macbeth* that stops the scientist from repeating the mistakes of the past, even though he has learned of the fate of the others who took the drug. Literary culture is thus raised to a position of ethical authority higher than that of empirical experimentation. Here we have an illustration not of the role of science in the formulation of culture, but of the role of culture in the formation of science. The inversion of fair and foul, so central to Levi's post-Holocaust understanding of culture, has become a double inversion, this time of methodology. His use of Macbeth as a figure to gloss his story suggests another kind of reversal as well: he uses science, in other words his versamine example, to reflect back on Macbeth.

Levi establishes a cultural continuum in his works that begins with his frequent evocation of Dante, continues through Shakespeare, and stops at Auschwitz. Levi cites from Macbeth in order to reflect on science. The citation deepens his analogy of knowledge run amok, drawn in this story of the moral and ethical price of medical experimentation. His cultural continuum serves to muse on the role of science after the Holocaust as well, by reflecting on the meaning of culture in general and literature in particular, both past and present.

Culture is for Levi a spectral enterprise, in which past is present and present is future. How important a collective memory is of that past is evident in his words about Macbeth in "Versamina," "never seen but better than seen" as the narrator remembers the heath of Scotland and its witches. And science is bound up in that enterprise as well, in its ever-present potential of confusing foul and fair. The role of science in the execution of the Holocaust has forever changed our notion that science is somehow confined to the good of people, not their destruction: in other words, a potentially evil nurse. Levi succintly explores this idea through his fictive recounting of the experiment of versamina and through his gloss of Macbeth, reminding us that history and the culture it produces, including scientific culture, exist in a continuum whose lessons can be learned only through a long memory and an examination of the past.

Notes

1. See Jo Ann Cannon, "Chemistry and Writing," in *Reason and Light: Essays on Primo Levi*, ed. Susan Tarrow (Ithaca, NY: Western Societies Occasional Paper Series, #25); Cesare Cases, "Sodio e potassio: scienza e visione del mondo in Primo Levi," in *Primo Levi as Witness*, ed. Pietro Frassica (Fiesole: Casalini libri, 1990); and Mario Petrucciani, *Scienza e letteratura nel secondo novecento*, (Milan: Mursia, 1978). Mario Porro, "Scienza" in *Primo Levi*, ed. Marco Belpoliti (Milano: Riga #13, Marcos y Marcos, 1997), and Giancarlo Borri, "Primo Levi tra scienza e letteratura", in *Primo Levi: Memoria e invenzione*, ed. Giovanna Iolo (San Salvatore Monferrato: 1995).
2. See Alberto Cavaglion, "Sopra una fonte dimenticata di Se questo é uomo", in *Primo Levi: Memoria e Invenzione*, ed. Giovanna Iola (San Salvatore Monferrato: 1995), for a discussion of Levi's first scientific writing and its relationship to the subsequent writing of "Survival in Auschwitz."
3. Promo Levi, "Beyond Survival," in *Prooftexts*, 1984, vol. 4, #1.
4. Ruth K. Angress, "Primo Levi in English," Simon Wiesenthal Center Annual, vol. 3 (Los Angeles: Simon Wiesenthal Center, 1986), pp. 317–330.
5. Primo Levi, "Writing a Novel," in *Other People's Trades*, trans. Raymond Rosenthal (New York: Summit Books, 1989), pp. 128–9.
6. Critics by and large have not paid as much attention to Levi's science fiction works as they have to his other, better known texts. One notable exception is Giuseppina Santagostino, who has written several excellent articles on this subject, including "Primo Levi e le facce nascoste del tempo" in *Primo Levi: Memoria e invenzione*, ed. Giovanna Iola (San Salvatore Monferrato: 1995).
7. Levi said in interviews that he chose to publish under a pseudonym because intially he felt that these stories were so different from his previous works, *Survival in Auschwitz* and its sequel, *The Reawakening*, that they would detract from the seriousness of the Holocaust experience outlined in the other works. He subsequently realized that in fact these fictional stories had been so influenced by his Auschwitz experience that the pseudonym was no longer necessary, and he dropped its use.
8. Primo Levi, "Versamina," in *The Sixth Day and Other Tales*, tran. Raymond Rosenthal (London: Michael Joseph. 1990), pp. 45–54.

9. All citations of *Macbeth* are taken from *The Oxford Shakespeare*, Nicholas Brooke, editor.
10. See for example, John K. Roth and Carol Rittner, *Different Voices: Women and the Holocaust* (New York: Paragon House, 1993).
11. Benno Muller-Hill, *Murderous Science* (Oxford and New York: Oxford University Press, 1988), p. 3. For a penetrating discussion of various scholars who have written on the topic of science and the Holocaust, including Muller-Hill, see Mario Biagiolo, "Science, Modernity, and the 'Final Solution'," in *Probing the Limits of Representation: Nazism and the 'Final Solution'*, ed. Saul Friedlander (Cambridge: Harvard University Press, 1992).
12. Primo Levi, *The Drowned and the Saved*, tran. Raymond Rosenthal (New York: Summit Books, 1988), p. 16.
13. Ferdinando Camon, *Conversations with Primo Levi* (Marlboro, VT: The Marlboro Press, 1989), p. 66.
14. Primo Levi, *The Periodic Table* (New York: Schocken Books, 1984), p. 181.

5

Moral Snares and Parables: Between Science Fiction and Midrash

Dr. Mirna Cicioni[1]

Primo Levi was always fascinated by the literary tradition which, from Thomas More to François Rabelais, Jonathan Swift, Jules Verne, and H.G. Wells to Aldous Huxley, used space and time travels as estrangement devices in order to articulate critical discourses on society. One of the stories in *Vizio di forma*, significantly entitled "Visto di lontano" ("Seen from Afar"),[2] explicitly defines itself as "a last reverent tribute to Lucian of Samosata, Voltaire, Swedenborg, Rostand, E.A. Poe, Flammarion and H.G. Wells" (III:219). Levi's 1981 "personal anthology" of the literary and non-literary texts most significant for his own development, *La ricerca delle radici*, contains what he defines as "many instances of things turned upside down": excerpts from *Gulliver's Travels* and from *Gargantua*, and the classic American short-short story "Sentry" by Fredric Brown. From the late 1940s until the end of his life he wrote short fiction texts which describe possible future scientific, technological or biological developments. These are usually referred to as Levi's "science fiction" stories.

Some scholars who have analyzed these stories in depth have mainly stressed Levi's humanist perspective, the need for science to be guided by humanist considerations (Klein) and the rejection of passivity in the face of the danger of dehumanization (Grassano). Dehumanization processes are, of course, the focus of most analyses connecting Levi's stories with his writings on Auschwitz (Cases; Mengaldo; Santagostino 1991 and 1993). An aspect which has not yet been fully explored, however, is whether, or where, they belong in the established parameters of science fiction. Levi himself was hesitant to refer to them as "science fiction" and always qualified the noun with the adjective "so-called".[3] In the letter to Einaudi which was reprinted on the cover of *Storie naturali* he called his texts *trappole morali*, "moral snares." This definition prepares his readers for his use of defamiliarization devices to alert them to the fact that, as he put it,

> in the world we live in there is a discrepancy, a small or large gap, a structural defect which cancels out one aspect or another of our civilisation or our moral universe.

Subsequently, in a paper which in English is known as "Beyond Survival," but which in Italian has the more revealing title "Itinerario di uno scrittore ebreo" ("Journey of a Jewish Writer"), Levi said that some of his stories "are linked (perhaps unconsciously) to the midrashic tradition of the parable" (385). The explicit moral focus on the structural defects, the *vizi di forma*, of our civilisation is what differentiates Levi's stories—even those closest to the readers' notion of "science fiction" texts—from conventional science fiction and implicitly connects them to *midrash*, the centuries-old tradition of interpreting sacred texts in order to draw lessons for the present and the future.

Darko Suvin, one of the main contemporary theorists of science fiction, has summed up the classical model of the genre in the formula "cognitive estrangement": the narrative logic of each text is determined by an innovation which deviates from the author's and implied readers' expectations of reality, yet is consistent with their empirical reality and with existing scientific knowledge (*Metamorphoses* 66–70). Suvin also maintains that "every meaningful science fiction text must always be read as an analogy" to situations and relations specific to the author's own time ("La fantascienza e il 'novum'" 35–7). Levi's texts, as well as being based on estrangement devices fully consistent with Suvin's formula, are also analogically transparent, in that they are generally very close to their author's place (technologically advanced societies, usually capitalist ones) and time (the present, or a fairly near future). Significantly, aliens are the only one of the main props of the genre—namely scientific and technological innovations; their impact on human behavior; catastrophes and mutations, either natural or provoked by people; contacts between technologically advanced species and so-called primitive cultures—which is absent from Levi's narratives.[4] In traditional science fiction, either as visitors to Earth or as species encountered by Earth travellers, aliens are the Other. Contact with the Other shapes human beings' perception of self; "primitive" races lead the "advanced" species who encounter them to question what counts as "progress." Levi's Others are other human beings, and his "primitive" cultures are all Earth-based. This keeps his "parables" firmly away from the realm of the transcendent, where much of the genre tends to stray, and gives them a more immediate didactic dimension.

In the earlier stories, the lesson is explicit rather than implicit. The Arunde in "Verso occidente" (Westward) are a contented native South American tribe.[5] They have no religious convictions and accept and encourage a painless form of suicide. When Western scientists ask them to be experimental subjects for a chemical antidote to self-destruction, which they also want to test on lemmings, the Arunde politely decline: "We prefer freedom to drugs, and death to illusion" (III: 205). In the later texts, the ethical lesson is conveyed implicitly, through irony, to question not only the notion of "progress" but that of knowledge itself.[6] Two consecutive stories, "La nutrice" and "Il rafter" ("The Nurse" and "The Rafter"), set in an unspecified Third World village called Recuenco, are a transparent ironic metaphor for some forms of piecemeal aid given by "developed" nations to "underdeveloped" ones.[7] The village is, once every two or three generations, supplied with a liquid vegetable food. The first story is told from the overawed point of view of the village people, who pass down the legend of a supernatural Nurse "who brings both repletion and death" (III:

317). The second story is told from the point of view of the bored, well-paid international crew of the space rafter which mechanically drops tons of food over starving areas without worrying about the concomitant destruction of people, animals, and property. The central characters of "Gli stregoni" (The Witch Doctors)[8] are two British ethnographers who come into contact with the Sirionos, inhabitants of the Bolivian jungle.[9] Left without most of their equipment after a fire, the two highly-educated representatives of technological civilization turn out to be unable to reconstruct any of their tools, and the Bolivian tribe decides to starve them to death as "useless" when they cannot manufacture something as deceptively simple as a knife or a match. Levi's recurrent theme, the need to be skilled with one's hands, introduced in *The Truce*, expanded in *The Periodic Table* and fully developed in *The Wrench*, is taken to its extreme logical consequences here: technological civilization has as an inevitable by-product the loss of skills which in any other context may prove vital.

This theme is also a familiar one in those classical science fiction texts which look at human survival after a worldwide catastrophe (usually a nuclear war), from *Brave New World* to George R. Stewart's 1949 novel *Earth Abides* to Pamela Sargent's *The Shore of Women*, written in 1987. However, earthwide ("end-of-the-world") catastrophes are almost absent from Levi's fiction. He does not share the belief of many science fiction writers that a new order can come about only after the old one has been destroyed. The writer J.G. Ballard said in 1977 that "the catastrophe story . . . represents a constructive and positive act of the imagination rather than a negative one, an attempt to confront the terrifying void of a patently meaningless universe by challenging it at its own game."[10] Levi's position is diametrically opposite: the world we live in is the only starting point we have, and imagination must be used to reverse existing trends rather than to envisage improbable new beginnings. He stated this in an interview when *Vizio di forma* was published:

> Some of my stories do end in catastrophes, but the catastrophes are, at least in my intention, ironic, and, so to

> speak, conditional: we are going to end up like this if we do not take steps in time, but we have the means, the intelligence and the strength to take steps.[11]

Brian Stableford in his essay "Man-Made Catastrophes" points out that at the heart of the catastrophist stream in English-language science fiction lies the notion of basic flaws in human nature, which he connects to the Christian concept of original sin (100–113). For Levi, the basic flaw, the "structural defect" is to be found, rather than in human nature, in specific practices: asking inappropriate questions or making morally unacceptable choices. Consequently, the narrative structure of his "catastrophic" texts follows a regular pattern, which in cinematic terms could be described as a track-out from a close-up to a long shot: the isolated problems of one individual are gradually revealed to be part of a much wider process of interconnected negative practices. These texts are the closest in Levi's writing to what is conventionally known as "science fiction," and they are the least original and powerful of his production. Some are variations on the hackneyed theme of the negative consequences of an industrial development which disregards human needs and emotions. "Protezione" ("Protection")[12] moves from the weary restlessness of an urban housewife to reveal that all city dwellers are bound by law to wear suits of armour, allegedly as a defense against a rain of micro-meteorites, in fact to keep the production of manufactured metal goods going after car sales have reached saturation point. The armour has also become a psychological defense against urban alienation:

> I feel protected . . . against everything. Against men, wind, sun and rain. Against smog and polluted air and radioactive waste. Against fate and against all the things we cannot see and foresee. Against evil thoughts and against diseases and against the future and against myself. (III: 193)

"Lumini rossi" ("Small Red Lights") recalls a bitterly satirical 1950s story, "Cost of Living" by Robert Sheckley.[13] In the American story a man's life at work and at home is reduced to a series of button-pushings, which he, and all workers like him, cannot escape because they are inextricably caught in a spiral of debts engineered by the consumer system. In Levi's text, a man's life is a series of red lights: the controls at work, the traffic lights on the road, and the small light bulb on his wife's breast, signalling her fertile days. "I gladiatori" ("The Gladiators"), written in the mid-seventies, starts with a man planning to take his girlfriend to the stadium on Sunday and gradually reveals that society has solved at the same time the problems of unemployment, vehicle obsolescence, and mass entertainment by re-inventing circuses where unemployed men and criminals are made to fight motor vehicles.[14]

One story, "Le nostre belle specificazioni" ("Our Fine Specifications"), has powerful connections with Levi's other works and exemplifies the strengths of his use of estrangement, showing the evil lurking behind the apparently humdrum.[15] A young white-collar worker, while revising the specifications for every item used in the factory where he works, comes across "Specification No. 366 478. Man," which defines this item's maximum and minimum acceptable height and weight and lays down ways to test its resistance to bending, twisting, heat and cold, its memory, its leadership skills, and its emotional stability. Any attempts to oppose the specification fail, and the conclusion ironically states that specifications like this thrive in any system "where due consideration is paid to normalization, amalgamation, standardization, and rationalization of production" (III:294). Readers familiar with *La ricerca delle radici* will recall that one of Levi's "roots" is "the proposed method for checking the resistance of dried adhesive films to attacks by cockroaches," published in 1955 by the American Society for Testing Materials. This is a totally factual text, which merely specifies the correct equipment and procedure for carrying out the required resistance tests, and in itself is anything but sinister. Levi introduces it by, on the one hand, admitting that "the foundations of our technological civilization must be consolidated by precise measures and definitions," and on the other hand expressing his concern that "the monstrous network of specifications is destined to grow, since every object mentioned in a specification must in turn be specified" (183). Thus the apparently neutral American technological guidelines and Levi's morality tale constitute the implicit discursive space of another of Levi's "roots," the conclusion of Hermann Langbein's *Menschen in Auschwitz*:

> This is the lesson of Auschwitz: the first step, the first surrender to a social structure which aims at total control over human beings, is the most dangerous. (qtd in *La ricerca delle radici* 227)

And all three texts—the one by the anonymous American author, Levi's, and Langbein's—are implicitly recalled in the reflections, in the chapter "The Grey Zone" of *The Drowned and the Saved*, on the collective dimension of all power relations and on the mechanisms of collaboration:

> From many signs, it would seem that the time has come to explore the space which separates (not only in Nazi camps!) the victims from the persecutors . . . Only a schematic rhetoric can claim that this space is empty. It never is: it is studded with foul or pathetic figures (sometimes both at the same time), and it is essential to know them if we want to know humankind, if we want to be able to defend our souls should we ever face a similar ordeal, or even if we only want to understand what goes on in a big industrial plant. (I: 677–8)

Levi's explorations of the internal contradictions within the contemporary world and his attempts to understand and interpret them—the constant in all his work—are deeply rooted in what Cynthia Ozick has called "the Jewish language of collective conscience [and] moral seriousness" (28). As is well known, Levi was what in Italy is known as "un ebreo di ritorno," someone whose process of retrieval of his Jewish heritage began after the anti-Semitic laws and continued in the seventies, when many Italian intellectuals, Gentiles as well as Jews, discovered Jewish culture through the fiction of Ashkenazi Jews from Eastern Europe and the United States. Levi's perspective is wholly secular: the aspect of Jewish culture which fascinates him is, as he put it in the essay "Il rito e il riso" ("Ritual and Laughter"),[16] "an intellectual flexibility which does not fear contradictions, in fact accepts them . . . [because] they may contain the seeds of all our tomorrows" (III: 766). Some of his stories belong in the tradition of *midrash*: they are parables which interpret the Jewish religious and historical heritage in the light of contemporary ethical and social problems, and use estrangement to attempt to make sense of the contradictions of life and to ask how one should live in times of change and crisis.[17] These parables are on the whole more imaginative and express Levi's sense of estrangement more powerfully than the stories based on conventional "science fiction" formulae. Three of them are particularly interesting: one is close to a traditional scenario ("Trattamento di quiescenza," "Retirement Fund"); one is, literally, a morality play ("Il sesto giorno," "The Sixth Day"); and one is a reworking of the Jewish legend of the Golem ("Il servo," "The Servant").[18]

"Retirement Fund"[19] is at the same time an anticipation of "virtual reality" and a *midrash* on Ecclesiastes I, 7-18, quoted at the end: "The eye is not satisfied with seeing, nor the ear filled with hearing . . . For in much wisdom there is much vexation; and he that increaseth knowledge increaseth sorrow." It elaborates on the traditional science fiction topos of the "lotus eaters."[20] An American company has perfected a helmet which transmits sensations and emotions and allows the wearers to relive, as often as they wish, experiences previously undergone and recorded by people or animals. The salesman who should test it on himself becomes hopelessly addicted to it, and stops living his own life altogether. The lesson is that knowledge and wisdom do not coincide, and knowledge is only the necessary, not the sufficient condition for progress: the recurrent theme of all Levi's reflections on science and on history.

In Genesis 1:26 God said: "Let us make man." As Holtz shows, rabbinical scholars saw a problem there: who is the "us"? To whom is God speaking? (191–2). A *midrash* from

Bereshit Rabbah, a sixth-century commentary on Genesis, answered these questions as follows:

> Rabbi Simon said: When the Holy One, blessed be He, came to create the first man, the ministering angels divided into groups and parties, some saying: Let him not be created, and others saying: Let him be created . . . Mercy said: Let him be created, for he will be merciful, and Truth said: Let him not be created, for he will be all lies. Righteousness said: Let him be created, for he will do righteous deeds; Peace said: Let him not be created, for he is full of strife. . . . While the ministering angels were still arguing and disputing, the Holy One, blessed be He, created man. Then He said to them: Why do you argue? Man is already made. (VIII, 5; qtd. in Holtz 191–2)

In Levi's "The Sixth Day," a supernatural Management Committee—where the economic and the moral viewpoints are expressed by two of the gods of Persian mythology, the god of darkness Ahriman and the god of knowledge Ahura Mazda—debate, in the perfectly reproduced register of committee procedures, the pros and cons, the feasibility and the cost-effectiveness of various projects for the creation of Man. They finally decide that the creature-to-be should be a bird, only to discover that a higher authority "upstairs" has already created the new being out of clay and has formed the female from one of his ribs. Levi does not mention *Bereshit Rabbah*, and it has not been possible to ascertain how much direct knowledge he had of it. His own *midrash*, whether original or not, is, however, an ironically relevant reference to contemporary industrial society: considerations of cost-effectiveness and efficiency are in inevitable conflict with the basic human properties ("being able to invent and use tools, to communicate in an articulate fashion, to live under extreme conditions, and to some extent, to live communally," [III: 147]). Man, rather than God, is at the centre of Levi's vision. "The one who is about to be born will be our judge," the god of knowledge says. "Not only our errors, but all of his, through centuries to come, will weigh upon our heads" (III:160).

"The Servant" is at the same time a *midrash* on knowledge and technology and a tribute to some elements of Jewish culture. The title is also an implicit tribute to the neologism *robot*, introduced by Karel Capek in 1920. Levi rewrites the traditional legend of the rabbi from Prague who constructs a golem, "a strong, faithful and not too discerning servant, in short what in his Bohemian language is called a robot." The process of construction involves reflections on the prescriptions of the Torah, on the precept to "build a hedge around the Law," and on *gematriya*, the ingenious computing of the numerical values of letters and concepts:

> The Golem . . . was ready in the year 1579 of the vulgar Era, the 5339th of the Creation; now, 5339 is not quite a prime number, but it almost is, and it is the product of 19, which is the number of the sun and of gold, by 281, which is the number of the bones in our body. (III: 341)

The Golem comes to life every time a scroll with the Name of God is inserted into its mouth. In Levi's version of the legend, however, its very first utterance is the angry question Job asks of God in Job 21, 7: "Why does the evil man thrive?" which Levi in *La ricerca delle radici* described as one of "the questions of all time, those for which man could not find an answer nor will he ever, but will for ever keep seeking one because he needs to in order to live, to understand himself and the world" (5). The Golem helps the rabbi and the Prague community until one Sabbath when the rabbi is late in taking the scroll with God's Name out of its mouth. Then it destroys everything around itself, and breaks into pieces. The rabbi acknowledges that he only, not God or the Golem, is to blame.

The relevance of this parable lies in the relationship between human beings and technology. The havoc caused by the human invention is due exclusively to inappropriate use, a notion which recurs in many of Levi's writings. "We have no choice—he stated on the cover of the first edition of *Vizio di forma*—we cannot go back to Arcadia. Technology, and technology alone, is what can restore order on our planet, and correct any 'structural defect'." Yet he points out, implicitly in "The Servant" and explicitly in later non-fiction texts, that, contrary to the claims of the rationalist philosophy of science, knowledge is never morally neutral. Golems can be sources of knowledge and joy, as he wrote in the 1984 essay "Personal Golem," an extended amusing comparison between the Jewish legend and his own experiences with a recently-acquired personal computer.[21] But Golems can also be sources of potential disaster. In the last months of his life Levi repeatedly proposed that science graduates be asked to swear something akin to the Hippocratic oath. In one of his last essays, "Covare il cobra" ("Hatching the Cobra"),[22] he told them:

> Within the limits that you will be granted, try to know the end to which your work is directed . . . Don't hide behind the hypocrisy of neutral science: you are sufficiently educated to evaluate whether from the egg you are hatching will issue a dove or a cobra or a chimera or perhaps nothing at all. (III: 977)

This tentative and limited proposal was the only concrete suggestion Levi believed he could offer. All his works end with unanswered questions. The conclusion of *The Drowned and the Saved* is "It happened, therefore it can happen again," and the conclusion of his essay "Eclissi dei profeti" ("Eclipse of Prophets")[23] is "Our future is not written, it is not certain: we have awakened from a long sleep, and we have seen that the human condition is incompatible with certainty. . . . We must build our own tomorrow blindly, gropingly; build it from the roots, without giving in to the temptation of putting back together the fragments of our shattered idols, and without building new ones" (III: 828–9). His stories also have no closure, and are limited to pointing out existing dangers: whether he knew it or not, he shared the view of the black American science fiction writer and theorist Samuel Delany, who said that "endings to be useful must be inconclusive."[24] The moral dimension of all knowledge, the need to keep questioning the beliefs and the contradictions of his time, and the unceasing attempt to clarify the nature of problems—all features common to science fiction and *midrash*—are part of Levi's legacy to his readers.

Notes

1. All translations from Levi's writings and interviews are my own. References to Levi's works are, except when otherwise specified, to the three-volume Italian edition of his collected works (*Opere*). Many thanks are due to Valery Burley and Chris Palmer for their comments on an earlier version of this essay.
2. Translated in *The Sixth Day*.
3. See, for instance, the answer to a question from a Swiss reader (qtd. in Poli and Calcagno, *Echi di una voce perduta. Incontri, interviste e conversazioni con Primo Levi* [Milan: Mursia, 1992], pp. 39–40).
4. The only encounter with an alien in Levi's stories occurs in the 1977 story "L'intervista" ("The Interview," published in *The Mirror Maker*).
5. Translated in *The Sixth Day*.
6. For a discussion of irony and ethics in Levi's writings see Gordon (1997).
7. Both translated in *The Sixth Day*.
8. Published in *Lilít* and not translated into English.
9. Levi actually informs the readers that his story is based on authentic data, and that the Sirionos still exist, although they are in danger of extinction (III: 536–7).
10. Qtd. in Wolfe, "The Remaking of Zero: Beginning at the End" (*The End of the World* edited by Eric S. Rabin, Martin H. Greenberg, and Joseph D. Olander. [Carbondale: Southern Illinois University Press, 1979]), p. 4.
11. "L'inquietante futuro," interview with Luca Lamberti, *La Provincia*, 12 January 1971, p. 3.
12. Published in *Vizio di forma* and not translated into English.
13. Translated in *The Sixth Day*.
14. Published in *Lilít* and not translated into English.
15. Published in *Vizio di forma* and not translated into English. A sophisticated analysis of this story, particularly its intertextual literary references, is developed in Santagostino, "Nuove prospettive."

16. Translated in *Other People's Trades.*
17. See Holtz, pp. 180–94 (*Back to the Sources: Reading the Classic Jewish Texts*, New York: Simon & Schuster, 1984).
18. All three are translated in *The Sixth Day.*
19. The English translation of the title is somewhat misleading. The term is a bureaucratic expression meaning "involuntary retirement"; it was used, as well as in other contexts, in the law of 5 September 1938 which decreed the enforced retirement of Jewish public servants.
20. The notion of "lotus eaters", from the well-known episode in *The Odyssey*, is used by Brian Stableford as a metaphor for the science fiction theme of people satisfied with ersatz technological experiences (pp. 109–115). "Man-Made Catastrophes" in *The End of the World*, edited by Rabin, et al.
21. Reprinted with the title "Lo scriba" (The Scribe) in *L'altrui mestiere*. "The Scribe" is translated in *Other People's Trades.*
22. Translated in *The Mirror Maker.*
23. Translated in *Other People's Trades.*
24. Qtd. in Wolfe, *The Known and the Unknown: the Iconography of Science Fiction* (Kent State University Press, 1979), p. 129.

Part III

Levi's Poetry

6

At an Uncertain Hour: The Other Side of Primo Levi

Nicholas Patruno

Surviving the atrocity of Auschwitz, and having the need to tell about it, proved to be for Primo Levi the beginning of an experience which would hold considerable reward as well as anguish.

Owing his survival to a series of circumstances, many of which, he acknowledges, were beyond his control and, at times, unwittingly "lucky"—to use Levi's own term in the interview with Philip Roth—Levi learned early that to communicate was vital to one's survival and as a man of science, whose inclination it was to understand by way of patient analysis and observation, he was able to absorb, and then to communicate the Holocaust, as a personally-experienced event as well as something from which a lesson is to be learned.[1]

In the chapter "Communicating" of his book *The Drowned and the Saved*, Levi writes at length on the importance of communication.[2] On the more immediate and practical level, within the confines of the concentration camp, the ability to communicate in German or to understand the language increased one's chances of survival. In both *Survival in Auschwitz* and in *The Drowned and the Saved*, Levi recalls how many prisoners, especially among his fellow Italians, were immediately put to death simply because, unable to understand German, they could not follow orders.

In the Lager, the suppression of language served as a cruel reminder that there will be no voice left to tell and to confirm to the prisoners that they were no longer human. If the word, the *logos*, is what distinguishes rational beings from animals, then, to reduce humans to the state of an animal it was necessary for the Nazis to strip them of their verbal power to communicate. When it came to reducing the intelligible language to incongruent sounds and to twist terms to the point of losing their intended meaning, as both Levi and George Steiner have noted, the Nazis did not even spare their own traditional vocabulary which, to the chagrin of many German writers, they sought to replace with the old Prussian of the barracks and the newly coined terms of the SS jargon.[3]

In light of this situation, in Auschwitz Levi soon concluded that his survival, in physical and moral terms, depended largely on his ability to oppose this Nazi scheme. In the camp, to allow that "highly evolved and noble form, which is language" to "eclipse"—to use Levi's own term—was a sign of falling into a state of "definitive indifference," and that was tantamount to conceding defeat.[4] To Levi, language could not be separated from humanity and to harm one of them meant causing damage to the other. ". . . . [W]here violence is inflicted on man it is also inflicted on language," he writes in *The Drowned and the Saved* (97).

Auschwitz confirmed to him how vitally important it was to communicate. He found unacceptable claims to the contrary, as clearly evidenced by his powerful statement in *The Drowned and the Saved*:

> Except for cases of pathological incapacity, one can and must communicate, and thereby contribute in a useful and easy way to the peace of others and oneself, because silence, the absence of signals, is itself a signal, but an ambiguous one, and ambiguity generates anxiety and suspicion. To say that it is impossible to communicate is false; one always can. To refuse to communicate is a failing . . . (89)

On a more profound level, then, to communicate, to relate by way of the intelligible word, was the weapon with which to counteract and obstruct the Nazis' intention of completely annihilating the Jewish population. If just one voice emerged from that hellish experience to recount it, the German master plan, euphemistically referred to as the "final solution," would have then failed. Levi was impelled, by inner experience, to become that voice, and a very clear and powerful one at that. It is a voice through which Levi spoke not only for himself but also for all his brothers and sisters who, having perished, were unable to speak for themselves. Moreover, in speaking out he confirmed to himself, and proclaimed to his oppressors, that indeed he had come out of that horrendous experience still a man. Parenthetically, this is the question Levi poses—with a decidedly affirmative reply, as evidenced by his actions in the book's final chapter— in the title of his first book, which is, in Italian, *Se questo è un uomo* (*If This Is a Man*), a far more revealing title than the bland, comparatively speaking, *Survival in Auschwitz*.[5]

Building his narrative texts from memories, Levi was faced with the need to construct an ethic to record his experiences in a form from which other humans could learn. Having been raised, in his pre-Auschwitz days, in an environment inhabited by what he calls "civilized Cartesian phantoms," where dreams and aspirations emerge from and are nurtured by reason and logic, and backed with a solid schooling in all the traditional literary texts considered to be fundamental to an education in the humanities and the sciences, the narrative mode on which Levi relies came naturally to him. (*Survival 9*). His concise, sober, lean style, is reflective of a mind that insists on being guided by reason and civility. His emphasis on clarity, his dispassionate approach, his accurate observations, honed by his scientific training, eschewed emotions, leaving them to his readers. He does so because he is a rationalist, not because he is lacking profound passion, pain, and frustration. He dignifies himself and the reader by allowing the facts to speak for themselves, so that each person may therefore experience and interpret them within one's own emotional framework. As a witness and spokesperson, he was neither swayed nor subverted by hatred, or revenge. Neither did he attempt to elicit this response from his readers.

Levi often likened his ongoing, compelling need to address the effect and consequences of the death camps to that of Coleridge's *Ancient Mariner* who could not repress the urge to tell his "ghastly tale" to all. The importance he placed on four verses of that poem is manifested by their presence in the opening page of his book *The Drowned and the Saved*:

> Since then, at an uncertain hour,
> That agony returns,
> And till my ghastly tale is told
> This heart within me burns. (vv.582–585)

The emotional charge of these verses may help understand how difficult it must have been for Levi to put into words, in such a controlled fashion, the unrelenting fire raging in him. So strong was his commitment to the sanctity of his mission that he could not yield to his emotions. This may help explain why he initially used a pseudonym when writing on subjects which he originally considered unrelated to the Lager experience. This was the case with his book *Storie naturali*, a collection of short stories with a marked leaning towards science fiction. He would admit that, initially, he felt uncomfortable placing the same signature next to two literary modes that originally seemed to him to run along two different and distinct tracks.[6]

There appears to be a similar feeling of apprehension with his poetry. This significant side of Levi's literary production has not been given the full attention it deserves. For this Levi himself must bear a good part of the blame. In the preface to *Ad ora incerta* (*At an Uncertain Hour*), his central and most significant collection of poems, Levi, besides underrating his poems by claiming virtual ignorance of theories on poetry, adds that someone who composes a poem every now and then, as he does, cannot truly be called a poet. He contends that his poems, which he does not consider "eccellenti," make up the part of him deemed "unnatural" by his other "rational" part.[7] As to his poems, his judgment is no kinder in the book *Dialogo* where, in a 1984 interview, he confesses that he places little faith in their quality.[8] It is more than a question of quality, however. More likely, in fear of tarnishing the "rational" aspect of his persona, which is now his trademark, Levi seems reluctant to expose his "emotional" side to the world.

The poems reveal Levi's more intimate side, the part in which he releases his bottled-up emotions. One detects in them his therapeutic need to vent his innermost sentiments expressive of, but not limited to, joy, love, anger, social and environmental concerns, irony, humor, frustration, sadness and solitude.[9]

Included among these is a handful of poems through which Levi relives and responds to the agonizing experience of the Lager. There is "Shemà," the poem with which he opens his book *Survival in Auschwitz*, where he places a curse on those who, living in the comfort and warmth of their homes, neglect to meditate on the suffering inflicted on their fellow human beings in the concentration camps. He has also a punishing wish for a very long, sleepless life for Adolf Eichmann, the son of death—a night for each of the five million he sent to their death—in the poem "For Adolf Eichmann." He is pungently ironic in the poem "Annunciation," where he, with no disrespect intended for Catholicism, gives voice to an angel, different from the one who at another time descended to earth to promise another Lord, to announce to the expectant mother the coming of a Hitler-like evil self-declared savior.

In other poems the lingering pain of the Lager experience is more evident. In "Reveille," the opening poem of his book *The Reawakening*, Levi, even now that he is living in relative comfort, continues to be haunted by the expression "Wstawać" This word, Polish for "get up," that feared and painful awaited wake-up call of the Lager not to be disobeyed, is a constant irritant as it keeps on reminding him of the ache and despair it brought, to him and to the other prisoners, in anticipation of the daily abuse and suffering they were to endure.

In the poem "Ostjuden," (*Ostjuden* being the official term attributed to the Polish and Russian Jews), Levi pays tribute to his brothers and sisters of eastern Europe who, despite their suffering and continuous persecutions, have remained a steadfast and tenacious people of "altera cervice" ("stiff-necked"). In the poem "The Girl-Child of Pompeii," the sight of the body of a young girl imprisoned in a wall of petrified ashes brings to Levi's mind the sight of another girl, Anne Frank, she too imprisoned by four walls and then being turned into ashes and scattered in the wind. He directs his cry of anguish and anger, reminiscent of that of Leopardi in "La ginestra," to those who have the power and the means to be ruthless and destructive and begs them to stop, for nature, as evidenced by the eruption of Mount Vesuvius, can spew out enough punishment on her own. In "Dark Band" the observation of an almost insignificant but laborious and struggling anthill close by the trolley tracks in Turin brings back to the poet the disconsolate scene of the prisoners in the concentration camps, they too were slave laborers considered no more important than ants by their oppressors. The image is so painfully overwhelming that it becomes impossible for him to continue writing the poem. However, in "11 February, 1946," a love poem to his wife, the reader does see, if only for a fleeting moment, Primo Levi the victor, the one who, when face to face with death, shouted "no" from "every fibre" of his being as he refused to bend to the will of his persecutors.

But torn he was by the nagging and lingering "guilt of survival." In the poem "The Survivor," which opens with Coleridge's verse (from the "Rime of the Ancient Mariner") "Since then, at an uncertain hour" and from which this collection of poems takes its name (*Ad ora incerta*), Levi touches the nadir of despair. By way of a description of their emaciated physical conditions, Levi alludes to the state of affliction of the detainees—and of his own—in the concentration camp and to their eventual death. But he, unlike them, has survived. Overcome by the sense of guilt, he feels the need to justify his fate by shouting—but, with little self-assurance—that his survival, unlike that of other prisoners, did not come at the expense of others.[10]

These verses of Coleridge, which Levi found so fitting to his own situation, appear now to plague him. While, at one time, they helped to stimulate in him the need to tell what he had witnessed, they now return to haunt him. The "agony" endures because, afflicted by this sense of survivor's guilt, he finds it increasingly difficult to justify to himself the self-appointed task to be a witness for those who could not speak themselves. How could he, a survivor, know what it meant to touch bottom and, that being the case, how trustworthy could his "ghastly tale" be?

The obsession with these self-doubts, counteracted by the rise in revisionist movements which questioned the reality of the Holocaust, gave Levi cause to question the success he was having in getting his message across. No longer convinced that reason is the proper channel to follow to explain the Holocaust, and with the need to tell still burning within him, he seeks an outlet by turning to his emotional side.

A clear manifestation of this is present in the closing pages of *The Drowned and the Saved*, his most psychologically incisive and last major work connected with his experience at Auschwitz. In this book he goes beyond witnessing. He "revisits"—to use Levi's own word—Auschwitz, for the last time, by way of a series of penetrating essays on the Lager and on its consequences. Following a close examination of the facts, he is now ready to accuse and, implicitly, to pass judgment. He reaches the moment of anger and extreme frustration following the essay "Letters from Germans." These letters, which he received from Germans following the publication, in Germany, of *Survival in Auschwitz*, confirm to him that they have not grasped the gravity of the offense, and most likely never will.

It is clear to Levi that, between those who barely acknowledge what happened, those who accept it but only conditionally, those who deny it outright, and those who in their ignorance and stupidity still take pride in what they have done, the German people, be it out of shame, embarrassment, simple obtuseness, or arrogance, are not willing to acknowledge the cowardice of their past behavior. Sadder still, as time goes on the memory of the Holocaust is fading with the deaths of those who did bear witness. If the skeptical younger generations acknowledge the event, they see it as a historical dinosaur with little or no relevance to their lives.

Confronted with this reality, Levi doubts his success in having made others aware of the Holocaust and of its repercussions. He fears that, in the long run, this horrible event has not made any great impact on those who were not victimized by it. Those same people who claim that another Holocaust cannot take place because times have changed reveal their skepticism when they sustain that wars cannot be avoided and that violence is sometimes needed to prevent more violence. To Levi, these are all obscene statements demonstrative of complete insensitivity towards all those who have been victimized by this kind of warped reasoning, and he vehemently denies them. There is nothing, he insists, that cannot be resolved by discussion. The only thing needed is a demonstration of good faith.

Here, Levi's tone is one of passion, something which, earlier, would have been out of character for him. He has realized that, in order to be heard, he must appeal to more than reason. Reason had not served him well enough to make a dent in indifference; and perhaps, he pondered, reason was not the proper vehicle to describe and analyze the Lager, which, as he had stated repeatedly, was the product of an evil aimed at defying human reason. For as much as Levi pleads that a heedless society sharpen its senses and not pay attention to "beautiful words" that are not supported by sound reason, the reader senses in these words a last ditch effort to avoid the unavoidable.

With his desperate cry "we must be listened to" (*Saved* 199) Levi expresses the pain of a man who fears that his story and, through his, that of millions who have paid with the ultimate sacrifice, will be forgotten. He owes it more to them than to himself to make sure such a tragedy never takes place again, even if he has to resort to emotional pleas to drive this point home. The younger generations must believe him when he says that, even if not carried to the point of a nuclear confrontation, the conflicts of more recent years (such as the ones in Vietnam, Cambodia, Afghanistan, the Falklands, Iran, and Iraq) are all examples of how devastating a war can be in an industrialized and technological age. Through these events, society must see that the potential of another Holocaust is always present. What has happened in the past can happen again if caution and vigilance are not exercised. One must stand guard because the tormentor has no distinguishing features. They are the product of an average education and are thus no different from most civil servants who obey orders without questioning them.

The Holocaust took place because most chose not to ask questions, because most chose not to be different from others. Implied in Levi's cry is his appeal to society to be ready to question and to hold those who govern accountable for their acts. Millions of lives were lost because an entire society refused to exercise those rights. In light of the sad events of more recent years wars, conflicts, doubts and denials of the atrocities of the past, Levi seriously questions if today's society has the moral courage to correct what is wrong. As he bursts forth with harsh, strong words, in a tone not to be found in any of his other works, understanding now gives way to severe judgment. The severe tone of his words "Let it be clear" (*Saved* 203) leaves no doubt about the firmness of his conviction that the blame for the Holocaust lies on the great majority of Germans who, "out of mental laziness, myopic calculation, stupidity, and national pride" (*Saved* 203), swallowed the "beautiful words" of "corporal" Hitler. Levi's mockery is plain in the juxtaposition of the rank and name.

Levi is enraged because he fears that, despite the collective stupidity, the Germans are about to have the last laugh. In his preface to this work he writes that the SS enjoyed cynically telling the prisoners that, no matter what, the Germans would have won the war because no one would be left to bear witness. Now, forty years later, Levi realizes that time is proving them right. Those who did bear witness are dying, and, with them, so is the memory of this century's most inhuman atrocity. At this point he has to ask himself if his own efforts, which have so far kept him alive and writing, will serve any purpose whatsoever.

There is a postscript to *The Drowned and the Saved* that should not go unmentioned. Levi died, presumably by suicide, a year after this book's publication. Among the many who accept that his death was a suicide, there are those who feel that it is merely a coincidence that this particular book was the last of his works to be published before his death. Were it not for other small but significant pieces of evidence derived from interviews and other minor works, the idea of a coincidence could be accepted with little argument. However, as Levi states in *Dialogo* (63) the mere fact that he temporarily interrupted this work to write *If Not Now, When?* gives cause for speculation. *Dialogo*, published in 1984, provides some revealing information on Levi's attitude toward his own writing. He admits, with obvious disappointment, to having exhausted his creative reservoirs and that he is writing poems to which he does not give much value. He states that perhaps the time has come for him to follow a new direction.

At the same time he returned to complete *The Drowned and the Saved*, he also discovered the computer which, impressed by how much it facilitated the mechanics of his writing, led him to state that to be without it would be tantamount to separating oneself from society and to insist on living at its margins. Rather perplexing is his claim that it is best just to use the computer and "repress the humanistic desire to understand "what's in it"" (*Dialogo* 64; my translation). These observations about the computer, as superficial as they might appear, reveal, one more time, a side of himself that seems out of character for the Levi who is familiar to his readers. Both as a scientist and as a writer, Levi placed the need to understand above everything else. Now, with that "to repress the humanistic desire," he appears to have changed his position. This remark, considered in conjunction with his overall dissatisfaction with his work, indicates that he has reached a critical point and that whatever he is producing comes more from sheer inertia than from—to use his own words—"humanistic desire."

Levi's emptiness and disillusionment are also reflected in his increasing references to the "black holes," which he uses as metaphors to express the dark void that history was and is making of the Holocaust. The pain this causes him is very much in evidence in the last article he wrote about Auschwitz, "Buco nero di Auschwitz" ("The Black Hole of Auschwitz") which appeared in the Turin daily *La Stampa* (22 January 1987) less than three months before his death.[11] In it he takes issue with several German historians (including Nolte and Hillgruber) and revisionists, if not deniers, who are attempting to distort and trivialize the Holocaust by raising inane questions concerning the accuracy of the number of deaths and, worse still, by questioning whether the Holocaust ever occurred. The title of this article suggests that nothing of importance seems to have come out of Auschwitz, no lasting lesson, and it is unlikely that any will. The "black hole," then, is a confirmation of his fear, raised in his essay "Stereotypes," (*Saved*, 165-66) that with the passing of time the mystery of the Holocaust will only increase and its impact disappear. At this point Levi sees a bleak future ahead with little promise for any improvement.

In light of this prevalent state of dismal indifference, Levi, who had come face to face with the demons of humanity and touched death in a way that few have, has the right to shout in his desperate, and final, attempt to shake humanity out of its complacency.

Notes

1. See interview with Philip Roth, "A Man Saved by His Skills," *The New York Times Book Review* 12 October 1986: 40. Levi states: "In my case, luck played an essential role in at least two occasions . . ."
2. Levi will make this point in several of his works. Also in "Sorgente di Vita," a documentary/interview in which Levi revisits Auschwitz in the early 80s.
3. George Steiner, "The Hollow Miracle," *Language and Science* (New York: Atheneum, 1967), p. 97.
4. *The Drowned and The Saved*, 89.
5. In fact, *Survival in Auschwitz* originally appeared in English under the title *If This Is a Man* (New York: The Orion Press, 1959).
6. Levi originally published this work under the nom de plume Damiano Malabaila. Several of these stories have been translated into English and are included in Primo Levi's *The Sixth Day and Other Tales* (New York: Summit Books, 1990).
7. Primo Levi, preface, *Ad ora incerta*, in *Opere*, vol. II (Torino: Einaudi, 1988), p. 521.

8. Primo Levi and Tullio Regge, *Dialogo* (Torino: Einaudi, 1984) 63.
9. All poems quoted in this paper are included in Primo Levi's *Collected Poems* trans. Ruth Feldman and Brian Swann (London-Boston: Faber and Faber, 1988).
10. In my view, this is confirmed by the closing line of the poem, loosely borrowed from Dante *Inferno*, Canto XXXIII, I., p. 141). With this line Dante questions, with disbelief, the identity of Branca d'Oria, a sinner in the ninth circle in Hell, since Dante claims to have seen him alive and well on earth. This suggests that Levi too sees himself breathing but that, in some ways, he is already dead.
11. This article has been translated into English under the title "The Dispute among German Historians" and is included in Levi's *The Mirror Maker* trans. Raymond Rosenthal (New York: Schoken Books, 1989), pp. 163–66.

Part IV

Levi and Language

7

On Language and Violence

Brian Cliff

Primo Levi was convinced that "where violence is inflicted on man it is also inflicted on language."[1] This essay will examine the violence done to humanity through the violence done to language, with a primary focus on the Lager jargon, and will attempt to show how language can be used as a weapon to form a vicious circle, wherein a definition leads to its own justification. In the context of the camps, this abuse of language was used to create a certain moral efficiency. This efficiency, in turn, proved a critical ingredient in the recipe for the violence done to humanity. George Orwell's argument about political language holds equally true for the language of the Third Reich and of the camps in particular: this language was "designed to make lies sound truthful and murder respectable."[2]

In his Afterword to *The Reawakening*, Levi elaborates on how this language was used in the Lager:

> Among other precautions, in order to keep the secret, in official language only cautious and cynical euphemisms were employed: one did not write 'extermination' but 'final solution,' not 'deportation' but 'transfer,' not 'killing by gas' but 'special treatment,' and so on. Not without reason, Hitler feared that this horrendous news, if it were divulged, would compromise the blind faith which

> the country had in him, as well as the morale of the fighting troops.[3]

These euphemisms, as Levi calls them, were part of a larger construction, the purpose of which was to eradicate the Jews. Specifically, such euphemisms contributed to this process insofar as they distorted and twisted the language. This linguistic violence simultaneously justified the physical violence and helped make it possible. The process of Auschwitz, then, begins by defining those designated as "the Other" as less than human, or simply as not human, as in the case of *Häftling* vs. *Mann*. When the Other is less than human, laws can be written and enacted that strip the Other of the rights reserved for human beings. When no longer human, either in the eyes of the law or in the minds of the general populace, the Other can be treated accordingly—as less than human. George Steiner aptly describes this process whereby "words lost their original meaning and acquired nightmarish definitions. *Jude, Pole, Russe* came to mean two-legged lice, putrid vermin which good Aryans must squash, as a party manual said, 'like roaches on a dirty wall.'"[4] In such a context as Levi carefully describes, those so categorized respond by taking on the role of the subhuman into which they have been placed.[5] Finally, the oppressors, who began the circle by defining the other as less than human, now see themselves and their actions, "taken in defense," as justified.

Within this vicious circular logic, they are right. In forcing the Other into a "subhuman" condition, the oppressors force them to behave as though they were less than human, and thereby to fulfill "all the expectations" of the oppressors:

> In fact, we are the untouchables to the civilians. They think, more or less explicitly—with all the nuances lying between contempt and commiseration—that as we have been condemned to this life of ours, reduced to our condition, we must be tainted by some mysterious, grave sin. They hear us speak in many different languages, which they do not understand, and which sound to them as gro-

> tesque as animal noises; they see us reduced to ignoble slavery, without hair, without honor and without names, beaten every day, more abject every day, and they never see in our eyes a light of rebellion, or of peace, or of faith. They know us as thieves and untrustworthy, muddy, ragged and starving, and mistaking the effect for the cause, they judge us worthy of our abasement.[6]

This abasement, as Levi continually asserts, was inextricably dependent upon the violence done to language. The abuse of language was morally efficient, and it cleared the way for the awful efficiency of the camps.

This Lager German was not the German of Mann or Rilke, but was rather, "skeletal, howled, studded with obscenities and imprecations . . . only vaguely related to the precise, austere language of my chemistry textbooks. [. . .]"[7] This comparison is indeed appropriate, for Levi the writer was as attentive to the building blocks of language, as Levi the chemist was to the building blocks of matter. Although Levi analyses this linguistic matter throughout his writings, let us, for the moment, focus on his discussion of Lager jargon.

The Lager term most often found in Levi's writings is *Muselmann*, a dated German word meaning, literally, Muslim. The term was applied to "the irreversibly exhausted, worn out prisoner close to death."[8] The most common explanation for this odd appellation relies on the imagery of the final physical collapse of the *Muselmänner*, which apparently reminded some of the Muslim prayer position. The brutality of this expression arises from its indication of a complete lack of concern for the dying. This single word, then, truly illustrates the isolation of the individual among the mass of people in the camps. In *Survival in Auschwitz*, Levi says that these *Muselmänner*

> form the backbone of the camp, an anonymous mass, continually renewed and always identical, of non-men who march and labour in silence, the divine spark dead within them, already too empty to really suffer. One hesitates to call them living: one hesitates to call their death death, in

> the face of which they have no fear, as they are too tired to understand.[9]

Note Levi's comment on the lack of a suitable vocabulary for these men: "One hesitates to call them living: one hesitates to call their death death . . ." Our words, the words of the world outside the Lager, are not fitted to this condition; they do not suffice. As Levi says in *Survival*, had the Lagers "lasted longer a new, harsh language would have been born [. . .]."[10]

Instead of a new language, however, the conditions of the Lager resulted in the violent abuse and manipulation of existing language. When the prisoners ate, they themselves used the word *fressen*, which normally refers to animals eating, rather than the verb *essen*, which has the standard connotations of "eat" in English:

> The Kapo comes to us periodically and calls: '*Wer hat noch zu fressen?*' He does not say it from derision or to sneer, but because this way of eating on our feet, furiously, burning our mouths and throats, without time to breathe, really is '*fressen*,' the way of eating of animals, and certainly not '*essen*,' the human way of eating, seated in front of a table, religiously. '*Fressen*' is exactly the right word, and is used currently among us.[11]

Unlike the use of *Muselmänner*, *fressen* here signals the application of an insidious and violent vocabulary to Levi and his friends. The object is no longer an external other, but now includes Levi himself. The language of this paragraph also exemplifies Levi's use of dramatic understatement. When he writes that the *Kapo* "does not say it from derision or to sneer," Levi does not do so to paint a generous picture of the *Kapo*. Instead, he leaves it unsaid, but distinctly implied, that the system in which the *Häftlinge* were living, and in which the *Kapo* was a complicit part of the power structure, had also reduced them to an animal-like state of existence. This condition was so pervasive that, as Levi tells us ("it is exactly the right word and is used currently among us"), the prisoners internalized the dehumanizing vocabulary that normally described animal behaviour and that the Nazis now applied to them. In this context, the *Kapo*'s use of "*fressen*" is neither hateful nor mocking, but merely "appropriate." Rather than an explicit absolution of the *Kapo*, the passage functions as an *implicit* condemnation of the system, and therefore, to a certain extent, an implicit judgment of those who were involved in maintaining it. Thus, the emphasis is not on the word "*fressen*" itself, but on the process that made it "exactly the right word."

These linguistic abuses were omnipresent from the very beginning of Levi's contact with the Germans. When the Germans held a roll call before loading Levi and his companions on the train to Auschwitz, an officer asked the corporal who had been counting the number of deportees a simple question: "*Wieviel Stück?*"[12] Here we have a prime example of the bluntness of this new language: the sentence is extremely clipped, lacking even the simple ornamentation of a verb. Levi literally translates the question as asking how many "pieces" are present. He does not comment on the significance of this vocabulary directly, but that is not to say he makes no judgment. By putting "pieces" inside quotation marks, Levi sets it apart from the rest of the text and marks it as alien, both from the text and from himself. In the very next paragraph, however, he repeats the phrase of the German corporal, "six hundred and fifty 'pieces,'" now with the significant substitution of "men," emphatically *not* in quotation marks, for the dehumanizing "pieces." In doing so, Levi quietly reclaims humanity for himself and for his companions.

Two sentences later, Levi again notes the vocabulary of the Germans: "Exactly like this, detail for detail: goods wagons closed from the outside, with men, women and children pressed together without pity, like cheap merchandise [. . .]."[13] In this deceptively simple sentence, Levi comments on and resists the linguistic strategies at work. "Strategies" is the appropriate word here, for the vocabulary of these Germans was far from incidental or accidental: as Steiner has noted, "A language being used to run hell [acquires] the habits of hell."[14] By insisting on the term "goods wagons"—it is the second time he has used it in three sentences—Levi subtly reinforces not so much the harsh conditions of the transport as he does the way in which the Germans viewed the deportees: *"stück,"* to be stacked in a train car. In the phrase "like cheap merchandise," Levi comes as close to a direct comment on this situation as he ever does. This is what the prisoners represent for the Germans, and Levi understands it only too well.

"Pieces" was, of course, a terribly and perversely ironic word for the Germans to use. Arno Mayer writes that,

> On the average, the life expectancy of the able-bodied Jewish inmates who were assigned to the constantly replenished pool of unskilled, heavy labor at Monowitz was between three and four months. They either collapsed and died at Monowitz, or were returned as 'unfit' to the SS for disposal at Birkenau.[15]

Echoing Levi's use of "pieces," Mayer places "unfit" in quotation marks within his own text. The effect of both words is the same. One, "pieces," initiated the prisoners' contact with the calculatingly dehumanizing language of the Nazis and signaled that, in the eyes and minds of their captors, the Jews were not human beings—just pieces for transport. The other, "unfit," completed the circle and brought a deadly end to that contact.

Later in *Survival in Auschwitz*, Levi describes a "selection," itself a deceptively innocuous word used for the process of weeding out the "fit" prisoners from such "unfit" prisoners:

> Each one of us, as he comes naked out of the *Tagesraum* into the cold October air, has to run the few steps between the two doors, give the card to the SS man and enter the dormitory door. The SS man, in the fraction of a second between two successive crossings, with a glance at one's back and front, judges everyone's fate, and in turn gives the card to the man on his right or his left, and this is the life or death of each of us. In three or four minutes a hut of two hundred men is 'done,' as is the whole camp of twelve thousand men in the course of the afternoon.[16]

Here, Levi employs the same register, the same diction, and the same use of quotation marks as in the case of "pieces." Levi's separation of "done" from the rest of the text via the quotation marks serves as the strongest commentary here, as above. We as readers are forced to make our own judgments, to face our own reactions to the events described in the text. Because Levi will not do that for us, because he will not make it easy, he does not comment on the process beyond noting that each individual's fate was decided "in the fraction of a second," and that two hundred prisoners were "done" in three or four minutes. On this aspect of his writing, Levi says, "It's true that I refrained from formulating judgments in *Survival in Auschwitz*. I did so deliberately, because it seemed to me inopportune, not to say importunate, on the part of the witness, namely myself, to take the place of the judge. So I suspended any explicit judgment, while the implicit judgments are clearly there."[17]

Undoubtedly Levi's most intensely harrowing example of the effect this defilement of language had on an individual human being appears in his second book, *The Reawakening*:

> Hurbinek was a nobody, a child of death, a child of Auschwitz. He looked about three years old, no one knew anything of him, he could not speak and he had no name; that curious name, Hurbinek, had been given to him by us, perhaps by one of the women who had interpreted with those syllables one of the inarticulate sounds that the baby let out now and again. He was paralysed from the waist down, with atrophied legs, as thin as sticks; but his eyes, lost in his triangular and wasted face, flashed terribly alive, full of demand, assertion, of the will to break loose, to shatter the tomb of his dumbness. The speech he lacked, which no one had bothered to teach him, the need of speech charged his stare with explosive urgency: it was a stare both savage and human, even mature, a judgement, which none of us could support, so heavy was it with force and anguish.[18]

This physical expression of the extreme will to communicate stretches the limits of the imagination as only something from within the boundaries of Auschwitz can. The vocabulary of this paragraph consists of words and phrases ("the will to break loose, to shatter the tomb of his dumbness," "the need of speech charged his stare with explosive urgency") the stark passion of which appropriately stands out, even in the midst of writing as strenuously clear as Levi's.[19]

Among the survivors present with Levi, only one could bring himself to work with Hurbinek. Henek, a fifteen-year-old Hungarian, spent hours upon hours at Hurbinek's bedside, caring for him and speaking Hungarian to him. Henek attempted not only to communicate with the boy, to let him hear warm words of human speech addressed to him, but also to teach Hurbinek to speak. Just as Henek cared for Hurbinek's physical needs by feeding and washing him, so he cared for his almost-physical and non-physical needs by making an extended effort to communicate with him. Levi sounds pained to admit that this fifteen year old boy was able to do what all the others thought should be done, but could not bring themselves to do. For Levi, Henek was the only one who could "support" this "stare both savage and human" which was "so heavy . . . with force and anguish."

After a week of this intensive care giving, Henek told the others that Hurbinek had learned a word. Everyone else responded to Hurbinek's effort, and tried not only to hear what Hurbinek was saying but also to identify the word and *understand* what he was saying. Everyone, Hurbinek included, strove to communicate. As long as Hurbinek lived, he kept saying that "word," but to no avail. At the end, Hurbinek died not having been understood, not having been able to communicate. In the incantatory paragraph in which he gives testimony to Hurbinek, one can hear Levi's voice straining with the anger and righteous indignation that he so rarely lets to the surface:

> Hurbinek, who was three years old and perhaps had been born in Auschwitz and had never seen a tree; Hurbinek, who had fought like a man, to the last breath, to gain his entry into the world of men, from which a bestial power had excluded him; Hurbinek, the nameless, whose tiny

> forearm—even his—bore the tattoo of Auschwitz; Hurbinek died in the first days of March 1945, free but not redeemed. Nothing remains of him: he bears witness through these words of mine.[20]

Unable to form his own words, Hurbinek lives on in the words of another: the absurdity, the indignity and the offense that was Auschwitz reaches one of its awful peaks in this story of a three year old boy. Hurbinek is representative of what Auschwitz produced; literally and figuratively, he is the extreme result of the subversion of communication and the perversion of language that contributed to the destruction of human beings. This three year old boy, created in a very real sense by the Nazis' brutal abuse of language, embodies the deathly silence that resulted. His will to speak mirrors and gives force to Levi's own compulsion to testify. When Levi wrote, he must have been urged on by the image of Hurbinek, crippled, struggling with what little life force he had to communicate, and dying, alone in the midst of a crowded room, unable to make that essentially human connection. To borrow from Coleridge, as Levi often did, Hurbinek and the way of his death and of his life were surely one of the fires that made Levi's heart burn until his "ghastly tale" was told.[21]

Notes

1. Primo Levi, *The Drowned and the Saved*, trans. Raymond Rosenthal (New York: Vintage International, 1989), p. 97.
2. George Orwell, "Politics and the English Language," *The Norton Anthology of English Literature*, ed. M.H. Abrams et al., sixth ed., Vol. 2 (New York: W.W. Norton, 1993), p. 2242.
3. Primo Levi, *The Reawakening*, trans. Stuart Woolf, Afterword trans. Ruth Feldman (New York: Collier, 1987), p. 199.
4. George Steiner, "The Hollow Miracle" in *Language and Silence* (New York: Atheneum, 1967), p. 100.
5. For example: "They looked around them with bewildered eyes, like trapped animals, and that is what they had in fact become" (Levi, *The Drowned and the Saved*, p. 96).

6. Primo Levi, *Survival in Auschwitz*, trans. Stuart Woolf (New York: Collier, 1961), pp. 110–111.
7. Levi goes on to say that the Lager German was "a variant, particularly barbarized, of what a German Jewish philologist, Klemperer, had called *Lingua Tertii Imperii*, the language of the Third Reich, actually proposing for it the acronym LTI with an ironic analogy to the hundred other acronyms . . . dear to the Germany of that time" (Levi, *The Drowned and the Saved*, p. 97).
8. Levi, *The Drowned and the Saved*, p. 98.
9. Levi, *Survival*, p. 82.
10. Levi, *Survival*, p. 113.
11. Levi, *Survival*, pp. 68–69. Levi frequently switches back and forth between the past and present tenses in *Survival*. Gabriel Motola describes this "seemingly unconscious use of verb tenses" as an indicator of "the process used to bring about the destruction of man: the present tense in *Survival* indicates an actual reliving of the particular experience while the past tense is indicative of a more general though no less terrifying communal experience or statistic" (Gabriel Motola, "Primo Levi: The Auschwitz Experience," *Southwest Review* 72 [1987]: 260–261).
12. Levi, *Survival*, p. 12.
13. Levi, *Survival*, pp. 12–13.
14. Steiner, p. 100.
15. Arno J. Mayer, *Why Did the Heavens Not Darken?* (New York: Pantheon, 1990), pp. 359–360.
16. Levi, *Survival*, pp. 116–117.
17. Ferdinando Camon, *Conversations with Primo Levi*, trans. John Shepley (Marlboro: The Marlboro Press, 1989), p. 13.
18. Levi, *The Reawakening*, p. 11.
19. This is Lawrence R. Schehr's phrase: "Primo Levi's Strenuous Clarity," *Italica* 66.4 (1989): 429–443.
20. Levi, *The Reawakening*, p. 12.
21. Samuel Taylor Coleridge, *The Rime of the Ancient Mariner*, line 584, qtd. in Levi, *The Drowned and the Saved*, 7.

8

On Language and Personhood: A Linguistic Odyssey

Patricia Sayre and Linnea Vacca

These are "ashes that once were men." Such is the bitter lament of the chorus in Aeschylus' *Agamemnon* when the remains of dead sons are returned from Troy.[1] These words could just as easily have been uttered as sober observation of fact in the Nazi death camps of our own era. Violence is the great transmuter of humans into things, death the ultimate step in the transmutation, and language the intimate handmaid in this grim diminishment. Much attention has been given to language as it figures into the destruction of personhood in the Lagers, and nowhere are the linguistic aspects of depersonalization better documented than in Primo Levi's works. But the use of language to undo persons is only half the story. Levi's works also offer compelling testimony to the capacity of language to reconstitute life and meaning, even for those apparently destroyed by its violent abuse.

In our essay, we offer a brief description of some of the Lager's dehumanizing techniques as they involve manipulating language to turn persons into objects. We then trace Levi's journey back to Italy from the Lager—a journey back to membership in a linguistic community in which persons are once again valued as such. We conclude with a summary analysis of elements contributing to the success of Levi's endeavor, as writer and Holocaust survivor, to reconstitute humanity through language.

Nazi Germany's Lagers turned persons into things by systematically destroying the structures framing human life. The family unit was forcibly torn asunder at the moment of arrival through segregation by sex and a process of "selection" that assigned the newly arrived to either slow death through slave labor or immediate annihilation in the gas chambers. Even when members of the same family or friends or people originally from the same community were among those chosen to work, in a camp the size of Auschwitz there was no guarantee of regular daily contact or, indeed, of any contact at all. Nor did circumstances in the Lager encourage the formation of new friendships or mutually helpful communities. Lack of food and appalling living conditions left prisoners with little energy for endeavors beyond those essential to individual survival. Cut off from the support of family and community, prisoners might still have found a structure in work that sustained their conception of themselves as human beings, but, as Levi tells us, work assignments in the Lager were arranged to minimize any sense of meaningful accomplishment. Tasks were repetitious and often appeared to accomplish no intelligible end—pure mindless labor.

Language sustains virtually all the social structures that form the matrix of human experience; it is vital to our capacity to construct a sense of self, and gives purpose and significance to our lives. It is no surprise, then, that prisoners were initiated into the Lager by having their names stripped away and replaced with serial numbers. What better way to undermine their familiar sense of self as having a recognized place in a linguistic community with rich and complex traditions? Levi laments, "They will even take away our name: and if we want to keep it, we will have to find ourselves the strength to do so, to manage somehow so that behind the name something of us, of us as we were, still remains."[2]

Employing language that reinforces the notion that prisoners are items to be processed is an effective first step in a policy designed to eradicate the personality of the individual.

The next step is to deprive prisoners of their own capacity to generate meaningful language by throwing together speakers of dozens of mutually unintelligible languages in circumstances so brutal and degrading that efforts to build linguistic bridges are kept to a minimum. "The confusion of languages," Levi notes, "is a fundamental component of the manner of living here: one is surrounded by a perpetual Babel, in which everyone shouts orders and threats in languages never heard before, and woe betide whoever fails to grasp the meaning. No one has time here, no one has patience, no one listens to you . . ."[3] In this Babel, guards issue life-or-death orders in German, a language that most do not comprehend, and severely punish those who do not obey:

> To those who did not understand them the [guards] reacted in a manner that astonished and frightened us; an order that had been pronounced in the calm voice of a man who knows he will be obeyed was repeated word for word in a loud angry voice, then screamed at the top of his lungs as if he were addressing a deaf person or indeed a domestic animal, more responsive to the tone than to the content of the message.[4]

In such interactions the prisoners' capacity to speak their own languages no longer has any value; without words, they are no longer persons to be reasoned with but mute beasts to be beaten into submission.

Destroying the prisoners' sense of linguistic efficacy was integral to the ideology of the Lager. Limiting their capacity to form linguistic communities not only reduced the likelihood of organized resistance but made it extremely difficult to sustain the sense of shared moral space that gives coherence and meaning to events and actions. Under conditions of extreme physical and moral deprivation, brutality readily becomes the norm. And here the suppression of language has yet another role to play: it is easier to do the unspeakable to other persons if they cannot speak, for it is easier to view them as objects indifferent to pain. Transforming persons into objects while they still live is a brutally efficient way to hasten them to their literal death. And death—creating ashes where once there were men—is the Lager's consummate contribution to the "final solution."

A corollary of Lager ideology and methods is that those who survive the camps have before them a horrendously difficult task: regaining their sense of themselves as human beings through reintegration into the structures the camps had set out systematically to destroy. It is a testimony to human resilience that so many Holocaust survivors have been so successful in this task. That so many have felt compelled to write about their experience is testimony to the importance of words when rebuilding a life in the Lager's despite. That the process of finding the right words should reveal a major literary talent, as it did in the case of Primo Levi, is a triumph over the Lager that no one (Levi least of all) could have foreseen. The role of language in reweaving the fabric of relationships and significances that constitute meaningful life is not only a subject of Primo Levi's work but is bodied forth in the very fact of the work itself. Small miracles of rebirth unfold on the pages of Levi's story of his journey back—literally to Italy, figuratively to life—but the great miracle is that the story could be told at all, and told with such grace.

If *The Truce* is an odyssey of language regained, it is fitting that the first and most moving in the series of vignettes comprising Levi's narrative should feature a linguistic anomally. Under the care of his Soviet liberators, Levi has just completed the shortest leg of what will be a long journey: leaving the work camp of Buna-Monowitz for Auschwitz proper. In the Auschwitz barracks he encounters Hurbinek, a small boy perhaps three years old, paralyzed from the waist down, about whom no one knows anything. His name has been given him by the other newly-released prisoners with whom he has been temporarily housed. He cannot speak and yet,

> his eyes, lost in his triangular and wasted face, flashed terribly alive, full of demand, assertion, of the will to break loose, to shatter the tomb of his dumbness. . . . [T]he need of speech charged his stare with explosive urgency: it was a stare both savage and human, even mature, a

> judgement, which none of us could support, so heavy was it with force and anguish.[5]

Due largely to the patient ministrations of Henek, a teenaged Hungarian who, unlike the others, seems to be "immune to the distressing power [the small child] emanated," Hurbinek eventually utters a word.[6] Or, more accurately, he produces several slightly different variations on an articulated sound. "In the following days," Levi reports, "everybody listened to him in silence, anxious to understand," but although among them were speakers of "all the languages of Europe . . . Hurbinek's word remained secret." Hurbinek, "who had fought like a man, to the last breath, to gain his entry into the world of men," died in Auschwitz, a month after the liberation of the camp, "free but not redeemed."[7]

The story of little Hurbinek can serve as a trope for the task of reintegration faced by all the prisoners on their release from the camps. Like Hurbinek, the newly-released prisoners were in many respects those about whom nothing was known. For many of them, no one who might know them was left in the world outside the Lager, entire families and communities having been wiped out as part of the Nazi purification schemes. Yet even for those for whom something might remain of their former lives, the world to which they would return had little knowledge of their ordeal. Information about the camps was fragmentary and uncertain during the period of their existence. The Nazis took considerable care to keep the evidence hidden from those outside Germany, while the "willed ignorance" of many inside Germany created a great cloud of unknowing that kept the truth at bay.[8] Nor, on Levi's account, was very much known even by those inside the Lagers:

> For knowledge of the Lagers, the Lagers themselves were not always a good observation post: in the inhuman conditions to which they were subjected, the prisoners could barely acquire an overall vision of their universe. . . . [T]he prisoner felt overwhelmed by a massive edifice of violence and menace but could not form for himself a

> representation of it because his eyes were fixed on the ground by every single minute's needs.[9]

These considerations aside, there is also a very real sense in which those who spent time in the Lagers became by definition unknowable, for what had happened to them lay beyond the pale of rational comprehension. From the first moment of arrival, Levi writes, "we became aware that our language lacks words to express this offense, the demolition of a man."[10]

If, like Hurbinek, the newly-liberated prisoners were essentially unknown, there were also those among them who, again like Hurbinek, desired to make themselves known. And this not only for personal reasons; much more was at stake. In *If This Is a Man*, Levi tells how his instinct for cleanliness left him after only a week in prison. In his despair, he bitterly chastises an older man who washes vigorously every morning for failing to see the futility of continuing to bathe. The older prisoner interrupts Levi in mid-sentence "and administers [him] a complete lesson." Levi much regrets he cannot reconstruct his teacher's exact words or manner of speaking: "But this was the sense, not forgotten either then or later: that precisely because the Lager was a great machine to reduce us to beasts, we must not become beasts; that even in this place one can survive, and therefore one must want to survive, to tell the story, to bear witness. . . ."[11] Time and time again in his works, Levi reports that it was precisely the desire to bear witness, to use language to tell the story, that sustained him in the camps. He adds that on his release, telling the story was a matter of as much urgency to him as uttering a word had been to Hurbinek; the things he had experienced in the camps "were things that I had inside, that occupied me and that I had to expel: tell them, indeed shout them out from the rooftops."[12]

It is one thing to desire to speak, however, and another actually to find words to communicate that which appears to be beyond the expressive powers of language. Although Levi had no Henek—no single individual devoted to helping him find his word—he did have the companionship of the diverse cast of characters with whom he made the journey back. The anecdotes Levi culls from these months of travel turn the Babel imagery of the camps on its head, so that linguistic diversity is no longer a life-threatening source of distress but rather provides a series of opportunities for increasingly creative efforts at communication. By the end of the journey, Levi is able to write that the months of wandering just past, "although hard," are nevertheless "like a truce, a parenthesis of unlimited availability, a providential but unrepeatable gift of fate."[13] This gift makes its first, tentative appearance while the newly-liberated prisoners are still in the main camp at Auschwitz. People start to speak to everyone and no one, in the case of Kleine Kiepura, "as if in a dream,"[14] or, in the case of Frau Vita, "with tearful eyes, starved of words,"[15] or, in the case of Olga, "by candlelight, with . . . eyes fixed on the ground."[16] Here there is certainly speech, although it is only a hesitant move in the direction of genuine communication. Still, it represents a reawakening of capacities that had been forced into dormancy by the Lager.

As Levi's odyssey continues to unfold, attempts to use words to reconstruct a world of human relationships become more confident. Consider Levi's report of his interactions with the extraordinary Mordo Nahum, whom he frequently calls simply "the Greek." The Greek is Levi's first real travel companion after leaving Auschwitz. An entrepreneur to the core, with a pitiful rag of a shirt his sole capital, he sets out to do business. Levi's knack for languages makes him usable; the Greek coaches him on what to say, and off they go to sell the shirt in a Polish-speaking marketplace. Despite linguistic obstacles, Levi reports that his awkward bartering awoke in him a "new and sapid willingness to converse, to open up human contacts."[17] The two sell the shirt, acquire some much-needed food, and continue their enterprises. As the day wears on, Levi tells us, "the tone of [the Greek's] discourse grew gradually warmer, and on a parallel plane the tie that united us changed: from owner-slave at midday, to employer-employee at one o'clock, from master-disciple at two o'clock, to elder brother-younger brother at three o'clock."[18]

These shifts in their manner of speaking reflect, in miniature format, the process of gradual reconstruction and expansion of modes of communication that characterizes the entire journey home. The starting point is the narrowly circumscribed owner-slave language of the camps, a non-reciprocal mode of speech in which on one side is the property owner, on the other the property. As the two men work together, however, the tone of their endeavor becomes real discourse, at first that of a rather impersonal business relationship, employer-employee, then the more personally invested one of master and disciple. By mid-afternoon Levi and the Greek have formed a fledgling family: elder brother and younger brother. Abbreviated into the compass of a half day, then, is the linguistic and relational regeneration that will enable former prisoners to reintegrate into a human community where persons engage in meaningful work and genuine learning and are sustained by familial relations.

The story of the day's work with the Greek is only one of a series of anecdotes featuring creative communication across linguistic barriers. Another work-related anecdote follows closely on its heels. Levi has found his way to the Italian transit camp at Katowice and has been given work in the camp infirmary. Every evening, he and his Russian co-worker, Galina, write up a set of medical minutes to satisfy a tightly defined but essentially irrelevant requirement of the Russian authorities. Much about the task renders it ludicrous, but the fact that Galina and he share little by way of common language introduces an added dimension of silliness. The elaborate gesturing they are forced to fall back on produces frequent peals of laughter—though more frequent from her than from him. Levi is still "painfully conscious of [his] miserable appearance" and "of Galina's glance, almost infantile . . . in which vague compassion was mixed with definite repulsion."[19] That glance, not unlike the glances of the female civilian laboratory assistants at Buna, surely served to remind Levi of the Lager. Even so, laughter that is shared, albeit self-consciously, represents yet another small step toward integration back into the world of the living.

As the odyssey moves the newly liberated farther from the Lagers and efforts at communication become less self-conscious and more flamboyant, the tone of Levi's reportage changes. The laughter that was so difficult with Galina now comes more easily in Levi's quite hilarious descriptions of the escapades of his fellow Italian, Cesare. An especially entertaining episode occurs on the trip north into Russia, as the group from the transit camp sets off on its round-about journey home. Cesare is determined to persuade some Russian villagers to trade a "little hen" for some plates the wanderers have picked up along the way. He struts and clucks and flaps, exerting all his imitative powers to convey to the villagers what he wants. Despite his dramatic, almost operatic, performance, Cesare receives only increasingly puzzled and eventually fearful stares in return. The problem with Cesare, as Levi sees it, is that "deep down [he] had never really accepted that Germans speak German, and Russians Russian, except out of gross malice; [and], in his heart of hearts, he was persuaded that they only pretended not to understand Italian through some refinement of the same malice."[20] Significantly, it is Levi, not Cesare, who in the end effects the trade—by drawing a picture of a chicken in the dirt.

The story of the little hen suggests that although Cesare may have had more self-assurance than Levi, Levi has something even more important. Despite traveling the same literal distance from the Lager, Levi has achieved a greater figurative distance, for he can appreciate that incomprehension need not always signal ill will. Where the will is good, incomprehension can almost always be overcome, and so, although Levi does "not intend to deny the utility of speaking the same language in business affairs," he

> can affirm from experience that it is not strictly necessary; each of the two knows exactly what the other wants, and although initially he does not know the intensity of the desire to buy or sell respectively, he can deduce it with excellent approximation from the expression on the other's face, from his gestures and from the number of his replies.[21]

The language of barter is limited, of course, and being restricted to this form of communication can over time produce "stunted and primordial relationships."[22] Levi laments that this was the best his Italian comrades ever managed with the Russians living in the surrounding countryside during the group's long stay at Starye Dorogi. Yet, within the encampment, the Italians finally find a meeting ground with their Russian cohorts on the occasion of an amateur drama revue held in an improvised concert hall.

In its creation, as well as in its particulars, the revue is a testimony to the progress the group has made toward forming a community with shared purposes and internally-generated goals. Significantly, the great success of the revue is an inspired performance of the "Three-Cornered Hat," a nonsense piece in which, with each repetition of the verse, a word is replaced by a gesture. The piece ends, eerily, in total silence—an "infantile whimsicality turned into sinister, obscurely allegorical pantomime, full of symbolic and disquieting echoes."[23] While this bit of play-acting represents with quixotic eloquence the destruction of language and hence life carried out within the Lagers, the silence in which the song ends differs in at least one crucial respect from the silencing within the Lager. In the Lager, speech was suppressed. At Starye Dorogi, speech is surpassed. A common space has been created in which all can grasp this tale of significant silencing.

The performance of the revue marks a turning point in the odyssey recounted in *The Truce*. The Italians leave shortly thereafter and, reversing their route, begin for the first time to travel south toward Italy. The work of the Lager has also at this point been so far reversed as to allow a community of shared meaning to re-emerge, one in which it is possible to communicate, through silence as much as through words, something of the experience of the Lager. And so on this final leg of the journey back, when Levi meets Galina unexpectedly at a station stop, he can reflect that although he has not changed much—"at least externally; a little less puny and under-nourished than before, though just as ragged"—still he is "rich with a new wealth."[24]

Not every prisoner who returned from the camps would or could talk about what happened there; that Levi was both willing and able is no doubt the result of a complex set of factors relating to character and circumstance. As Levi himself would affirm, speculating on how his writing might have been different had he returned directly home to Italy rather than traveling the circuitous route he did is "futile"—for "the business of reconstructing the hypothetical past, the what-would-have-happened-if is just as discredited as that of foreseeing the future."[25] Even so, and without making any claims regarding cause and effect, we notice that the occasions for overcoming linguistic obstacles described by Levi as an integral part of the journey home also presage quite accurately the almost insurmountable linguistic challenge he would face as a writer: finding a way to sensibly depict that which makes no sense.

Levi's writing is effective precisely because it is so sensitive to the enormous difficulties inherent in constructing a coherent narrative about life in the camps. Levi reports that in a dream he and many of his fellow prisoners had with some frequency during their stay in the Lager, the dreamers "had returned home and with passion and relief were describing their past suffering, addressing themselves to a loved one, and were not believed, indeed were not even listened to." This dream is but one manifestation of Levi's "keen awareness of the enormity and therefore the noncredibility of what took place in the Lagers."[26] Only if the difficulty of credibly bearing witness to the offense in all its enormity is overcome will it be possible to render the mature and forceful judgment the prisoners shrank from in the eyes of little Hurbinek. For in matters of justice, Levi writes, the task of the witness is "preparing the ground for the judge."[27]

An extremely effective way to convey enormity in bearing witness to the Lager is, paradoxically, to attend closely to the particular. Levi's technique of narrowing his focus from the broad spectrum of the Holocaust to individuals and events he personally observed not only lends immediate credibility to his account, but provides us, his readers, with a way of entering into the concrete reality of the offense without at once sinking beneath its weight. At the same time as he restricts himself to the particularities of his own experience, however, Levi carefully crafts his descriptions so as to invest them with a meaning pointing beyond the personally observed. We have already alluded to one example of this technique in the story of little Hurbinek, which moves us all the more once we recognize it as emblematic of the difficulties all survivors of the Lagers will face in transforming speech back into genuine communication. It is present too in Levi's recounting of his time with the Greek, where changes in modes of speaking during the course of a day recapitulate the linguistic transformation of dehumanized objects back into human beings. This mythologizing technique, far from diminishing the weight of Levi's testimony, enhances its moral and emotional significance by revealing in the details something of the enormity of it all.

Unlike Cesare, who shows an angry impatience with those who do not immediately understand, Levi cultivates a measured patience that manifests itself throughout his writing as an untiring faith in the possibility of communication—even when that which must be communicated is so much larger than the words available. He describes this faith, near the end of his career, in the pages of *The Drowned and the Saved*.

> I never liked the term *incommunicability*. . . . According to a theory fashionable during [the 1970's], which to me seems frivolous and irritating, "incommunicability" supposedly was an inevitable ingredient, a life sentence inherent to the human condition, particularly the life style of industrial society: we are monads, incapable of reciprocal messages, or capable only of truncated messages, false at their departure, misunderstood at their arrival. Discourse is fictitious, pure noise, a painted veil that conceals existential silence; we are alone, even (or especially) if we live in pairs. It seems to me that this lament originates in and points to mental laziness. Except for cases of pathological incapacity, one can and must communicate, and thereby contribute in a useful and easy way to the peace of others and oneself, because silence, the absence of signals, is itself a signal, but an ambiguous one, and ambiguity generates anxiety and suspicion. To say that it is impossible to communicate is false; one always can.[28]

We must speak, Levi is arguing, because silence is an ambiguous signal. Yet it is neither necessary nor possible to say everything. The real task is harnessing speech so as to create silences that produce "more closeness than distance."[29] The writer's art that Levi has so successfully mastered is thus a "saying and a not saying" of precisely the sort powerfully prefigured in the performance of the "Three-Cornered Hat."[30]

The skillful interplay between what is and what is not said gives Levi's stories a power that is difficult to dismiss. His indirection reinforces the fundamental unintelligibility of what happened while his matter-of-fact reportage makes it impossible to deny that it did happen. Furthermore, in resisting the temptation to try to make sense of and sum up the horror of the Holocaust by offering us explanations and generalities, Levi simultaneously anticipates and short-circuits attempts to discredit by counter-example. He thus responds in advance to the letters he received from Germans who, on reading his work, wrote him to suggest various explanations of how the Holocaust could have happened while at the same time exempting themselves from responsibility by citing this or that extenuating circumstance.

If telling his tale is to facilitate the truly mature judgment he intends, it is important that Levi avoid the sort of oversimplification his German correspondents displayed. In *The Drowned and the Saved*, Levi warns against the dangers of oversimplification, especially concerning life within the Lagers. "[T]he network of human relationships inside the Lagers was not simple," he tells us; "it could not be reduced to the two blocs of victims and persecutor."[30] Rather, there existed a complex "gray zone" in which prisoners collaborated with authorities either explicitly, by accepting, for example, positions as Kapos, or implicitly, by allowing the dehumanizing conditions imposed on them to result in bestial behavior on their part. And so, although "[e]very victim is to be mourned, and every survivor is to be helped and pitied . . . not all their acts should be set forward as examples."[32]

Levi takes care throughout his writings never to put himself forward as a model. Both *If This Is a Man* and *The Truce* are characterized by descriptions of places, other persons, events; yet Levi spends little time detailing his own subjective states. This stylistic—or perhaps characterological—decision serves to capture the variety of human responses to the extreme tension in the Lagers in a way that subverts any easy presumption we might be tempted to make about what our own responses would have been. It also highlights yet another sense in which Levi successfully captures the essential unintelligibility of the Holocaust. Not only is it impossible to explain how the Holocaust could have happened in a "civilized culture," and not only does the enormity of the event exceed our capacity to sum up through generalization but even at the level of individual action there is no way of rationally predicting in advance how a person will react when placed in such extreme circumstances.

Levi's attention to complexity, particularity, and unpredictability also serves the following critical function: it keeps his readers from slipping into the very abstractions that turned persons and cultures into problems to be solved and thus made the camps possible in the first place. Well aware of "the essential inadequacy of documentary evidence" to affect us in any deep way, Levi presents us with living (and dying) persons rather than mind-numbing statistics.[33] In a telling anecdote, he remarks how the special-squad prisoners assigned to the crematoria try to hide and care for a young girl who, by some fluke, survived the gassing. These men are "transformed" once "they no longer have before them the anonymous mass" but rather "a person."[34] In reading Levi's work we are similarly transformed, compelled by the "calm, sober language of the witness" to pay the kind of attention to concrete evidence that is required if we are to render mature judgment.[35]

To return to an earlier theme, maturity of judgment in this case must also involve recognizing the impossibility of ever offering a final summation of the evidence. In bearing witness as he did in *If This Is a Man* and *The Truce*, Levi set himself a task with no definite end. Although on finishing these first two books he did not then "feel the need to write anything else," he eventually found that his experience of Auschwitz was far from exhausted.[36]

> I had described its fundamental features . . . but a host of details continued to surface in my memory and the idea of

> letting them fade away distressed me. A great number of human figures especially stood out against that background: friends, people I'd traveled with, even adversaries—begging me one after another to help them survive and enjoy the ambiguous perennial existence of literary characters. This was no longer the anonymous, faceless, voiceless mass of the shipwrecked, but the few, the different, the ones in whom (if only for a moment) I had recognized the will and the capacity to react, and hence a rudiment of virtue.[37]

If the journey back from the Lager is, as we have argued throughout this essay, a journey of linguistic reintegration, then it is a measure of Levi's grasp of the profoundly social character of language that the words his odyssey inspired should be largely words about others—and not just one or two close associates. In his works Levi recreates a rich and densely populated world of human interaction, rescuing with language an assemblage of persons varied and alive. No longer a voiceless mass, they have been given the chance to address us, Levi's readers, and tell us their tales.

And so it is that little Hurbinek, free and at last redeemed, finally speaks.

Notes

1. Aeschylus. Agamemnon. *Aeschylus 1: Oresteia*. Ed. David Grene and Richmond Lattimore. Trans. Richmond Lattimore. (Chicago: University of Chicago Press, 1953).
2. Levi, Primo. *If This is a Man*. Trans. Stuart Woolf (London: Abacus, 1987), p. 33.
3. Ibid., 44.
4. Levi, Primo. *The Drowned and the Saved*. Trans Raymond Rosenthal (New York: Vintage Books, 1989), p. 91.
5. Levi, Primo. *The Truce*. Trans. Stuart Woolf (London: Abacus, 1987), p. 197.
6. Ibid.
7. Ibid., p. 198.
8. *The Drowned and the Saved*, 15.
9. Ibid., p. 16–17.

10. *If This Is a Man*, p. 32.
11. Ibid., p. 47.
12. *The Drowned and the Saved*, p. 168.
13. *The Truce*, p. 378.
14. Ibid., p. 201.
15. Ibid., p. 204.
16. Ibid., p. 205.
17. Ibid., p. 221.
18. Ibid., pp. 223–224.
19. Ibid., p. 237.
20. Ibid., p. 305.
21. Ibid., pp. 321–22.
22. Ibid., p. 329.
23. Ibid., p. 344.
24. Ibid., p. 359.
25. *The Drowned and the Saved*, p. 167.
26. Ibid., p. 12.
27. Levi, Primo. Afterword. *If This is a Man, The Truce*, 382.
28. *The Drowned and the Saved*, pp. 88–89.
29. Levi, Primo. *The Monkey's Wrench.* Trans. William Weaver (New York: Penguin Books, 1987), p. 47.
30. Ibid., p. 52.
31. *The Drowned and the Saved*, p. 37.
32. Ibid., p. 20.
33. Levi, Primo. *Moments of Reprieve: A Memoir of Auschwitz.* Trans. Ruth Feldman (New York: Penguin Books, 1987), p. 67.
34. *The Drowned and the Saved*, p. 56.
35. Afterword, p. 382.
36. *Moments of Reprieve*, p. vii.
37. Ibid., pp. vii–viii.

V

Levi's Legacy

9

Bridging the Narrative and Visual: Primo Levi as a Source of Inspiration for Contemporary Artists

Stephen C. Feinstein

Primo Levi's narratives and messages about survival during the Holocaust usually evokes powerful and introspective responses among readers. There is no doubt that Levi, perhaps more than other Holocaust survivors, comes closer to certain truths about human relationships in the camps. In his poetry and works like *The Periodic Table*, Levi suggests how the memory of those past events are never erased, and continually intrude into attempts to restore a "normative" existence after persecution. For artists, Primo Levi and Anne Frank represent the most potent personalities of the Holocaust, and are often represented in visual works. Unlike Anne Frank, whose figure and message has become iconographic, Levi's messages continued to evolve until his death in 1987. In an interesting way, many artists have acknowledged that Levi, more than any other survivor, has been of significant influence for their understanding of the Holocaust, an event that they did not experience but seek, nevertheless, to comprehend. The result has been that much of Levi's writing has been used as a springboard for a creative visual investigation of the Holocaust by contemporary American artists, who have sought to transfer the images of Levi or his messages into art. The following group of contemporary artists have responded to the life and work of Primo Levi, using his work both as a way of exploring the meaning of the Shoah and as a vehicle for expressing their comprehension of that dark event.

The work cut out for artists who seek to use Levi in representational work is difficult. The individuality of Levi's testament as found in his memoirs and novels is undoubtedly unique, and deals with a personalized form of memory which he could not elude. The image of the Dantesque world which Levi conveys, however, can become the basis for artistic metaphor and creation just as Levi's use of scientific logic and analysis is a springboard for memory. Also, as Levi is so focused on language as a means of conveyance, with long and probing analysis of the German language and its sadistic misuse in the camps, and the inversion of daily language, it is almost logical for his struggle with questions of civilization and barbarity to become a focal point for further discussion. For many artists, it is Levi's description of the Lager and what it represents for contemporary civilization, a challenge to an ethical world without heroism, that is disquieting and the basis for a dialogue.

All of the artists discussed in this paper are American. Several are children of Holocaust survivors. The rest are "empathizers," individuals who were not touched directly by the Holocaust but as Jewish artists were driven in some way to deal with the Holocaust and especially the works of Primo Levi. None, however, are survivors themselves. There exists a large core of talented survivor artists who have made a strong impact on the artistic world and have conveyed their own response, representation, or illustration of the Shoah. However, none have been found who use Levi or anyone else's testimony. Their own memories are too strong to necessitate using even a powerful literary figure such as Levi.

Larry Rivers: *Mainstream Artist*

Larry Rivers, an internationally-known New York artist, has done a series of paintings as responses to reading Primo Levi and seeing Nazi photographs of Jews awaiting selection at Auschwitz-Birkenau. These he saw first in *The Auschwitz Album*, but also obtained "better photos" from the Parisian historian, Serge Klarsfeld. Earlier, Rivers had entered the Holocaust as a subject for visual representation in his large series, "The History of Matzah," which is composed of three large canvases that describe the history and wanderings of the Jewish people. In each work, a large map provides the backgrounds onto which Jewish wanderings are appended. "Part II" includes scenes of pogroms and Russian Cossacks attacking Jews. "Part III" includes both routes and scenes of immigration to America, while in the center are six Jews sitting on a park bench, in front of which is montaged the sign *"Juden entriit in der parkanlagen Vertboten/Zydom wstep do parku wzbroniony."* Rivers' interest in the Shoah was intensified in 1985 when he was commissioned by *The New York Times* to do a cover for an article, "Erasing the Past." Two colored pencil and lead pencil drawings were submitted, both entitled "Erasing the Past." One showed a concentration camp inmate from a 1945 liberation photo, with part of the drawing erased by the artist. The other depicted a group of Jews with their yellow stars, with parts of the painting literally "erased" as a technique, except for the memory of the stars. Here, the technique of drawing evokes the question of memory of the camps, both by survivors and the outside world. The Holocaust, however, is not a major part of Rivers' oeuvre. But the subject well fits the artist's larger themes that have dealt with political questions of other victim groups and how memory is made and revised.

The number of Rivers' works about the Holocaust generally is impressive, especially four portraits of Levi. They suggest an attempt by the artist to comprehend Levi's life in the Lager, aspects of his memory, his use of science as a methodological inroad to specific memory, as in *The Periodic Table*, and restoration of dignity for the survivor and author. Rivers prides himself on having read every one of Levi's works. He has found all of Levi's works powerful and attractive, tragic because of his apparent suicide, and containing an "odd series of cross currents linked to the events of Levi's life and the fact that he never left the camp."[1] Several paintings were done as commissions. In 1987, Rivers was approached by Furio

Columbo, director of FIAT, USA, (who himself had written several books on labor history and was a friend of Levi's), to go to Turin to paint Levi's portrait. Levi's death prevented the journey. Rivers created the piece by working from photographs.

The result of this 1988 endeavor was the portrait which served as a elegy, *Primo Levi-Periodic Table*. It is an oil painting of Levi, based on a 1980 photograph, with the title derived from the book of the same name, mounted on sculpted foamcore. As art critic Sam Hunter has noted, the use of foamcore has the effect "to increase the image's poignancy by projecting it into the viewer's space."[2] This work is dominated by charcoal and gray colors and two open doors of the crematorium. Even the use of charcoal as a medium is significant here in the context of the vision of crematorium. Levi sits with what appears to be a great deal of ease and contemplation. Most of his face and part of his body are complete, as if it was the portrait of a contemporary, living person. Parts of the head and body, however, recede into the charcoal and gray of the background crematoria, suggesting the power of the past on memory of the author. That past, as witnessed in all of Levi's works, cannot disappear from memory. At times it became vividly real, not only for Levi, but for all survivors. Thus, in one small area around Levi's head, as if a halo, true color returns to the crematoria wall, enhanced by the sculptural qualities of the foamcore. In various parts of the painting, particularly the top and bottom, starting from top left, are written the names of the chemical elements that Levi uses as chapters in *The Periodic Table*: Argon, Mercury, Vanadium, Potassium, Iron, Gold, Zinc, Chromium and Phosphorus. Hunter has noted that "the exquisite finish of Levi's face stands in sharp contrast to the sketchy, more expressionistic brushwork of the ovens, and the almost provisional nature of his arms and shoulders, which appear to be mottled with fallen ashes."[3]

Rivers continued with what appears to be an attempt to understand Levi's inner and outer transformation through two other portraits in 1988. "Primo Levi (Double Head) II," like the first portrait was done with oil on canvas and mounted on sculpted foamcore. The foreground is dominated by a contemplative older Levi in white shirt. Montaged in the background and over part of his face is a portrait of a concentration camp survivor, based on a 1945 liberation photograph. Rivers had used that photograph earlier for the 1985 charcoal drawing entitled "Erasing the Past I." The two figures are one, even though the face of the liberated survivor is not Levi himself. The striped prisoner's uniform creates a dramatic effect of becoming part of the elder Levi's face and beard, suggesting the power of Levi's own memory and the view of outsiders toward him, and that the images of the camps could never be erased. In an abstractly painted background, a bookcase stands with one legible title, *The Periodic Table*. The painting is exceptional as an expression of medium. The foamcore and the overlay of images creates a tension between past and present, and raises the question of dignity and imagination. The viewer seems to be asked by the artist if Levi's memory was always clouded by the image of the Lager. Rivers' interpretation is that "the Auschwitz prisoner in the photograph was never able to escape Levi's mind." In reading *The Drowned and the Saved*, the answer appears to affirm Rivers' speculation about Levi.

A third portrait of Levi, also from 1988 and done in two variations is "Primo Levi: Witness Drawing." One variant is done with pencil and colored pencil, the other "Primo Levi: Witness" was done with oil on canvas mounted, like the earlier works, on sculpted foamcore. Both works are divided into three sections visually and are essentially the same with different media, but are powerful in different ways. In the center of each is the older Levi as survivor, who is posed in the position of a storyteller-prophet, appearing to speak with his hands in animated gestures. Dominating the background is the chimney and crematoria of Birkenau. In the center to left foreground are scenes of children wearing yellow stars within the perimeter of the distinctive electric fence at Birkenau. Although not indicated, the artist appears to ask the viewer to "listen" to Levi, evoking the poem "Shema" which appears as the frontispiece of *If this is a Man: Survival In Auschwitz*. Three of the portraits are now owned by the newspaper, *La Stampa*, and are in Turin. The fourth, "Primo Levi-Witness" in the pencil and colored pencil version was sold to an Italian collector by the artist early in 2000.

In assessing the power of Rivers' Levi portraits, one must underscore the importance of portraiture in the eighteenth and nineteenth centuries, and its relative decline from a content point of view in the twentieth century in favor of visual techniques involving deconstructive processes. The eighteenth century produced mainly academic and vanity portraits, while the nineteenth century, especially in the age of realism, eventually sought to introduce a type of psychological introspection. This is well demonstrated by the Russian painter Perov's "Portrait of Leo Tolstoy," Ilya Repin's "Portrait of Modest Mussorgsky," or Valentine Serov's "Portrait of Ivan Morozov." All three works by Russian artists suggest personality aspects of the subject's past. From the nineteenth century Russian view, the title of the painting was sufficient. Portraits were, of course, also the subjects of the Impressionist- to Post-Impressionist artists, from Renoir to Van Gogh. Recent portrait painting, however, often appears academic, even "official" in nature, while others are concerned with the medium and some mild abstraction. In this respect, Rivers' portraits of Levi are unique and important, as they provide us with a vision of the Levi the man, and a slight inroad, perhaps enough to make us curious about finding out more about the subject and his body of work. Rivers has also completed a portrait of Claude Lanzmann using similar background techniques, as a commission from the French Embassy in Washington.

As a painter of Holocaust-related themes, Rivers might be termed an "occasional user." There are many interesting subjects which the artist has tackled, and his technique and subjects are often provocative. But Rivers' use of the Holocaust mirrors Levi's own struggle with his own memories. It is significant enough for a modern and financially successful artist to come back with some frequency to a subject which has raised many questions about representation and authenticity of artistic vision by those who did not experience the event directly.

Joyce Lyon: *Conversations with the Past*

Joyce Lyon is a Minneapolis artist whose father was a refugee originally from Rzeszow, Poland. Most of his family were killed in the Belzec death camp. Lyon's position as a member of the second generation led her to inquire about relatives who disappeared, about literature and testimony around the Holocaust, and ultimately to her own expression, "Conversations with Rzeszow: A Dialogue exploring different kinds of knowing." "Conversations" is a series of paintings that were also transformed into an artist's book of the same title. It is, as Lyon points out, "a dialogue between what is familiar to me . . . and experiences that I do not—and cannot—know first hand."[4]

The artistic aspect of "Conversations" juxtaposes paintings around Rzeszow, including scenes of mass graves in the Glogow Woods, with remarkably similar landscapes from Minnesota and New York. The message is clear, and suggestive of the terrible burden that memory imposes: the similarity of landscape between Poland and parts of North America are indications that memory about genocide can be induced particularly from non-political sources. Lyon's father, when questioned about the memories of his youth in Rzeszow, did not remember forests in the area. When the artist arrived at the same place as a tourist, she was startled to find it was surrounded by dense forests. In translating the images of Poland to a meaningful metaphor, Lyon used a bird sanctuary, woods near Tofte, Minnesota or the remains of a razed hotel from a New York resort, all of which have a magical potency of evoking images of isolation and death in Poland's camps and forests. Gerda Weissmann Klein, a Holocaust survivor from Germany, was particularly taken in seeing Lyon's rendition of a bird sanctuary as it evoked for her an episode in the camps when a bird flew in, sang on the roof of a barracks, and then flew out through the barbed wire. Lyon's paintings suggest that the Holocaust's landscape was very much like places we know and enjoy.

Primo Levi is an important element in "Conversations with Rzeszow," not only as an influence but through the use of text in the artist's book and in installation of her paintings. Lyon also used the prose of Marge Piercy and *Protecting the Dead* by Francine Prose, and was further influenced by, but did not include *A Scrap of Time* by Ida Fink and the diary of Etty Hillesum. Lyon first became aware of Levi through an article in *The New Yorker*, which analyzed his presumed suicide and the link between it and the publication of *The Drowned and the Saved*, Levi's last published work. During summer, 1989, Lyon journeyed to Poland to visit the area of Rzeszow, as well as Warsaw, Krakow, and Auschwitz. She carried with her a copy of *The Drowned and the Saved*, and a book of short stories by I. B. Singer. However, she did not read Levi on this occasion, as she "was afraid of being swallowed by despair."[5]

Upon returning from Poland, the artist read most of Levi's writings, some critical essays, and finally, *The Drowned and the Saved.* Of her encounter with Levi's works, Lyon has written:

> I have heard Levi described as cold, analytical, unemotional, but that's not how I read him. Rather, I find Levi to be vigilant, urgent, clear-eyed, and deeply human/humane. The emotion is quiet, but intense; I find it revealed in his sense of human connection. He is also a wonderful writer who, in his continuing attempts not to miss—and not to simplify—the point, pares and shapes language and forms an essence. I find this to be true in the translations, and to the limited extent that I can now penetrate the Italian, I find it there as well. Often his perceptions are very visual . . . It is the quality of these perceptions and voice that makes me see.[6]

Lyon sees the clarity of Levi as part of his urgency which cuts three ways. She sees him as being first dedicated to the complexity of his experiences, both in Auschwitz and in his recovery; secondly, he invites and establishes, as much as possible, a connection with the reader, "whom he addresses almost intimately without presuming agreement or understanding;" and third, "while acknowledging the difficulty (impossibility) of understanding, he makes clear the absolute moral necessity of trying."[7] In addition, Lyon as an artist sees Levi as inviting the reader into a dialogue, to probe, to question, but not to describe, like himself, what is not known. In "Conversations with Rzeszow," Lyon used a quote from Levi's *Opere I* as a "coda" for the entire work:

> Perhaps what happened (The Holocaust) cannot be understood, because to understand is almost to justify . . . We cannot understand it; but we can and must understand, whence it was born, and be alert. If understanding is impossible, knowing is necessary, because of what happened can return, human consciences can be seduced and darkened again: even our consciences.[8]

Lyon, who approaches the enormity of the Holocaust in a meek way and is fully aware of the taboos of Holocaust representation, understood Levi's words as "permission to try" to approach the subject visually. Early on in the development of "Conversations," Lyon felt that she wanted to integrate not only images, but also quotes from Levi, other authors, and her own responses to the process of artistic discovery. The relationship between image and text is described by Lyon as "synergistic." Levi's poem, *Pliny*, was discovered when she was beginning to contemplate "Bird Sanctuary I." In *Pliny*, Levi had written:

> Don't hold me back, friends, let me set out
> I won't go far; just to the other shore.
> I want to observe at close hand that dark cloud
> Shaped like a pine tree, rising above Vesuvius,
> And find the source of this strange light . . .[9]

For Lyon, it was as if Levi himself gave the artist permission to search for her own visual answers, even if the results could be devastating emotionally. This is also close to an analogy Eli Wiesel made in a talk about Lot's wife, from the story in Genesis. In contemplating why Lot's wife was turned into a pillar of salt, Wiesel suggested that the fire of Sodom and Gomorra were as hot as Auschwitz, and more than fifty years after liberation, it is still difficult to touch and see, and might have the same effect on those who get too close to it.[10] Once the structure of Lyon's work was established, "the images and books took turns leading." *The Wine of Purim* suggested for Lyon the glow in her painting, *Bird Sanctuary III*, and the painting of Mt. Oberg was related to her reading in *If Not*

Now, When? Lyon is certain that without Levi, her project would not have had the same form, for he, even more so than the female voices, was not exclusive and "the rhythm of studio and reading took on its own life."[11]

Mindy Weisel: *Imagining Auschwitz*

Mindy Weisel, as a Washington-based, second generation painter, has moved her work in the direction of abstraction. The medium involving abstraction, intensive color washes and infusion of small signs of the ever-presence of the past, is suggestive of varying levels of emotional coping with events that were connected with her parents' survival in Auschwitz. Born in the Bergen-Belsen DP camp in 1947, Weisel has noted that she struggled for recognition from her parents, who seemed to have established a psychic and real distance from her during childhood, which was a function of their own problems of survival and loss. Painting, for Weisel, has become a method of coping with the emotions she inherited from her parents' survival. She has noted that she did not read much about the history of the Holocaust, or even memoirs, because her father spoke so much and often about his experiences. But she was drawn to Primo Levi's writings because his works "allowed for a visualization of bleakness, of void, of darkness."[12] Levi's writings, however, did not create a psychological satisfaction in knowing, "but only added to my horror and sadness and pain as it made it all so much more real."[13] Recently, Weisel found some relief from the debilitating effects of being a child of Holocaust survivors by her mother's death, in the sense that she feels she will "no longer have to physically, mentally and emotionally carry her pain."[14]

Weisel began showing her art in 1977 and a 1980 exhibit was entitled *Paintings of the Holocaust*, a series of works done in pastel, oil paint, crayon and pencil on paper.[15] Her father's Auschwitz number figures prominently in some of the works, and most of them have a sense of brooding, although some optimism may be detected. Above all, Weisel's art can be appreciated on a purely aesthetic level as abstraction, and the

Holocaust-related symbols may evade the inattentive viewer. Weisel's painting raises important questions about how specific "Holocaust" art needs to be defined versus more generalized or abstract concepts of human suffering. The greatest difficulty is for the artist to avoid clichéd symbolism based on photographic images from the substantial film and photographic legacy of the Holocaust. With abstraction, however, there is often a tendency of the audience to read too much into the work, or perhaps not enough. The problem lies with the artist providing sufficient detail and symbol to suggest meaning. Weisel's abstractions have been used by Collier Press to illustrate front and back covers of 1993 editions of Primo Levi's *Survival in Auschwitz* and *The Reawakening*.[16] The paintings used were not commissions for the books, but had been completed already with titles derived from her reading of Levi. She has been in dozens of solo and group exhibitions since 1977 and is represented in the permanent collections of the Smithsonian Institution, Hirschorn Museum, National Museum of American Art, Jewish Museum of New York, and Yad Vashem in Jerusalem. Her work is considered to be successful, and has sometimes been compared to that of Mark Rothko and Mark Tobey.

The primary medium of Weisel's works are watercolors, although other types of paint, such as acrylics and oils have been used. Weisel's paintings have a spiritual feel to them, especially with color choice: strong blacks, blues and aquamarine colors prevail in most of her works, often with yellowish/tan backgrounds or intrusions. Symbols abound, be they concentration camp numbers, Hebrew words, or visual references. "Lost Flowers" (1979) is a dark, altar-like work with a multicolored, dabbed brush stroke of dark colors that serves as a frame leading into the painting's interior which is black, except for a blue square. Inside the square is the inscription in Hebrew: "Shemà." In this context, "Shema" may be a shout to the viewer to "listen," or it may be an intonation of Israel's belief in God, despite utter catastrophe, or a reference to Levi's poem, "Shemà," which serves as a preface to *If This Is A Man*, and contains dire warnings about the consequences of not listening to the cries of those who suffer indignity. Within the brush strokes of the painted frame is the Auschwitz number of the artist's father. In "Kiddush Wine" (1980), the canvas is divided into three vertical sections, with two on the right in yellowish hue and the far left in black, blue and green wash. A black object loosely associated with a Kiddush cup hangs suspended in the middle of the far right panel, with another black rectangular form intruding on the second panel. Throughout the entire painting are blue lines which appear to be random, but occasionally create stars of David. The result is an altar-like effect with strong emotional overtones, integrating "annulled images" into the entire work as well as smaller symbols, such as the Jewish star. The two lighter sections may be read as a window on Jewish destruction, which is remembered by the second generation survivor on occasions when strong familial support is visible, such as the ushering in of Shabat. Pearl Oxorn has suggested this work is also evocative of "the fires and splintering glass of Kristallnacht" which reflects "a tormented sensibility."[17]

"Ovens" (1980), also from the Holocaust series is an abstract work that draws the viewer into an inner space which moves in a color scheme from lighter at the outside to darkness within. Above the darkened interior are lighter gray washes, which appear as images of smoke. Scratching and other types of broken images enter the painting. A small blue patch in the center right of the work suggests some optimism, but this is obscured by the smoky gray above. The painting's border contains a repetitive and partially embedded text of her father's Auschwitz number, A3146. "Waiting" (1980) is a dark work, almost entirely in black. To one side is an inset that appears to be a view into a closed room, perhaps a barracks. Lines of paint run down vertically, suggestive of prison garb. Lest the viewer be confused into another interpretation, the number A3146 appears twice in the canvas.

Other works in Weisel's Holocaust series of the late 1970s and 1980 contained similar but no less dramatic elements. The text may be inferred from some of the titles of the 1980 works: "Barbed Souls," "Remembrances," "A3146," and "Ani-Maamin." The first is an abstract work with an altar-like black object using more horizontal characteristics than vertical in the center, with a Rothko-like quality. It is suggestive of the doors of a crematorium. Around the black object in a brownish wash of color are small Jewish stars, which give the appearance of being sucked into the black object. At the outermost limit is a square line framing the inner space with A3146, her father's Auschwitz number repeated. In the center of the black space, we again encounter the Hebrew word *shema*. The "Ani Maamin" paintings carry the title of a memorial song sung on Yom HaShoah, the day of Holocaust Commemoration, and Yom Kippur, the Day of Atonement. Weisel's themes continued beyond her specific Holocaust works of the late 1970s through 1980. The 1984 series, *Black Gifts*, were reflective of "the way I see my life. I was one of the first children born at Bergen-Belsen. Life was such a gift. But then, look at what I was born into: such anxiety, such tragedy, such heartache. . . . There is no question that I touch very old, old places. That is what my painting is about."[18] The title "Black Gifts" is also evocative of the first lines of Paul Celan's poem, "Todesfuge":

> Black milk of dawn we drink at dusk
> we drink it at noon and at daybreak
> we drink it at night
> we drink and we drink . . .[19]

The abstraction of this series is more intense, and the effect is darker, although some windows on both the past and future are implied visually.

In 1994, Weisel produced a large abstract blue and green canvas entitled "The Drowned and the Saved." The title, taken from Primo Levi, deals abstractly with the difficulties of survival, the absence of direction and ambiguous future for some of those who survived. Outside the large blue and green abstract canvas is a suitcase, which sits on the floor. Around the outside of the suitcase is the artist's father's Auschwitz number. On the right side, again the word *shema*, and in a small, lyrical landscape painted in a two inch square area, one can detect, only upon close scrutiny (the viewer must get down on hands and knees to see it clearly) is a Hebrew text of the prayer for travellers, "Tefilat HaDerekh." The prayer is particularly poignant in this context, as the wayfarer asks God to "make us reach our desired destination for life, gladness and peace. May you rescue us from the hand of every foe, ambush, bandits, and evil animals along the way, and from all manner of punishments that assemble to come to earth."[20] The cruel reality is the abstraction in orange, red and yellow on the left side which seems to symbolize the chaos of Auschwitz and probability of annihilation for those who "travelled" there. The abstraction of Weisel's canvas provides us with some of the mystery and unintelligibility of the Lager as Primo Levi describes it, and the fact that anyone entering the world of the Holocaust kingdom faced an unfathomable darkness. Levi has made it clear that those who survived were not necessarily those with the highest moral fiber:

> The "saved" of the Lager were not the best, those predestined to do good, the bearers of a message: what I had seen and lived through proved the exact contrary. Preferably the worst survived, the selfish, the violent, the insensitive, the collaborators of the "gray zone," the spies. It was not a certain rule (there were none, nor are there certain rules in human matters), but it was nevertheless a rule. I felt innocent, yes, but enrolled among the saved and therefore in permanent search of justification in my own eyes and those of others. The worst survived, that is, the fittest; the best of all died.[21]

Linking Weisel's abstractions on canvas with Levi's descriptions of survival provides an interesting insight into the survival process, and how abstraction as a form can possibly communicate more to the viewer of a painting than a realistic representation. The question among many survivors is how to represent that which cannot be described. For Mindy Weisel, being a member of the second generation, the task is even more difficult.

Pearl Hirshfield: *Shadows of Auschwitz*

Pearl Hirshfield was born and raised in Chicago from East European immigrant parents. Hirshfield has been exceptionally involved in political movements since her youth. Much of her early political thinking was molded by the Holocaust, where members of her family, including grandparents, disappeared. Anti-Semitism also existed in Chicago, as the artist recalls many incidents from her youth. In the 1960s, Hirshfield helped organize the first Peace Center in Evanston, Illinois, as a response to the growing violence she saw in society. In 1971, Hirshfield conceived, organized and produced "Conspiracy: The Artist as Witness," a limited edition portfolio of the works of thirteen major artists for the Center for Constitutional Rights. Much of her art is politically directed and deals with charged subjects: First Amendment rights and the United States Constitution, violence inflicted by racist groups and police brutality, and questions around women's rights and issues.

During her visit to the Nazi death camp at Auschwitz-Birkenau in 1985, Hirshfield came face to face with the grim landscape of death that may have been the place where her mother's relatives disappeared. Hirshfield found in Poland a series of contradictions: there were young Poles who still openly hated Jews, while, on the other hand, the artist learned of entire Polish Christian families who had been executed by the Nazis for hiding Jews. Ultimately, the experience at Auschwitz would inspire several major works. The first was "Shadows of Auschwitz," a moving installation that recreated an Auschwitz-like environment with lights, mirrors, shadows and Auschwitz identification numbers.[22] Hirshfield embarked on a long, academic project as part of the process of this installation, contacting Holocaust survivors and recording both their stories and their numbers. A significant stimulus for this installation room were the writings of Primo Levi.

In this installation, the viewer enters a "Z"-shaped space, twenty-two feet long by eighteen feet wide, identified by the German word "Engang." A dark interior reveals an array of lights, including one producing the effect of a rotary beacon or watchtower light from a concentration camp. Vertical slats approximately six feet in height each provide the Yaakov Agam-like illusion of a German deportation cattle car, marked with Reichbahn numbers. The viewer walking through this first section of the "Z" sees their own shadow cast onto the car, while light projecting through the vertical slats provides an illusionary concentration camp fence as a shadow on the wall. Thus, for the viewer, the illusion of the fence is the reality that Primo Levi could never forget. A chalk-written inscription on the wall in front of the viewer provides a variant of Primo Levi's warning from the short story "Story of a Coin" in *Moments of Reprieve*, and also in *The Drowned and the Saved*: "beyond the fence stand the lords of death, and nearby the train is waiting," providing the unsettling reality that the legacy and memory of the Holocaust lives beyond 1945, and the continued inhumanity of the contemporary world suggests that genocide, if not another Holocaust, continues in terms of presence.[23] As the viewer turns the corner of the "Z," he is confronted by the reverse side of the vertical slates making up the railroad car on the entry side. This side is covered with vertical mirrors, with actual Auschwitz numbers of Holocaust survivors written across it. The first number is that of Primo Levi—174517. The lighting allows the viewer to see themself with an array of numbers across their own body, as if they have suddenly, like Levi, been "baptized" as a Häftling.[24] The floor contains a simulated railroad track and ties, and barbed wire maintains the tension of the walk-through installation. The tension and darkness of bringing the viewer close to the concentration camp experience is barely relieved. "Ausgang" marks the exit for the museum goer, which is not a deception as it may have been for inmates at Auschwitz. The last wall, lit with single-hung bulbs, has an array of testimony from Auschwitz survivors, collected in part by Lydia Vago, director of the Holocaust Survivors' Association in Israel. The artist herself keeps the actual numbers of Auschwitz survivors at home wrapped in a tephillan pouch.

"Shadows of Auschwitz" does not pretend to be a recreation of Auschwitz, nor a memorial space, but an environment that picks up on many of the symbols of the camp which have become part of the post-Holocaust symbolism in both literature, art and popular culture: the image of the deportation car, the ambience of the camp, the darkness, and the potentiality for the ordinary person to become the victim. Implied is the reverse, with what historian Christopher Browning has described as "ordinary men" who could perpetrate the most insidious crimes and maintain their lives as if nothing extraordinary was happening in the victimization with which they were involved. Aesthetically, "Shadows of Auschwitz" comes off very well as a work in a controlled space where the viewer feels the claustrophobia and uncertainty of what to expect. The two display walls, ever changing because of the movement of lights or movement of the viewer, create a highly charged atmosphere and a work uniquely related to the Holocaust. Lest the viewer think another Holocaust cannot occur, one might return to Primo Levi's writings, where he indicates that "these factors can occur again and are already recurring in various parts of the world. The convergence again of all of them within ten or twenty years . . . is not very likely but also not impossible."[25]

In constructing "Shadows of Auschwitz," Hirshfield was strongly influenced by Levi's *The Periodic Table*, followed by most of his other books. She has written that "the writing was different from novels and short stories I'd read. The straightforward, beautifully written, personal accounts touched me deeply."[26] In describing her particular reaction to Levi's description of Chaim Rumkowski, Hirshfield has suggested that the quote contains "basic truth on the human condition." Hirshfield has also noted that "when I read that (quote), it was like an epiphany (and I admit I rarely epiph) but it's the truth, there was an instant recognition of what my work was about and I knew I had to use that quote."[27]

Hirshfield, however, is not bound totally to Levi, and to suggest some contrast, a second Holocaust work, "Shadows of Birkenau—Zur Disinfektion. Verordnung," focuses on the *Diary of the Warsaw Ghetto* by Emmanuel Ringelblum, and was completed in 1995. This installation included two large milk cans, symbolizing the hiding place of Ringelblum's diaries, which were dug up after the end of World War II. The work also included copies of original documents from the Warsaw Ghetto and an audio tape with readings from the diary of the Ghetto. Bricks in this installation are from synagogues burned by arsonists in Skoke, Illinois during 1993. This established a real connection in the artist's work between the past and present.

All of Pearl Hirshfield's works are suggestive of the power of the multimedia installation, and the immense potential for application of artistic motifs for entering politically charged subjects. In the case of each installation, the artist has involved herself in spaces which deconstruct and try to understand the atmosphere of the camps and ghettos, without becoming involved in a form of mimicry. If some viewers come away offended, the artist would probably suggest that the viewer consider the impact of the real event described in the art, rather than the provocation of the art itself.

Susan Erony: *Levi as a Basis for Understanding Ethnic Cleansing*

Susan Erony, a painter based in Boston, is involved in a large project about the Holocaust grounded in her sense of responsibility as a Jewish artist to retell the story visually. She focuses specifically on the technological aspects of modern barbarism, dehumanization, and statements against genocide and its recent variant, "ethnic cleansing." During the period beginning in 1989, Erony made several trips to Germany and Poland. In Thyssen, she photographed the legacy of older German industry as well as some aspects of the new. While visiting Poland, she photographed the same product of technology applied to a negative end. Erony's works are dark, using heavy applications of oil and acrylic, often framed with tin or lead, which extend the metaphors of Auschwitz and enclosure into the painting itself. Additional works in the series deal with destroyed Jewish communities—Lodz, Prague and others. Some of the materials are photographic, while others are in some respects relics of the Jews themselves. Erony's visit to Lodz, Poland in 1989 came after a fire at the only synagogue there, where burned prayer books were being thrown away. She took them and integrated the charred remains into several works as memorials to the victims. Erony is sensitive to certain limits of politically-oriented art. The work must retain its artistic qualities while avoiding trivialization.

Primo Levi's writings have figured strongly in Erony's research and her attempt to understand the Holocaust, Levi's scientific analysis of the Lager and survival. In her series of painted works on the Holocaust, Erony entitled one work from 1993, "Hier ist kein warum" ("Here, there is no why"), which was a quote from *Survival in Auschwitz*, a guard's response to Levi's questioning him as to why he was not permitted to suck an icicle after being deprived of water for days. The reference comes near the beginning of Levi's camp experience:

> Driven by thirst, I eyed a fine icicle outside the window, within hand's reach. I opened the window and broke off the icicle but at once a large, heavy guard prowling outside brutally snatched it away from me. 'Warum?' I asked him in my poor German. 'Hier ist kein warum' (there is no why here), he replied, pushing me inside with a shove.[28]

Erony's work relating to this section of Levi, a visual attempt to convey rather than an illustration, is a dark work of mixed media, using photos, pastel, acrylic and ashes. The background, where the phrase "Hier is kein warum" can be discerned across the center of the work. Below are two sets of ovens from Buchenwald, one set inverted. Around the ovens are six hands (those of the artist), while one set of tracks goes directly into the oven. The visual representation is undoubtedly a reference to the prior paragraph in *Survival in Auschwitz*, when Levi explains: "And this is the refrain that we hear repeated by everyone: you are not at home, this is not a sanitarium, the only exit is by way of the chimney."[29] A subsequent work in the same series, "WARUM," depicts technological images of destruction and the word "WARUM" in block letters, with multiple repeats, as if the artist was in a frantic search herself for an answer to the dilemmas posed by Levi.

Ted Hirsch: *Memory Logs*

Ted Hirsch is another Boston artist who has produced two interesting forms of sculpture as his personal way of trying to understand the Holocaust. One was to make memory-logs, actual trees into which are placed slate-paged books inscribed with messages and writings about the Holocaust. The small granite markers, simply called "Holocaust Markers" are a work in progress that use a second medium to convey memories of the Holocaust.

Hirsch and his family were not affected directly by the Holocaust. His family has German-Jewish roots, but all had immigrated to America before the rise of Nazism. For Hirsch, Primo Levi's works were a strong stimulus for both understanding and for producing art about such a difficult subject:

> I am sure that artists will always use Primo Levi's work as a benchmark for art about the Holocaust. He is someone, through his work, who is so easy to love and feel close to and yet in his poetry he expresses an anger and a truth that grounds you. He has been my guide to the whole subject . . .[30]

Hirsch was affected strongly by the directness of Levi's writings, especially *If This Is A Man* and *Poems*. Hirsch has said that it is hard to comprehend how a writer like Levi could be so "quiet and self-effacing." For Hirsch, it was the non-exaggeration of Levi's writing that made it real. The fact that Levi saw himself as Italian first and a Jew second also had meaning for the non-affiliated artist Hirsch.

In a 1994 show entitled "Mediated Memory," Hirsch submitted a group of sculptures, each made from cross-sections of tree trunks cut down the middle with carved niches. The artist explained that "[i]n two of the pieces, "Memory Log" and "Shema," I have made slate books which fit into the carved depressions and which can be stored in the logs." Hirsch views his use of logs as something archeological, as examination of the rings of the tree defines age and time, while the cut limbs suggest a trauma. In "Holocaust Marker," I have cut blank slate tablets in the size of burned squares." Hirsch has explained that his distancing from Judaism, typical of American Jews of the post-war generation, led him to only gradually become aware of the enormity of the Holocaust as an event. For Hirsch, the log converted into a sculpture became the symbol for his own sheltering from both Judaism and the Holocaust.

> The log may look from the outside like a simple piece of fire wood, but it is also the ark for my story . . . I hope we can heal the way a tree can heal. When a branch is cut the tree grows around the wound and eventually over the cut limb. The tree always shows a swelling marking the change, but it continues to grow.[31]

One of Hirsch's log sculptures is entitled "Shema," after Levi's poem which serves as a preface to *Survival in Auschwitz*. The log, after being cut down the middle is held together with leather straps. Inside, the left side is cut to form an ark for a book to be inserted, while the right side exposes a similar ark burned and painted orange. The book enclosed in this sanctified space is a hand-copied, slate version of Levi's poem from the Ruth Feldman and Brian Swann edition. The cover reads "'Shema: Primo Levi 174517," which forms a miniature tombstone and book cover, while the text of the poems is repeated with illustrations. Levi's grave marker in Turin contains his Auschwitz number as well as name. Thus, "You who live safe in your warm houses," is written over the illustration of a house, while "Carve them into your hearts," is illustrated with a human heart, and "going to bed, rising," with a children's bed marked "Ben and Cleo," which is a reference to the artist's children.[32] One might certainly argue that Levi's "Shemà" needs no illustration, as the power of the poem speaks for itself and leaves the reader to imagine their own response. Hirsch's desire is to try to comprehend the Holocaust, however, and for him Levi's works are a principal vehicle. As far as the artist is concerned, illustrating them was a method for him to convey the message to others, carrying out Levi's instruction to "repeat them to your children." It would appear that two interesting questions are raised here: one relating to the general question of Holocaust-related art, and the other on the ethics of maintaining the sanctity and integrity of Levi's work. Hirsch's "Memory Log" may be only partially successful. The idea of a tree never totally repairing itself is a valid metaphor, as well as its becoming the repository for knowledge. However, the images used by the artist may seem a bit simplistic in light of the power of "Shemà" as a poem.

Pearl Hirshfield, *Shadows of Auschwitz*. Room Installation. Entrance with representation of deportation car, revolving light creating shadow images on far wall, and inscription from Primo Levi on wall. 180 × 288 × 144 inches. 1989. Reproduced with permission of the artist.

Pearl Hirshfield, *Shadows of Auschwitz*. Room Installation. Reverse side of deportation car with mirror array painted with numbers of Auschwitz prisoners, collected by the artist. 180 × 288 × 144 inches. 1989. Reproduced with permission of the artist.

Pearl Hirshfield, *Shadows of Auschwitz*. Room Installation. View looking back toward mirror array, Primo Levi's message from "The Coin," and exit with wall of documents written by survivors. 180 × 288 × 144 inches. 1989. Reproduced with permission of the artist.

Pearl Hirshfield, *Shadows of Auschwitz*. Room Installation. View of group of visitors moving through the installation. 180 × 288 × 144 inches. 1989. Reproduced with permission of the artist.

Larry Rivers. *Primo Levi, Survivor*. 1988. Oil on Canvas mounted on sculpted foam board. 72 1/2 × 61 × 4 inches. Reproduced with permission of the artist.

Larry Rivers. *Primo Levi: Periodic Table*. 1987–1988. Oil on Canvas mounted on sculpted foam board. 75 1/2 × 68 × 5 inches. Reproduced with permission of the artist.

Larry Rivers. *Primo Levi: Witness*. 1988. Oil on Canvas mounted on sculpted foam board. 75 1/2 × 68 × 5 inches. Reproduced with permission of the artist.

Susan Erony. *Warum*. 1993. Photos, acrylic, pastel on canvas. 24 × 24 inches. Reproduced with permission of the artist.

Joyce Lyon. *Chimneys at Birkenau II* from *Conversations with Rzeszow*, 1991. Oil stick. 43 x 60 inches. Reproduced with permission of the artist.

Mindy Weisel. *The Drowned and the Saved*. 1994. Oil on canvas with suitcase. 66 × 78 inches. Reproduced with permission of the artist.

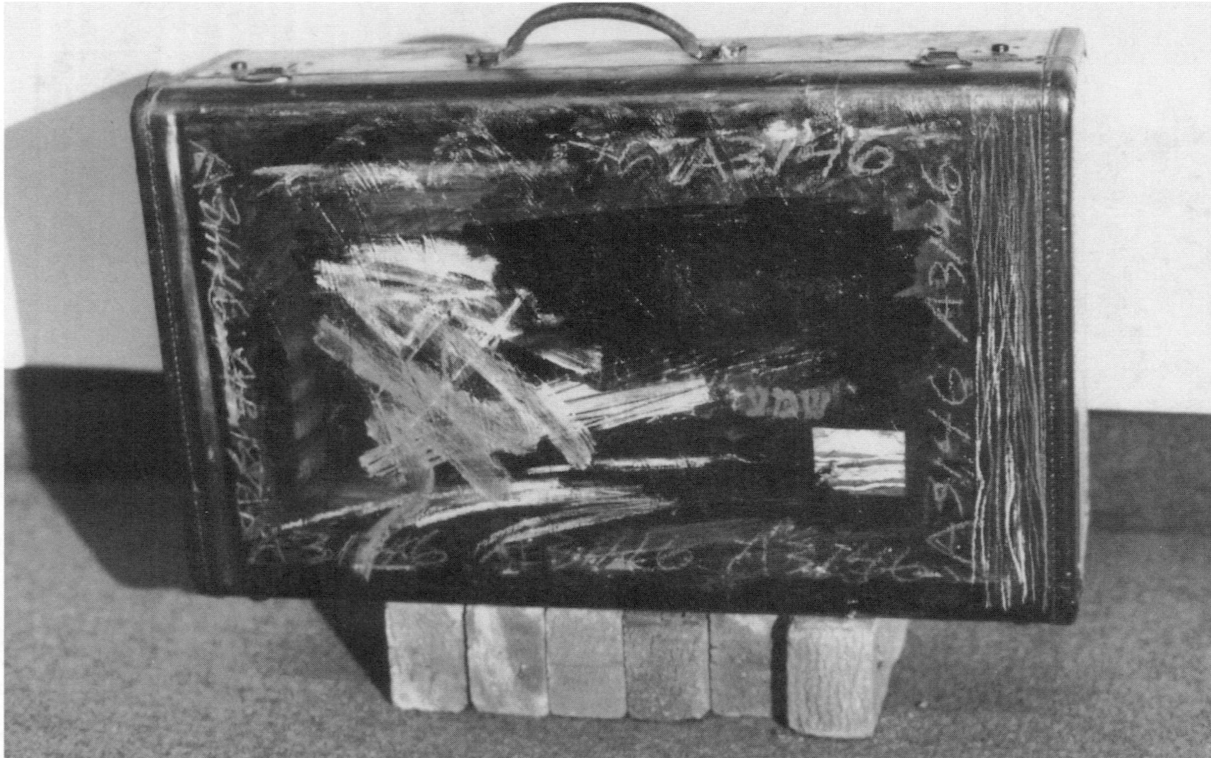

Mindy Weisel. *The Drowned and the Saved*. 1994. Detail of suitcase depicting Auschwitz number of the artist's father, *Shema* ("Listen") in Hebrew, abstract painting, and *Tefillah ha Derekh*, the "Prayer for Jewish Travelers" inscribed in a small postage stamp-sized landscape. Reproduced with permission of the artist.

Jack Wolsky. *Bringer of Light I.* 1988. Encaustics. 13 × 18 3/4 inches. Reproduced with permission of the artist.

Ted Hirsch. *Memory Log* (open). 1994. Wood, slate and paint. 18 × 12 × 12 inches. Reproduced with permission of the artist.

Jack Wolsky: *Bringer of Light*

Jack Wolsky is a Professor Emeritus of Art from the State University of New York at Brockport, and resides in Rochester, N.Y. Wolsky's works may be familiar to those who have studied Primo Levi's works, as he was a participant in the 1989 "Bringer of Light" Symposium organized by Susan Tarrow at Cornell University. Like many artists, Wolsky did not consciously enter the Holocaust as a subject. Once confronted by it, however, he "decided to pursue it."[33] Wolsky's artistic approach has been to synthesize photographic documents of Nazi atrocities with acrylic paint, glazes and collage. The result is a reinterpretation of some traditional images from the Holocaust with strong color, which is occasionally disarming to the viewer. Thus, while many of Wolsky's works contain some photos from the Warsaw Ghetto or the ramp at Birkenau which seem familiar, artistic manipulation can and does provide some new interpretations and observations, especially through techniques of repetition and montage.

Wolsky was extremely motivated artistically by reading Primo Levi. He was introduced to Levi by a June 1987 article by Richard Cohen in the *Washington Post*. The artist noted that "reading Primo Levi brought a different me back to the easel; different in the sense that new sensibilities, triggered by Levi's writings, entered my psyche and aesthetic reflection."[34] The "Bringer of Light" series was inspired by Wolsky's reading of *The Periodic Table*. Drawn to the word "phosphorus," meaning "bringer of light," Wolsky created a series of twenty paintings with this title. He has described the paintings as "a visual equivalent to Primo Levi's writings."[35] His work on "Bringer of Light" coincided with his use of new materials and techniques, especially encaustics, a mixture of beeswax and pigment with heat. In a certain sense, Wolsky appears to have viewed himself as a scientist creating art, just as Levi spent his time as a chemist. Wolsky actually referred to Levi frequently as he painted the series.

The essential motif Wolsky used in "Bringer of Light" is the glass test tube, which provides a geometric center and balance to the paintings. The pale colors and textured surface used in these works suggest a process that has been open to chemical experimentation, with degrees of mutation present. The series may also be likened to the works of Mark Rothko, whose brooding altars have been interpreted to represent an abstract expressionist and post-war response to the Holocaust. More than anything else, the title of the series and the chemical nature of the encaustic process used suggests that Wolsky may be trying, through his understanding of Levi, to use an alchemical process which exorcises darkness from the world and replaces it with light. In the most direct sense, Levi may have been the inspiration for the "Bringer of Light" theme seen in his deft use of chemical elements as a means of probing the immense darkness of the Holocaust. In Levi, however, we see this process drawn out in a literary sense. Artistically, the task is more difficult. Wolsky provides some direction for the viewer by the title appearing in many of the works, and the visual suggestion of light emerging from darkness, thus providing an aesthetic suggestion of optimism for renewal of the world. However, the darkness is never totally eluded, suggestive of how we might succumb to it.

All of Wolsky's paintings are beautiful, especially in his control of surface. Judith Reynolds has suggested these works are aerial, with an overlay of geometric lines and that "unswerving symmetry and formal structure hold the biomorphic flux in check."[36] Reynolds also correctly identifies an essential monumentality and stillness in Wolsky's paintings, which she equates with Levi's philosophy of determination—"a determination and will to live." The use of titles such as "Bringer of Light," "A World Ablaze with Splendor," "The Periodic Table," "A Place of Refuge", and "Sanctum II" suggest motifs of the Holocaust. One visible textual reference, perhaps taken directly from Levi, is "how filled with awe is this place, and we did not know it."

Conclusion

Representation of the Holocaust through the visual arts is an ongoing and a difficult subject for artists. Entering the world of the Holocaust, especially for those who were not in the camps provides the same barrier that novelists and even some historians face—the need to interpret, but not falsify information and narratives about the event. As difficult as the subject is, like other events centered on violence, the Holocaust will continue to be a subject for artists. This paper has been an attempt to suggest that Primo Levi has been one of the most significant sources of understanding of the Holocaust for a number of American artists. The manifestation of that understanding is seen in various forms of visual representation, from painting to installation art, but also in the use of Levi's texts in the art itself. While Levi has always been viewed as a survivor and writer whose works challenged basic precepts of understanding the Nazi death camps, artists have provided new understanding of Levi's work for themselves as well as their viewing audiences through their own work . The artists discussed have all been stimulated by some aspect of Levi's language, whether, as in the case of Hirshfield, a single quote about the potential for violence and destruction that still surrounds us, or Lyon, who sought out Levi's "permission" to enter the subject, or Wolsky's work influenced by Levi's scientifically-based narratives.

Rivers' portraits, in this respect, are different in that they are elegies or commissioned works. However, in discussing the impact of Levi on these artists, it is an intellectual journey that brought the artist to Levi as a source and inspiration, even after the writer's death in 1987. The potency of Levi's language becomes clear when the same sections of Levi's works are quoted by literary critics and scholars, as well as artists. The critics and scholars, however, have a different framework for analyzing and discussing Levi's life and language. For the artist, the problems are more difficult, as visually representational works are completed in smaller spaces, do not contain a total narrative as a written work, and leave it to the viewer to complete the metaphor. Nevertheless, it appears that for those artists who have experimented with some artistic endeavors based on Levi's potent language, the result has been, sometimes in odd ways, beneficial to the audience who may obtain a deeper understanding of the enormity and subtlety of Nazi brutality. If nothing else, the repetition of Levi's words on canvas and in installations suggests the potential for bridging between narrative and visual representations of the Holocaust. If there is a limitation, it is that no artistic work examined is a match for Levi's own testimony. Therefore, it is important for the viewer to understand that artists are using Levi as an inspiration in attempting to explain, by telling it to their children, but they cannot hope to reproduce him or the world he describes.

Notes

1. Larry Rivers, in a telephone conversation with Stephen Feinstein, October 22, 1995.
2. Sam Hunter, *Larry Rivers* (New York, Rizzoli, 1989), p. 43.
3. Ibid.
4. Joyce Lyon, *Conversations with Rzezsow*, p. 2.
5. Joyce Lyon, Letter to Stephen Feinstein, September 24, 1995.
6. Ibid.
7. Ibid.
8. Primo Levi, *Opere I*, as quoted by Lyon, ibid.
9. Primo Levi, as quoted in Lyon, *Conversations*, op. cit.
10. Speech by Eli Wiesel, Dartmouth College, Conference on the Holocaust sponsored by Educational Holocaust Foundation, Willamette, IL., October 1994.
11. Lyon, Letter, op. p. 3. Lyon also indicated the following excerpts were important for the formulation of her art: Excerpts from *Survival in Auschwitz* and *The Reawakening*:

> "(The night before deportation from Fossoli to Auschwitz) the mothers stayed up to prepare the food for the journey with tender care; . . . and at dawn the barbed wire was full of children's washing hung out in the wind to dry."
>
> "Facing the roll-call square (in Monowitz-Buna Lager) there is a bit of grass, carefully mown, where the gallows are erected when necessary."
>
> "Clausner shows me the bottom of his bowl. Where others have carved their numbers, and Alberto and I our names, Clausner has written: 'Ne pas chercher a comprendre.' (Don't try to understand')."

[Description of Primo Levi's recurrent dream:] "It is an intense pleasure, physical, inexpressible, to be at home among friendly people, and have so many thing to recount: but I cannot help noticing that my listeners do not follow me. In fact, they are completely indifferent: they speak confusedly of other things among themselves, as if I were not there."

"But only after many months did I lose the habit of walking with my glance fixed on the ground, as if searching for something to eat or to pocket hastily or to sell for bread: and a dream full of sorrow has still not ceased to visit me at sometimes frequent, sometimes longer intervals.

As the dream proceeds, slowly and brutally, each time in a different way, everything collapses and disintegrates around me. . . . Now everything has changed to chaos; I am alone in the center of a gray and turbid nothing, and now, I know what this thing means and I also know what I have always known it; I am in the Lager once more, and Nothing is true outside the Lager. All the rest was a brief pause, a deception of senses, a dream, a family, nature in flower, my home. Now this inner dream, this dream of peace is over, and in the outer dream, which continues, gelid, a well known voice resounds: a single word, not imperious, but brief and subdued. It is the dawn command at Auschwitz, a foreign word, feared and expected: Get up, 'Wstawach!' "

12. Mindy Weisel, letter to Stephen Feinstein, September 19, 1995.
13. Ibid.
14. Ibid.
15. For an extended discussion of Weisel's background with longer personal statements, see Vivian Alpert Thompson, *A Mission in Art* (Macon, GA., Mercer University Press, 1988), pp. 94–95.
16. See Primo Levi, *Survivial in Auschwitz and The Reawakening* (New York, Collier Books, 1993), both paperback and clothbound editions.
17. Pearl Oxorn, "Mindy Weisel, working out Memories of the Holocaust Through Painting," in *The Washington Star*, January 27, 1980.
18. Mindy Weisel as quoted in Cynthia Jaffe McCabae, *Black Gifts* (Washington, Baumgartner Galleries, 1984), brochure.

19. Paul Celan, "Todesfuge", in *Speech-Grille and Selected Poems*, tr. Joachim Neugroschel (New York, Dutton, 1971), p. 28.
20. Sidur Ahvat Shalom, *The Complete Artscroll Siddur* (Brooklyn, NY., Mesorah Publications, 1993), p. 222–223.
21. Primo Levi, *The Drowned and the Saved* (New York, Vintage International, Simon and Schuster, 1988), p. 82.
22. "Shadows of Auschwitz" was most recently displayed at the Minnesota Museum of American Art, Saint Paul, MN. as part of the show, *Witness and Legacy, Contemporary Art About the Holocaust*, January 29–May 14, 1995.
23. Levi's exact quote is: "Willingly or not, we come to terms with power, forgetting that we are all in the ghetto, that the ghetto is walled in, that outside the ghetto reign the lords of death, and that close by the train is waiting." Primo Levi, *The Drowned and the Saved* (New York, Vintage International, Simon and Schuster, 1988), p. 69., also Primo Levi, *Moments of Repreive* (New York, Penguin Books, 1987), p. 172.
24. See Levi, *If This is a Man* (New York, Summit Books, 1985), p. 16.
25. Primo Levi, *The Drowned and the Saved*, op. cit., p. 87.
26. Pearl Hirshfield letter to Stephen Feinstein, October 3, 1995.
27. Ibid.
28. Primo Levi, *Survival in Auschwitz* (New York, Collier Books, 1993), p. 29.
29. Ibid.
30. Ted Hirsch, Letter to Stephen Feinstein dated March 18, 1995.
31. Ted Hirsch, "Artist's Statement" for show, *Mediated Memory*.
32. Hirsch in this representation uses a structure almost identical with Joel Shapiro's sculpture for the plaza at the United States Holocaust Museum. Shapiro, however, has inverted the house.
33. "Wolsky's 'The Holocaust Series' Exhibit Opening at Oxford Gallery," *The Arts* (Rochester, NY, February 1979), np.
34. Barbara Ulfsparre, "Artist Jack Wolsky to Exhibit New Series," *Brockport Post* (Brockport, NY, Wolf Publications) September 8, 1988, n.p.
35. Jack Wolsky, "Primo Levi: Bringer of Light," in Susan Tarrow, ed. *Reason and Light: Essays on Primo Levi* (Ithaca, Western Societies program, Occasional Paper #25, Cornell University, 1990), p. 148.
36. Judith Reynolds, "Chiarenza's Paradox and Wolsky's Prayers," in *City Newspaper* (Rochester, NY), September 29, 1988, p. 9.

10

The Duty and Risk of Testimony: Primo Levi as Keeper of Memory

Franca Molino Signorini

My Lord had said to me:
"Go, set a watchman
let him declare what he seeth."

—Isaiah 21:6

"Have we, we who have returned, been able to understand and to make others understand our experience?" This question opens the second chapter of Primo Levi's *I sommersi e i salvati* (*The Drowned and the Saved*) published only a few months before his death.[1] This book brought to a close and sealed Levi's lifelong effort to describe what is beyond description, a task Levi first embarked upon in 1946, with *Se questo e' un uomo*, written soon after his return home from a year spent in the death camp of Auschwitz-Monowitz.[2]

The title *Se questo è un uomo* has been translated into English in two different ways. Of the two, I opt for *If This is a Man*, the one that is closer to the Italian original. In my opinion, *Survival in Auschwitz* does not do justice to the purpose of a book that was not meant to be simply a memoir. Primo Levi wrote explicitly in the foreword, that its aim was to confront the reader with a radical question: Is this a man? Is someone who has been divested of his humanity, degraded, tortured, brutalized and finally killed—is he still a man? And someone who can conceive, carry out or let others carry out the total and cold-blooded destruction of other human beings—is this still a man?

If This is a Man was not an immediate success. There were of course reasons for this. After being rejected by the Italian publishing house, Einaudi, it was finally accepted by a smaller publisher, Antonicelli, who printed 2,500 copies, 600 of which remained unsold and were eventually destroyed by the flood in Florence in 1966. The war—and we must keep in mind that in Italy it had been a civil war as well—was just over, and people were eager to return to their normal life. They longed to forget bereavement, ruins, individual and collective guilt. They had had their fill of hate, crimes, and destruction and the last thing they wanted was to read about crimes so atrocious they appeared unbelievable. Moreover, the book was not easily categorized. It was neither a novel nor an essay, its terse and essential style had nothing in common with the rhetoric that had imbued Italian letters during twenty years of fascism. Even though it received a few positive reviews, the book was soon forgotten.

The author himself, as he was to say in many interviews after its republication, almost forgot it for some years. When he wrote *If This is a Man*, he did not think of himself as a writer, but only as someone haunted by a secret too cumbersome to bear and felt the urge to disclose it so he could forget it. Levi later said that had written the book in a rush, whenever he had time to spare, with no claims to style or literary ambitions, more, one might say, for the sake of writing it, than for the sake of having it read. While in the Lager, Levi became convinced that he had a moral obligation to bear witness to what had happened. He writes: "Already in Auschwitz I knew that if I survived, I would have to tell what I had seen, that I would not be able to avoid it. And not only that; I knew that this telling, this bearing witness, was a purpose that made it worth staying alive."[3] For a time, however, Levi believed that it would be enough to do this only once, just as a person who is called to the witness stand before a court knows that after giving their testimony the trial will be carried out by others.

> I had returned from captivity three months before and I was living badly. The things I had seen and suffered were burning inside me, I felt closer to the dead than to the living and felt guilty about being a man . . . It seemed to me that if I told my story I would be cleansed, and felt like Coleridge's Ancient Mariner, who waylays in the street the wedding guests on their way to the feast, inflicting on them his tale of woe. I was writing brisk and bloody poems, and was caught in a frenzy of telling my story by talking to people or by writing it down, so that gradually a book was born. As I wrote I attained peace and felt myself becoming a man again, a person like everyone else . . . one of those people who form a family and look to the future.[4]

Just a few years later, as society and especially young people began to feel the urge to know more about the recent past, Levi again submitted *If This is a Man* to the publisher, Einaudi, who had rejected it eight years earlier. This time its success was immediate. Reviews were favorable, and *If This is a Man* became a literary event.

Some Italian critics maintain that Levi's entire corpus is actually nothing but an amplification of that first book, which through its narrative unravels the poem (originally of the same title, but changed later to "Shema") placed as its epigraph.[5] I do not entirely agree that all Levi's later work expounds on this book. However, it is true that over the years he kept adding to this first story through comments, details, annotations and more stories. In placing greater emphasis on his role as witness to the Shoah, rather than on his more extensive activity as a writer, it appears that subsequent books issue from the first. Eventually, in *The Drowned and the Saved*, his last book, he rearranges the strands of his testimony, completes and restarts it from the beginning, as a meta-testimony that probes and ponders over itself, and raises new questions.

Having devoted forty years of his life to recounting his experience as a victim of the Nazi camps, Primo Levi, shortly before the final silence, felt the need for assessment:

> There comes a time when one feels the natural wish to draw a balance: what one has received and what one has given: how much has been gained, how much had been dispersed, and what is left. Satisfying such a need may be pleasant, but the very fact one feels it is a signal.[6]

Levi had written this in his preface to *The Search for Roots*, one of his so-called "minor" books, in which, at his publishers request, he set up a personal anthology of key texts that had most influenced him, that, in effect, described his cultural roots from a literary point of view.

First and foremost there is Job, the archetype of a man suffering unjustly, who from the depth of his misery hurls questions but receives no answers, "nor will he ever receive any, but will continue to search for them because he needs an answer in order to live, to understand himself and the world."[7] Job's questions—which are also the philosophical foundation of existentialist theodicy—are those asked by righteous people oppressed by injustice. A single question sums them up: "Why the evil?" The righteous man suffers because a tacit pact between nature and creator has been broken. This breach tears the human being from his axis and hurls him away from the coordinates that confer a meaning to his existence.

Just as at the time of Creation, out of the original cosmogonic chaos day was parted from night, so justice separates good and evil thus creating an order. Injustice flings us back into confusion, into the ethical chaos where there is no discrimination, and where man loses himself, because he no longer has a frame of reference that also includes his pain. As the philosopher Salvatore Natoli points out:

> Suffering is not universal: the injury suffered by mankind is universal, but not the sense of that injury. And man is the one being who experiences events through the meaning he confers to them. The innocent man who is perse-

> cuted and oppressed experiences a pain that has no justification, because it is absurd (existential). Absurdity can be understood only as impossibility to exist and therefore as impossible existence. The existence of absurdity can occur only as a declaration of impossibility. From this point of view it exists because there is someone who bears witness to its being a livable experience. . . . The search for meaning is a way to give a meaning to suffering, a way to keep a grip on oneself in the face of events that tend to disperse body and reason. Being able to keep up the questioning is a means of finding oneself again.[8]

Job is surrounded by "friends" who are incapable of seeing beyond the frame of their own existence, who cannot share, because they have not experienced it, the suffering that comes from absurdity. Unable to share this experience they fail to communicate: instead of questioning themselves, they give partial, misleading, even accusing answers. Their inability to understand each other leaves Job alone in the face of God. Alone but not speechless. As long as he suffers and continues his questioning, Job is a witness.

Testimony arises therefore from the need to give meaning to suffering and endeavors to communicate *so as to give meaning to suffering*. Man, who is an essential part of civilized society and is integrated into it, finds himself ejected from it. The manner of his ejection causes suffering but has no justification and is, therefore, absurd. When, as in Auschwitz, suffering surpasses all human bonds, thus dehumanizing all, the victim becomes a *Geheimnistraeger*, a bearer of secrets, from which he must be released in order to regain his humanity.

Levi has repeatedly taken up the issue of communication within and without the camp. During imprisonment the confusion of tongues and the fact that speech is reduced to a brutal and incomprehensible jargon are parts of the process of stamping out the prisoners' human traits. Not only does understanding what is said become a "watershed between life and death," but understanding an order at once helps to avoid blows and to decipher the rules of the camp and therefore to survive, but also because communicating through speech implies the use of a code of expression, that is of shared rules and signs.[9] When people are able to understand and be understood, they become less alien to each other. In a context where people are alienated from each other, and forced to revert to a purely biological survival, speech allows human contact. Speech as a means to express thought, "this necessary and sufficient mechanism for man to be a man," remains the last relic of those superior mental functions that the camp tends to nullify[10] "To accept the eclipse of speech—Levi writes—was an ominous symptom: it signaled the approach of the ultimate indifference.[11]

In the camp one also tried, at least in dreams, to keep up communication with the world left outside the gate. In a dream, shared by many prisoners, they told their experience to those who had remained at home. This occasioned an "intense pleasure, physical, inexpressible."[12] It also demonstrates how the need to build verbal bridges is for man an almost physiological need, whereas the impossibility to communicate (symbolized in the dream by the indifference shown by relatives, who turn their backs without listening), causes a "desolating grief, like some barely remembered pains of our earliest infancy: it is pain in its pure state. . . ."[13]

After leaving the camp, communication is as necessary to the survivor, as it was in captivity, and takes on different meanings. This communication is more personal, we might call it therapeutic, and is expressed in the psychological need to tell one's story so as to be relieved of an unbearable load, distanced emotionally from the events lived through, by repeating one's tale over and over again. This need goes hand in hand with the need to be welcomed, accepted and understood by the listener who has not lived through the same experience.

A less subjective meaning takes on the quality of testimony. The dialogic and dialectical relationship that springs up between the witness and interviewer acquires a social and ethical function. The experience passed on by the witness is not just something that concerns him alone, something that is or could be considered alien to the listener. The witness, even the one who is unable to find words, is aware that those events have left an everlasting mark on him, having deprived him of his innocence. But at the same time he knows that those same events have also marked forever the society to which he has returned, for the simple reason that "A crime [has been] irrevocably introduced into the world of existing things."[14] Not only those who knew and have allowed them to happen are involved, but all have become contaminated, as if from the fallout of a nuclear explosion, because mankind as a whole has lost its innocence. This means that a change has been wrought in our individual and collective existence, a change that bars us from any possible return to the previous condition.

Like actors in this historical tragedy, the Jews were the victims, Nazi's the executioners, yet unquestionably neither contemporary nor future generations can claim the role of mere onlookers.

The Nazi's slaughter is a crime of a kind previously unknown, a crime against humanity. As such it places every one of us—because we are human beings—in a twofold condition: that of indirect victim, because mankind as a whole has been maimed, and that of offender, since it is man who has committed such a crime against himself. Wlodek Goldkorn writes: "Once we have ascertained the concrete, empirical, proven possibility of annihilating mankind, all we can do is to develop new modes of behavior, new values, in short a new ethos, based on the criteria of individual responsibility for the destiny of all mankind. It is an ethos as old as monotheism. And yet it has now been discovered anew. 'If one kills a life, it is as though he had killed all mankind' recites the Talmud (and further: 'If one humiliates a man, it is as though he killed him'). This truth . . . has been rediscovered in the light of the totalitarian experience."[15]

Bearing witness therefore fulfills two tasks: that of affirming, proving and making visible the factual and historical reality of the Shoah, and that of preserving its memory to serve as an admonishment. The witness takes upon himself the role of "sacral instrument" for society, so that two rites of atonement can be celebrated. On one hand, there is *the trial*, both the one which actually takes place in a court of law against the (few) executioners brought to justice, and the collective, symbolic trial, of moral condemnation, so as to restore the sense of justice. On the other hand, there is *the memory*, as an everlasting acquisition of social shared consciousness. We can thus talk about two kinds of testimony, a judicial and a prophetic one. With regard to the Auschwitz crime, they complete each other and are both necessary: the richer in detail and more widely known the first is, the more powerful the later can be. Trial and memory, on the other hand, usher in another issue, that of the contemporanity of this event and of the risk that, once the trials have lost their usefulness because victims and executioners have disappeared from the scene, the event itself will become outdated and even its memory will fade and eventually disappear.

Being typically averse to obscure and oracular language and distrustful of false prophets, Levi has always preferred the role of judicial witness, who describes events as they have taken place with the unassuming accents of the faithful reporter, leaving judgement to others. His first and foremost concern is that his testimony shall be complete, truthful, and in no way distorted by emotions. In his foreword to *If This is a Man* he declares that the purpose of his book is to "supply documentation for a quiet study of certain aspects of the human soul."[16] The horrors he relates are so evident that there is no need to employ querulous or apocalyptic accents, which would in any case be alien to his temperament and to his mental outlook. Restraint and understatement are typical of the Piedmontese temperament, which differs in this peculiar way from the Italian character. Levi writes in *Terza paginz, racconti e saggi* (*Short novels and essays*) that the distinctive traits of the Piedmontese are "their rejection of display, of all that is abstract, monumental, bombastic and showy, and their respect for human rights."[17] It is almost a self-portrait, especially in the rejection of display, above all the display of suffering.

Levi himself and many of his critics have tended to stress the tendency of the chemist to look at facts, however disturbing, with the detachment of the scientist who observes, takes apart, and analyses his laboratory specimens. This to me seems to be one of Levi's contradictions and paradoxes. I believe that this attitude of his, which in fact exists, hides much deeper chords linked to reserve rather than to science. The desire to understand, which is at the root of the search for meaning, does in fact require an unbiased outlook and therefore necessarily distances the observer from the object of his research. In this case, however, the use of rationality does not ward off suffering because as the rationalist, he employs the only tool he has, reason, to dissect his memories, using his analysis as a scalpel, but the memories he exposes are made of living, wounded flesh.

In Auschwitz—as Levi never tires of reminding us—those who were not killed at once were killed gradually, by systematically destroying their individuality until they were nothing but mass, reduced to mere matter, and eventually to inert flesh. Levi writes in *If This is a Man*: "Nothing belongs to us any more: they have taken away our clothes, our shoes, even our hair. . . . Imagine now a man who is deprived of everyone he loves, and at the same time of his home, his habits, his clothes. In short, everything he owns: he will be a hollow man, reduced to suffering and need. He will be a man whose life and death can be lightly decided, with no sense of human affinity."[18]

On arrival, as we know, the deportees had to submit to the ritual of shower and shave, which cancelled the last exterior signs of individuality, clothes and hair. Nudity and promiscuity meant a constant violation of that intimate and private sphere every human being is entitled to. Among the many thousands of bodies crowded together, the prisoner was paradoxically always alone, and never by himself. Stripped of their clothes, prisoners were left for a long time waiting, naked and shivering. Collective nudity—a routine procedure in the camp—literally divested all traces of civilisation. It is significant that in the myth of Eden, when Adam departs from the original state of nature, his first cultural gesture is to hide his naked body. The Nazi's, on the contrary, humiliated their victims by depriving them of their privacy, until they were stripped of their sense of shame:

> One entered the camp naked. Public and collective nudity was a recurrent condition, typical and laden with significance. A naked and barefoot man feels as if all his nerves

> and tendons were severed: he is a helpless prey. Clothes, even the filthy rags that were handed out, are a feeble yet indispensable defence. Anyone who has been deprived of them no longer perceives himself as a human being, but rather as a worm: naked, slow, despicable, prone on the ground. He knows that he can be crushed at any moment.[19]

As noted earlier, Levi's reserve prevents him from screaming or groaning. He keeps his feelings buried in his inner self, letting us catch, at the most, an echo of them in other forms of writing, as in his poems. When one has to tell of the annihilation of one's dignity as a man, only muted, composed and tranquil accents can restore the dignity one is ashamed of having lost. "Lo pudor e' uno ritraimento d'animo da laide cose, con paura di cadere in quelle" ("The sense of shame is a recoiling of the soul from four things, for fear of falling into them") writes Dante.[20] If a sense of shame means respect for oneself that is maintained by preserving one's privacy, decency can be described as the moral condition in keeping with, but not above, the elementary rules of respect for one's own and other people's dignity. Levi uses the expression "decency/decent" on at least two occasions. In *If Not Now When?* the watchmaker Mendel, faced with the decision of taking up arms against the Nazis, says: "On the one hand there was the weariness of many centuries, and fear, and a loathing of arms. . . . On the other there wasn't much: just a silent need for decency."[21] In his short essay "Itinerario di uno Scrittore Ebreo" ("Itinerary of a Jewish Writer"), Levi uses almost the same words to describe his decision to become a partisan: "The use of arms was alien to me, but to join the Resistance was the only decent choice."[22] Here his use of "decent"—as in Eugenio Montale's *Intermezzo*,[23] where he speaks of "everyday decency"— means ethical, in the sense of the elementary and indispensable condition needed to maintain one's dignity, or in the sense of imposing limits on oneself and therefore of assuming responsibility. "We became men once again, that is people with responsibility," Levi wrote in *The Drowned and the Saved*."[24]

With all due respect for the courage displayed in ruthless analysis, we can see the restraint, which is the stylistic trait of Levi the writer as well as of Levi the witness that evolves as a sense of shame and decency, is a great deal more complex and meaningful than the sharp, cold examination of a scientist hiding behind the lens of his microscope. Moderation is a barrier against overstepping the bounds surrounding the human condition. No one understands the importance of moderation better than those who have themselves felt the devastating effects of what the Greeks called *hybris*, the sin that led the Nazi's to believe they could rise beyond the highest bounds of humanity. Thus, with their mistaken and pernicious doctrine of the *Uebermensch*, they dragged millions of people, the *Untermenschen*, below the lowest of those bounds. When the occasion arose some years later to meet one of his persecutors, Levi welcomed the thought of this encounter, as he tells in Vanadium" in *The Periodic Table*, not with a spirit of vengeance, but in order to "re-establish the right proportions." His answer could not but be "sincere, balanced, dignified."[25]

Subsided accents are essential to the task of bearing witness as Levi understands it. When requested to write a foreword to the German edition of *If This is a Man*, and, thus to directly address the people to whom the one-time persecutors belonged, he declared: "I was asked to add to the book, that is to the testimony, a direct appeal to the German people, a peroration, a sermon. I was expected to raise my voice, to step on a dais, to change from witness to judge. . . . All these were tasks that went beyond me, tasks I would gladly have delegated to others, perhaps the readers themselves, whether German or not."[26] Elsewhere he adds: "for me judging is painful."[27]

Fearful that his testimony may be biased or limited, Levi is driven to constantly revise that first "disposition," adding to it, amending it, always searching for ever greater accuracy. To avoid simplification, which alters the complexity of events and generates stereotypes, he endlessly probes, ponders and questions again the truth that on each telling seemed established once and for all. He fears twists of memory, does not shun awkward questions, nor does he try to push away unwelcome thoughts but questions himself again: "Have we, who have returned, been able to understand and make others understand our experience?"

Levi does not limit his testimony to a description of that hell, as other witnesses, even important ones, have done. For instance Hermann Langbein, from a technical point of view has probably given us the most complete and detailed description of how Auschwitz as a whole was run.[28] Levi is not simply a witness who, having been called to the stand, gives a detailed account of the crime. The greatness and uniqueness of *If This is a Man* probably lies in the author's choice to describe Auschwitz from a deliberately narrow angle. One is easily reminded of Leopardi's poem *L'infinito,* in which the very hedge that hides part of the horizon from view allows the poet to grasp the immensity of the universe, which would otherwise be inconceivable.[29]

Levi does not tell us of the millions of human beings destined for the gas chambers, of the vastness of the death factory, of the stacks of dead bodies and of all the atrocities we have seen in documentaries and read about in books on the Shoah. He tells us instead what he saw with his own eyes, what one single prisoner underwent day after day. He tells us *what* was experienced and *how* it was experienced, and *the how* allows us to appraise *the what*. Many witnesses, for instance, have told how the selections were carried out. But Levi describes the days preceding the selection, the resumption of the routines in the barrack after selections, where those condemned to the gas chamber and those for the time being who have escaped, wait together for the soup. Lets us experience from within the fears, the false hopes, the relief, the despair, the hunger even more real than death.

It is precisely because the "normal" aspects of the absurdity of that world are horrifying, that Levi manages to convey the monstrosity of that horror through small sketches, all the more poignant because of their apparent insignificance. Nazis and kapos are not bloodthirsty fiends, nor are victims saints aspiring to martyrdom. They are—all of them, on both sides—normal, ordinary people, "whose humanity is buried underneath the outrage they have suffered or have inflicted on others."[30] Typical in this respect is the episode in which the kapo escorting the prisoner, Levi, to the chemistry examination, carelessly and unthinkably wipes his greasy hand on Levi's overall: in his eyes Levi is no more than a rag. This commonplace gesture, apparently trivial in comparison to all that is happening nearby, allows us to feel sympathetically—more perhaps than other situations that are harder for us to relive—the inhumanity of the "experience of those who have known days when man was but a thing in the eyes of man."[31]

Levi's testimony remains unique precisely because of the intellectual courage and honesty he displays in describing "that common inner misery," paradoxically shared by both the executioners and the victims, although their responsibilities are and remain separate; their roles are not interchangeable, nor could they ever be. To the former belongs the entire guilt (however seldom associated with a sense of guilt), while the latter retain the shame for having been irreparably "broken, conquered . . . because part of our existence resides in the souls of those who approach us."[32]

I believe that the evocative power of Primo Levi's testimony also lies in his having understood how people's feelings for empathy are inevitably overwhelmed by the frenzy of numbers about the slaughter: the small shoe shown in the Museum of the Holocaust at Yad Vashem touches and distresses us more than the vast numbers of the genocide. To multiply by millions the destruction of one single life makes our mind reel. By showing us what a single individual can be reduced to, Levi speaks to us of mankind, and succeeds in rising from the particular to the universal by describing what human beings can turn into if certain conditions arise. He admonishes us: "It has happened, therefore it can happen again. It can happen everywhere . . . precursory signs already loom before us."[33]

Levi thus fulfills his second role as well, that of prophetic witness: I too have the blood of a prophet in me, like any son of Israel" declares Mendel, the writer's alter-ego in *If Not Now, When?*[34] It should perhaps be stressed here that in the Bible the prophet is not at all a seer who reads the future and discerns truths ignored by his fellow men. He is quite simply a man who is able to interpret the present in the light of knowing the past. The Jewish prophet is not a clairvoyant, but simply a man who sees more clearly, who has the ability to perceive signs. He is the watchman who proclaims what he sees and alerts his fellow-men, who points out the dangers of actions fraught with consequences. The prophetic testimony is a mirror reflecting an image of ourselves that we would otherwise be unable to discern. It is a disturbing and disquieting mirror, since the reflected image is anything but pleasant since it reminds us that victims and executioners are not monsters or aliens, nor saints or demons, but people like us. What Levi is telling is that we all, one way or another, belong to that grey area, to that continuum leading from the persecutor to the persecuted, because this is nothing but normality.

Our identity is shaped by the memory of our past. In the camp annihilation caused loss of memory (because thought, or what was left of it, was forcefully constrained because of the immediacy of physical needs), and the loss of memory in its turn caused loss of identity, until people no longer knew who they were, nor who they had been. But even outside the camp, those who do not know themselves, those who have neither identity nor awareness, are destined to lose themselves.

Let us now try to reconsider Levi's poem "Shemà," which, as we have said, condenses in a few lines all that Primo Levi has ever written about the Shoah:

> You who live secure
> In your warm houses, You who coming home at night
> Find hot food and friendly faces:
> Consider *If This is a Man*
> Who toils in the mud
> Who knows no peace
> Who fights for a scrap of bread
> Who dies because of a yes or no.
> Consider if this is a woman,
> Without hair and without name
> With no strength left to remember
> Her eyes empty and her womb cold
> Like a frog in winter.
> Meditate that this has been:

These words to you I command.
Engrave them in your heart
At home, walking the streets,
Going to bed, rising;
Repeat them to your children,
Or may your house fall apart,
May illness hinder you,
May your children avert their faces from you.[35]

What strikes the reader here is the solemn, scriptural tone. The poem addresses those who have not themselves experienced destruction, but nevertheless are called upon to shoulder a moral obligation: "Consider *If This is a Man*. . . . Consider if this is a woman. . . ." The verse recalls Dante's "Considerate la vostra semenza, fatti non foste a viver come bruti, ma per seguir virtute e canoscenza" ("Consider your seed/ For brutish ignorance/ your mettle was not made: you were made men/ to follow after knowledge and excellence").[36] This poem is also evocative of Lamentations 1:12: "Consider and behold, if there was ever a suffering equal to mine." It is as though Levi is saying, meditate that this has been; these words to you I command. It is not enough for the listener to remember inertly, the memory must always be present, engaging all spiritual faculties. It is a duty, a new commandment.

In Jewish culture, in particular, history is not a manifestation of the cyclical quality of nature. History is seen as a collective and linear path that the generation of man travels on. It moves in only one direction, forming a chain that uncoils from a beginning (*bereshit*) toward a final end: the coming of the messianic era. The Hebrew word *Toledot*, commonly translated as "history," literally means "generations." As André Néher explains so clearly, this word

> implies the function and the act of generating, the logical succession which leads from father to son, from mother to child, marking a progress that cannot be reversed. The chain of generations can be broken, the umbilical link can be severed, but the direction cannot be reversed. Time cannot ascend again from son to father, it descends from

> father to son. The sense and meaning of the present are functions of the memory of the past and of the hope for the future.[37]

The main Jewish prayer "Hear, oh Israel: the Lord is the One and Only" is a profession of faith that the Jewish people address to the Deity and confirm themselves by perpetually recalling and restating the covenant binding them to God. In the same way, the memory of the destruction must engrave itself in the hearts of men, in private and in public life, to be handed from one generation to the next. Otherwise—here imperative can be converted into indicative and curse into prophecy—that same destruction will rise again to wipe out our uncertainties and privileges, which are but an illusion and cannot save us because "we are all in the ghetto, the ghetto is enclosed by walls, outside the walls are the masters of death and the train is waiting nearby."[38]

The words found in Isaiah 21:6 "My Lord said to me: Go, set a watchman, let him declare what he seeth" can fittingly be said to apply to the keeper of memory. The witness of the past becomes living memory, for himself and for others:

> If we die here in silence as our enemies want us to, if we do not return, the world will never know what man has been capable of, what he is still capable of, the world will not know itself, will be even more liable than it already is to a repetition of nazi barbarity, or of any other equivalent barbarity, whatever its actual or proclaimed political source[39]

Memory thus becomes admonition. It is after all significant that the Latin verb *moneo* (I admonish), from which comes *monumentum* (monument), and *memini* (I have memorized and therefore I remember), from which comes *memoria* (memory), have the same Greek root *mimésko*, (I remember). And in the other Latin verb for "I remember," *recordor* (whence the English "to record"), we can still easily trace *cor, cordis*, the heart. To remember means indeed to pass back through the heart; that is to relive emotionally a past experience by recalling it in the present. Thence arises the difficulty to keep alive, and therefore present, the memory of an experience lived by others and not felt as one's own.

The risk of testimony nowaday is that it may end up being considered anachronistic and it may become difficult to find anybody willing to listen to it. We are becoming increasingly aware of the sense of boredom and staleness all too often occasioned by the recalling of the memory of Auschwitz, which nowadays also is no longer perceived as a universal and absolute event. For too many people remembering is more often than not seen as an obsession haunting those people who are still unable to free themselves from the experience. I believe this is due to the fact that the memory of Auschwitz no longer raises a sense of scandal. It is as if all the atrocities after Auschwitz that have happened in the world and that we can watch daily on television had wiped out its paradigmatic value and its current relevance. It is as though we have formed a habit that cancels emotional responses. For the new generations even the Shoah probably is in the process of vanishing into the past like so many other events.

That means *memory* is becoming history. Maurice Halbwachs claims that memory ends where history begins.

> Memory might be defined as the living recollection of an event and of an experience that accompanies those who have lived through it. History, on the other hand, is the resumption of a severed thread, of events seen impersonally, in the third person. Memory and history each have their own logic, although they can be intertwined: interiority and exteriority, first and third person.[40]

According to neurophysiologists, our mind collects memories in a temporary depot containing plentiful information, and then stores them in a long-term depository in the shape of semantic groups. It is with growing uneasiness that we are now forced to watch how the Shoah, made commonplace and undoubtedly faced, at least in Europe, with an ever lowering attention, is often undergoing a process of semantic transformation. Generally speaking, one might say that the communication flow although not yet severed, is nonetheless showing signs of breaking up.

Twelve years ago Levi's keen prophetic eyes had already discerned this process. In an interview he gave on January 27th, 1983 he confessed that he no longer liked visiting schools to tell the youngsters of his experience. He felt that his words had become "inadequate"; he was afraid he was speaking "a different language" and that his young listeners were no longer interested.[41] He had been particularly upset by a question asked by two boys: "Why do you keep coming and telling us these things, after forty years, and after Vietnam, after Stalin's camps, after Korea, after all this, why?" Levi owned that he had felt "pushed to the wall, a veteran at any cost, embarrassed." "Although I know, that I have told important things," he concluded, "and I have no doubts at all about the significance of my books, I have the feeling that they are stale, that they have grown old." Elsewhere he added, "I feel as if I had exhausted the store of things to say."[42]

The loneliness of potential listeners inevitably occasions in the witness a crisis of identity, making him doubt himself. It seems significant for me that shortly before his death Levi expressed to his doctor the fear, entirely unjustified, however, of suffering from Alzheimer's disease. Once again it is true that "part of our existence resides in the souls of those who approach us."

As Yerushalmi writes;

> A people remembers, when his past has been actively handed down to the present generation and has been accepted as meaningful. On the contrary, a people forgets when the generation who holds the past does not pass it on to the next generation, or when the later rejects what it has received and does not in its turn pass it on, which after all is the same.[43]

The memory of the Shoah also requires two conditions in order to live on in collective memory: witnesses who continue to recall its memory and a community that continues to accept their testimony, converting it into something of their own. Now, while the ranks of direct witnesses keep getting thinner, several signs seem to indicate that the community is also approaching a transition from one era—what might be loosely termed the post-war period—to another in which geopolitical and ideological systems as well as the emotional link with those events are undergoing a deep transformation.

The debate as to whether rifts, all too hastily labeled as "old" should be overcome was heralded in the early eighties by several important episodes, whose main characters have been political leaders and German and French academic historians. For instance, I would like to mention briefly former U.S. President Ronald Reagan's visit to the cemetery at Bittburg, where SS soldiers are buried, and more recently the ceremonies held in 1995 on the fiftieth anniversary of the liberation of Auschwitz. On this occasion Polish authorities in Warsaw at first conveniently forgot the importance of the slaughter of the Jews in order to better emphasize, for political purposes, the suffering of the Polish people. But at an academic level, even dismissing the negators, there have been attempts on the part of some historians to deny the uniqueness of Auschwitz by putting stress on the historical context ("the foul effort of the revisionists" as Levi called it).[44] This has had immediate side-effects on common opinion, by spreading doubts, if nothing else. It must be said, however, that without a change in collective sensibility it would not have been possible in academic circles to openly vent ideas that only a short time ago would have been considered unacceptable.

The increasing emotional distance of ordinary people is often echoed by the mass media, which give voice to a wish, almost a need, to turn over the page and close a painful chapter of history by banishing it to an ever more distant past. Thence derives this false syllogism: Time in itself brings justice, wiping out wrongs and injuries: the time has therefore come to forget; but in order to do so we must forgive (and forgive ourselves); Jews do not forget because they cannot forgive; they don't want justice, but revenge. The desire for justice is temporary, the wish for revenge is everlasting. In other words, once forgotten, the memory of the slaughter is destined to become something "private," belonging only to those who have been directly affected by it, and it does not concern others. Eventually, the memory itself is perceived only as an irritating manifestation of a desire for vengeance. This is how the wish to dismiss unpleasant thoughts gives birth to and feeds new and old prejudices.

Levi's was only one response to the sliding away of memory, nor could it have been otherwise. He began to question himself over again, beginning from the very fallacy of memory, which causes the recollection of the witnesses to fade and is the alibi of the torturers. He questioned fallacy in collective memory as well, which misrepresents the reality of the past by replacing it with imaginary and stereotyped representations.

Levi's response has been called "revolutionary" because it gives new impulse to a careful reflection on the Shoah, starting from the very risk of failure of testimony. Actually, in *The Drowned and the Saved* there is nothing that was not to be found in any of Levi's previous books, but here everything is pushed to the extremes. It is the outlook that is new: against mummification and stereotypes Levi suggests a different point of view, that of corruption wrought by power, both on those who exert it and on those who are the victims of it, unless the use of power is placed within bounds.

If human nature, as the atrocious historical "experiment" of the Shoah has demonstrated, does not produce by itself the antibodies that are needed to avoid its aberration, we can and indeed we must, watch out for the conditions (historical, political, sociological) that can allow it to take place again. Levi's essay is therefore a political statement against all forms of totalitarianism, which feeds on propaganda—both direct and disguised as educational—on the control of information and on terror. He never forgets that these conditions are connected to the society where it manifests, because it needs varying degrees of complicity, that grey area made of silences, displacements, silent nods, passive acceptance. In short, lack of individual responsibility.

While he tears down the museum-like celebration of the Shoah, Levi rebuilds the memory of it to its full extent and complexity, inviting us to use that slaughter as a point of reference, in order to understand and possibly avoid the present massacres and those still to come. He does so by giving great attention to the importance of education. He reminds us that the SS in the camps, educated to violence, "had been submitted for several years to a school whose moral was upside down. In a totalitarian regime, education, propaganda and information find no obstacles in their way. They have unlimited power. Nazi's were mediocre human beings . . . but they had been badly educated."[45]

"The memory of that slaughter" writes Stephano Levi Della Torre "can live on and continue to be a warning to us if we continue to investigate those events."[46] I would add, if we are able to grasp how that slaughter has been at once a turning point and a point of departure. Levi felt strongly the duty to bear witness, yet he also perceived its many risks: "It is the awful privilege of our generation and of my people to bear witness to the incurable nature of the offense, that spreads like a contagious disease."[47] The Shoah has been unparalleled because of its vastness, violence and destructiveness, yet this does not mean that it cannot be imitated: on the contrary, if we look around we can easily perceive its devastating effects still lingering and proliferating. The boundaries, the Pillars of Hercules, which were crossed at the time have not become more secure but, on the contrary, more frail. Like an infection the genocide has lowered our immunity response against further relapses. The memory we maintain through testimony can work as a vaccine only as long as it is kept alive and succeeds in being formative, not just informative. This means that memory must be shared, constantly related to the present, and never deprived of its semantic force. In this aim may become limited, but it will never become useless.

Primo Levi left us thirteen years ago, and the void he has left behind is all too tangible: the alarming and unforeseeable things that have happened in the world during this time are before everyones' eyes. Almost in confirmation of his warnings we have seen scenarios arise which we thought had been buried forever in the past. Let me only mention the "ethnic cleansing" in former Yugoslavia, to see with our own eyes how—now and then—the slaughter of a people guilty only of existing can be imagined and put into practice amid the indifference or the impotence of the world's community.

It is consoling that despite this change in the general climate, Levi's books continue to be among the most widely read, both in Italy and abroad. The *Times Literary Supplement* even lists *If This is a Man* and *The Drowned and the Saved* among the hundred books that have most influenced European culture in the second half of our century. To those willing to listen, Levi's books have not ceased to speak and what they tell us remains true and not at all obsolete.

I would like to end by recalling the words that Levi gives to Faussone, the workman in *The Wrench*. These words about a work well done apply equally well to Levi's forty years of work as a writer and a witness who has delved deeply into the memory of the Shoah:

> [There is] the pleasure of seeing your creature grow . . . solid, necessary, symmetrical, suited to its purpose, and when it is finished you look at it and think that perhaps it will live longer than you and perhaps it will be of use to someone you don't know and who does not know you.

Notes

1. Primo Levi, *I sommersi e i salvati*, Torino: Einaudi, 1986, p. 24.
2. Primo Levi, *Se Questo è un Uomo*. Torino: Einaudi, 1958.
3. Primo Levi, *Itinerario di uno scittore ebreo*, on "La Rassegna mensile di Israel" no. 5–8, May/August 1984, p. 379.
4. Primo Levi, *Il sistema periodico*, Torino: Einaudi, 1975, p. 155.
5. Among them Alberto Cavaglion, see "Primo Levi *Sequesto è un uomo*" Torino: Loescher, 1992.
6. Primo Levi, Preface to *La ricerca delle radici*, Torono: Einaudi, 1982, p. VII.
7. Ibid., p. 5.
8. Salvatore Natoli, *L'esperienze del dolore*, Milano: Feltrinelli, 1988, p. 199.
9. Primo Levi, *I sommersi e i salvati*, p. 70.
10. Ibid., p. 70.

11. Ibid., p. 79.
12. Primo Levi, *Se questo è un uomo*, p. 82.
13. Ibid., p. 83.
14. Primo Levi, *La Tregua*, Torino: Einaudi, 1963, p. 15.
15. Wlodeck Goldkorn, *La memoria ambigua*, on "Micromega" n. 3, 1989.
16. Primo Levi, Preface to *Se questo è un uomo*, 1947.
17. Primo Levi, *Terza pagina: Racconti e saggi*, Torino, editrice-La Stampa, 1986, p. 158.
18. Primo Levi, *Se questo è un uomo*, p. 37.
19. Primo Levi, *I sommersi e isalvati*, p. 90.
20. Dante Alighiere, *Il Convivio*, ed Nuova Italia, 1970.
21. Primo Levi, *Se non ora, quandro?*, Torino: Einaudi, 1982, pp. 17–18.
22. Primo Levi, *Itinerario di uno scritotre ebreo*, p. 381.
23. Eugenio Montale, "La Bufera", da *Tutte le poesie*, Milano, Mondadori.
24. Primo Levi, *I sommersi e i salvati*, p. 381.
25. Primo Levi, *Il sistema periodico*, p. 227.
26. Primo Levi, *I sommersi e i salvati*, p. 142.
27. Primo Levi, *Itinerario di uno scrittore ebreo*, p. 381.
28. Hermann Langbein, Uomini ad Auschwitz, Mursia, Milano, 1984.
29. Giacomo Leopardi, *L'infinito*, in *Canti*.
30. Primo Levi, *Se questo è un uomi*, p. 31.
31. Ibid., p. 225.
32. Ibid., p. 225.
33. Primo Levi, *I sommersi e i salvati*, p. 164.
34. Primo Levi, *Se non ora, quando?*, p. 103.
35. *Voi che vivete sicuri / nelle vostre tiepide case, / voi vhe trovate tornando a sera / il cibo caldo e visi amici: / considerate se questo è un uomo / che lavora nel fango / che non conosce pace / che lotta per mezzo pane / che muore per un sî o per un no. / considerate se questa è una donna, / senza capelli e senza nome / sensa più forza per ricordare / vuoti gli occhi e freddo il grembo / Come una rana d'inverno. / Meditate che questo è stato / Vi comando queste parole. / Scolpitele nel vostro cuore / stando in casa andando per via, / coricandovi, alzandovi: / ripetetele ai vostri figli / O vi si sfaccia las casa / la malattia vi impedisca / i vostri nati torcano il viso da voi.*
36. Dante Alighieri, *La Divina Commedia, Inferno,* canto XXVI.
37. André Neher, *L'esilio della parola*, Marietti, Casale, 1983, p. 42.

38. Primo Levi, *I sommersi e i salvati*, p. 52.
39. Primo Levi, Preface to *La vita offesa,* Anna Bravo e Daniele Jalla, Milano, Franco Angeli, 1986.
40. Maurice Halbwachs, *La memoria collettiva*, Milano, Unicopli, 1987.
41. Cereja F. e Bravo A., interview to Primo Levi, in "Archivio della deportazione," 1983, p. 19.
42. Interview to Primo Levi by Roberto De Caro in "L'Espresso" del 26.4.87.
43. Yosef Hayim Yerushalmi, *Usi dell'oblio*, Pratiche editrice, Milano, 1990, p. 13.
44. Primo Levi, Preface to *La vita offesa*.
45. Primo Levi, *I sommersi e i salvati*, op. cit.
46. Stefano Levi Della Torre, *Eredita di Primo Levi*, on "La Rassegna Mensile di Israel" n. 2/3, May 1989, p. 191.
47. Primo Levi, *La tregua*, pp. 15–16.
48. Primo Levi, *La chiave a stella*, Torino, Einaudi, 1978, p. 52.

11

Legacy in Gray

Lawrence L. Langer

In measuring the enormous achievements of Primo Levi, I am struck first of all by the way American publishers have tried to twist his intentions as a writer into an affirmative direction by altering the titles of his books. His first and most famous work, *If This Is a Man*, appeared as *Survival in Auschwitz: The Nazi Assault on Humanity*, changing a hesitant inquiry into a confident manifesto, even though Levi to the end of his life continued to explore the morally uncertain meaning of the experience we call "survival." Its sequel, *The Truce*, appeared as *The Reawakening*, once again giving a positive spin to a decidedly neutral term, since an armistice between Auschwitz and the future can hardly be considered a revival from the realm of permanent sleep. And the anecdotal volume about Auschwitz published in Italy simply as *Lilith And Other Tales* is changed in America into *Moments of Reprieve*. Such revised titles might easily deceive readers into believing that Levi's main interest was to mine gleaming nuggets of human fellowship from the barren landscape of Auschwitz.

It was not. In a series of interviews conducted during the closing years of his life, Levi described precisely the varied population he found upon arrival in the camp:

> This was the human material I had around me. Among these unfortunates, there was not solidarity, none at all,

> and this lack was the first and biggest trauma. I and the others who'd been transported with me had thought, naively, "However bad it may be, we'll find comrades." It didn't turn out that way. We found enemies, not comrades.[1]

Of course, Levi was not pleased to reach this conclusion. He remembered his close friend Alberto in Auschwitz, who shared equally whatever scarce provisions he could find, or the "free" Italian bricklayer Lorenzo, who every day for many months sneaked Levi a large extra portion of soup. But he also recalled that the general spirit of Auschwitz reflected rivalry rather than unity. And he never ceased to be troubled by this memory of strife.

Throughout his writings on Auschwitz, Levi conducted an ongoing but ultimately futile quest to find a bond linking physical and moral survival. He believed in the value of community, while confessing that staying alive in the camp required the privileged to oppress the unprivileged. He strove to remain decent while admitting that survival "without renunciation of any part of one's own moral world" was conceded only to martyrs and saints, not the majority of inmates—presumably including himself.[2] He was too honest to insist that survival was a tale of spiritual triumph. The camp experience sabotaged the ethical vision that he cherished as a human being. Unwilling to abandon that vision, he tried in vain to restore a moral balance to the post-Auschwitz universe in which he lived. But like so many other survivors, he had to admit the dismal truth that the world had learned virtually nothing from the mass murder of European Jewry. Until his death, he wavered between the same hope and despair about the human condition that had assailed him during his year in the camp. He left us with a legacy neither shining nor bleak, only gray, dimmed by the similar doubts that still hang over the last moments of his life.

One of Levi's major tasks as a writer was to remind his readers, as he quaintly put it, that "Auschwitz etiquette was different from ours."[3] He tells amusingly of how he "corrupted" an innocent new Hungarian arrival who at first believed that work in Auschwitz must be carried out with the same discipline and rigor as work anywhere else. Levi resolves to "convert" his disciple by undermining the integrity that is sure to doom him:

> I tried to convince him of a few recent discoveries of mine (in truth, not yet well digested): that down there, in order to get by, it was necessary to get busy, to organize illegal food, dodge work, find influential friends, hide one's thoughts, steal, and lie; that whoever did not do so was soon dead, and that his saintliness seemed dangerous to me and out of place.[4]

These are among the commandments inscribed on the Tables of the Law in Auschwitz, and we still flinch at the image of honorable men and women being forced to endorse them in order to stay alive. Levi's disciple soon absorbed the wisdom of learning to steal.

Did this represent a temporary adjustment in values required by an abnormally oppressive situation, or a permanent inroad on integrity that would leave its scars long after the end of the war? Levi wrestled all his life with this question. Unlike Viktor Frankl, he avoided heroizing himself by finding formulas for spiritual vigor to let him rise above his lapsing fellow prisoners. He never insisted on unique personal strengths that distanced him from others. He offered instead a group portrait of diminished human beings who were compromised by their special knowledge:

> There was little feeling of camaraderie among us. It was confined to compatriots, and even toward them it was weakened by the minimal life conditions. It was actually zero, indeed negative, with regard to newcomers. In this and many other respects we had greatly retrogressed and become hardened. And in the "new" fellow prisoner we tended to see an alien, an oafish, cumbersome barbarian who took up space and time, and bread, who did not know the unspoken but ironclad rules of coexistence and survival, and who, moreover, complained (and for the wrong reasons) in an irritating and ridiculous manner because just a few days back he was still at home, or at least outside the barbed wire.[5]

These are not the words of a man still seething with recent memories of his painful encounter with moral disorder, but the feelings of a writer more than thirty years after the event. For Levi, the memory of atrocity never faded, nor did it dwindle into a sentimental tale of communal resistance against a ruthless foe. He stifled all temptations to allow the haze of time to obscure his initial view that the offense of Auschwitz was an "inexhaustible fount of evil."[6]

One of the greatest values of Primo Levi's work is that it permits us to measure the impact of chronology, both temporal and moral, on the original deeds of atrocity. Because he returned again and again to the ordeal of Auschwitz, Levi could pursue the truths of the camp down the twisting corridors of history, as well as into the dark recesses of his own inner life. To be sure, freedom followed imprisonment, for those lucky enough to survive, just as efforts at justice followed the hideous crime. But Levi quickly learned that they were not enough to decontaminate or redeem the evil spewed forth by Nazi Germany. In the opening pages of *The Truce* he had described how the moment of liberation had filled the souls of survivors with joy, but also with a painful sense of shame:

> so that we should have liked to wash our consciences and our memories clean from the foulness that lay upon them; and also with anguish, because we felt that this should never happen, that now nothing could ever happen good and pure enough to rub out our past, and that the scars of the outrage would remain within us forever, and in the memories of those who saw it, and in the places where it occurred, and in the stories we should tell of it.[7]

Although *The Truce* is Levi's account of the long journey back from the camp to his place of birth, he does not end it with a celebration of reunion, but with a report of a "dream full of horror" that continued to visit him after his deliverance. For me, it persists as the most frightening image in any of his works. In that dream, he writes, sitting amidst family or friends in a peaceful environment,

> I feel a deep and subtle anguish, the definite sensation of an impending threat. And in fact, as the dream proceeds, slowly or brutally, each time in a different way, everything collapses and disintegrates around me, the scenery, the walls, the people, while the anguish becomes more intense and more precise. Now everything has changed to chaos; I am alone in the centre of a grey and turbid nothing, and now, I know what this thing means, and I also know that I have always known it; I am in the Lager [the camp] once more, and nothing is true outside the Lager. All the rest was a brief pause, a deception of the senses, a dream; my family, nature in flower, my home.[8]

Levi was not the only survivor haunted by this kind of recurrent dream. Its dark verdict that "nothing is true outside the Lager" remained in constant conflict with the post-Auschwitz hopes of man and society, a conflict Levi returned to throughout his career.

If nothing is true outside the Lager, we need to explore Levi's version of what was true inside it, and the text of his first book, *If This Is a Man* (or *Survival in Auschwitz*) provides ample material for such an investigation. There, he developed a doctrine of multiple possibilities to clarify the varied responses to the threats that Auschwitz imposed on the self struggling to stay alive. Readers seeking simple explanations pounce on isolated lines or episodes as if they were hidden keys to the mystery of why one Jew survived, while another did not. But Levi's strategy duplicates the experience of a novice entering an unfamiliar milieu whose rules he has not yet understood. He offers us the "lessons" as he learns them himself; part of our education is to discern that what we master one day we may have to abandon the next, since no successful gesture can be separated from others that may subvert them.

One of the first rules Levi digests is not to ask why something is so. Reason does not reign in Auschwitz. Yet if one cannot fathom the rituals that replace it, one is doomed. Suffering from thirst soon after his arrival, Levi reaches out of a barrack window and breaks off an icicle; a prowling guard brutally snatches it away from him. *"Warum?"*

("Why?") Levi innocently asks with his limited German, and the guard's reply—*"Hier ist kein warum"* ("There is no why here")—exposes the basic nature of the place: questions have no answers, so it is useless to ask any. There are ways of behaving that hasten death, and other ways that postpone it: between these narrow margins lay the zone where the prisoner in Auschwitz was able to manuver.

Today we take for granted the role of a common language in helping us to express needs, form bonds, and define the moral frontiers of the universe we live in. But Levi discovered in Auschwitz what he called "a perpetual Babel, in which everyone shouts orders and threats in languages never heard before, and woe betide whoever fails to grasp the meaning."[9] He invites us to share this confusion of tongues by threading through his text foreign words, phrases, and sentences that pile up until they form a new global lexicon of Holocaust discourse. Only by feeling some ease with such discourse can readers, together with Levi, find their way amidst this confusion of tongues. Levi understood that we could not share the physical distress of the new arrival, who quickly learns that "the Lager is hunger: we ourselves are hunger, living hunger."[10] He realized that his audience would have trouble embracing this cramped view of the self. So he offered entry into the world of Auschwitz by extending his doctrine of multiple possibilities from human behavior to the words that described it.

Readers of *If This Is a Man* may wish that they had brought to the encounter an armful of dictionaries. The polyglot vocabulary is exasperating: *Lager. Häftling. Blockälteste. Muselmann. Klepsi, klepsi. Menaschka. Wäschetauschen. Wstawach. Wer hat noch zu fressen? La propreté, c'est la santé.* Without an interpreter, what average reader can make his or her way through such a colloquial maze? Either you adapt to the peculiar idiom of this multilingual domain, or you falter—and soon, you die. What better way to confront the reader with the potentially fatal verbal challenge that Levi and his comrades faced every day? In a few places, he accentuates this Babel of tongues by giving the options for a single word: "bread-*Brot-Broid-chleb-pain-lechem-keynér*,"[11] initiating us into his macrocosm not only in Italian, but also in English, German, Yiddish, Polish and Russian, French, Hebrew, and Hungarian. Levi is not playing linguistic games, but stressing the importance of translating Auschwitz into terms unfamiliar to our native ear. If naming stabilizes reality, continual renaming unsettles it, and the deeper meaning of Levi's Babel of tongues is that not only verbal but also moral values mutate in this volatile realm. Outside Auschwitz, what sense can we assign to the decree that "Death begins with the shoes," or to the reminder that "everything can be stolen, in fact is automatically stolen as soon as attention is relaxed"?[12] Like a voracious beast, camp routines consume prized laws of conduct, leaving an ethical void into which seep cynical maxims like the ones Levi lists. The prisoner who could not adapt to such unorthodox principles—Levi himself said they inspired stories for a new Bible—speedily perished. And the reader who cannot adjust to the impact of such a system on otherwise decent men and women will never cross the border into their world—one that eroded their spiritual stamina and reduced them to primitive means for staying alive, unseemly, at least in our eyes, for civilized human beings.

But Levi is not interested in judging, and he discourages us from doing so. His chief goal is to report the way it was, an existence full of uncertainty and contradictions. He manages to furnish us simultaneously with a chronological and durational narrative, the one beginning with arrest and deportation and ending at the point of liberation, and the other full of harsh moments and episodes that will remain engraved in memory, untouched by the passage of time. In the central narrative of *If This Is a Man*, the inmate in Auschwitz lives from hour to hour, meal to meal, evening to dawn, the normal rhythms of temporal existence having been upset by the demands of keeping the body intact through one more roll call. Only after the Germans flee the approaching Russians, leaving Levi and a few hundred other ill prisoners behind, does the text return to the daily flow of time: suddenly, Levi begins to date his entries.

With the future restored, the reader breathes a sigh of relief, though Philip Roth has described the interval between

German departure and Russian arrival as a version of Robinson Crusoe in Hell. Weakened by illness, Levi and a comrade nonetheless leave the crude infirmary where they and other starving patients are recovering from scarlet fever to scavenge the landscape for provisions: turnips, frozen potatoes, whatever is edible. Later they will seek a source of heat, and build a makeshift stove. But their human quest is framed by an event that casts lurid shadows over their effort: as the Germans leave, an air raid strikes the camp. Levi's description confirms the aptness of Philip Roth's portrayal:

> Two huts were burning fiercely, another two had been pulverized, but they were all empty. Dozens of patients arrived, naked and wretched from a hut threatened by fire: they asked for shelter. It was impossible to take them in. They insisted, begging and threatening in many languages. We had to barricade the door. They dragged themselves elsewhere, lit up by the flames, barefoot in the melting snow.[13]

If we did not know that we were facing victims rather than sinners, we might mistake this for a setting from Dante's *Inferno.* Despite the return of chronological time and the promise of liberation, the spirit of Babel prevails. Auschwitz still prohibits the shift to universal fellowship, because on the brink of freedom those stricken by scarlet fever fear further contagion from those infected with typhus or diphtheria.

As Levi records in his calendar the march toward rescue, he cannot avoid entries which impede that progress, as if moments of duration threaten forever to taint the restoration of chronology to the lives of those lucky enough to survive. In the ward adjoining Levi's hut lie wretches suffering from dysentery; their cries can be heard through the thin wall:

> Naturally I would have liked to have helped them, given the means and the strength, if for no other reason than to stop their crying. In the evening when all the work was finished, conquering my tiredness and disgust, I dragged myself gropingly along the dark, filthy corridor to their ward with a bowl of water and the remainder of our day's

> soup. The result was that from then on, through the thin wall, the whole diarrhea ward shouted my name day and night with the accents of all the languages of Europe, accompanied by the incomprehensible prayers, without my being able to do anything about it. I felt like crying, I could have cursed them.[14]

The principle of selective caring that allowed a few to help each other while the rest were left to die was a flawed compromise bequeathed by the evil of Auschwitz itself. Even after the Germans have fled, Levi is left with the sorrowful paradox that each advance is accompanied by a simultaneous retreat.

No section in the text of *If This Is a Man* stresses that legacy more than the one immediately preceding the narrative's return to the chronological rhythm. The last episode Levi records before he begins to date his entries highlights the crucial role of durational time in the memory of those who outlived the ordeal. The chapter itself is called "The Last One," and it refers to the final cry of the doomed man whose hanging Levi and his friend Alberto are about to witness: *"Kameraden, ich bin der Letzte!"* "(Comrades, I am the last one!"). The victim was one of the group who destroyed a crematorium abutting the gas chambers in October of 1944. But instead of being heartened by this futile deed of heroism, Levi and Alberto are only reminded of their own inertia and submissiveness: like everyone else required to watch the execution, they remain silent, "bent and gray, our heads dropped."[15]

The juxtaposition of the closing chapters of Levi's account of Auschwitz, "The Last One" and "The Story of Ten Days," forces us to consider the twin temporal possibilities for reading the text and for reflecting on its contents. Passage of time and fixation in time, movement toward release and memory anchored in scenes like the hanging tug at our responses, seeking affinity where perhaps none exists. But one thing is sure: durational moments send their roots into unexplored depths of the self, where they continue to feed in ways which even Levi may never have completely understood.

This does not mean, however, that he was unaware of the dilemma. Being a helpless spectator to the murder of others will remain for him a constant reminder of personal defeat, a source of shame that nothing can erase. Nowhere is the meaning of his title, *If This Is a Man*, more clearly invoked than in the lines he wrote following the report of the hanging:

> To destroy a man is difficult, almost as difficult as to create one: it has not been easy, nor quick, but you Germans have succeeded. Here we are, docile under your gaze; from our side you have nothing more to fear; no acts of violence, no words of defiance, not even a look of judgement.[16]

In Levi's ongoing saga of Auschwitz, this joint paralysis of the physical and moral will both is and is not the sign of a final state of being. Chronological time allowed Levi, through the chance of survival, to free himself from this paralysis and to rejoin the human community as a productive chemist and a successful writer. But durational time plunged him back into the chaos of his Auschwitz past, where even forty years after the event he was still exploring the meaning of shame and judgment, and that gray zone where man's vaunted moral self had lost its dignity and never found a way to reclaim it.

As I said at the outset, Levi could never equate the accident of survival with any form of triumph. In the next-to-last entry of his closing calendar in *If This Is a Man*, the day before the Russians arrive, Levi wrote:

> It is man who kills, man who creates or suffers injustice: it is no longer man who, having lost all restraint, shares his bed with a corpse. Whoever waits for his neighbor to die in order to take his piece of bread is, albeit guiltless, further from the model of thinking man than the most primitive pygmy or the most vicious sadist.[17]

These are among the somberest words that Levi ever wrote, but they should not be mistaken for an expression of reproach, either of Levi himself or of others. As a witness to the demeaning atmosphere that surrounded him, he was too honest to alter it for the sake of a posterity that needed to salvage some message of hope from this quagmire of despair. But he was wary about one crucial issue: though the victims may seem crushed by their ordeal, the fault lay not with them, but with "you Germans," the agents of the evil that consumed their moral strength and, for most, their physical lives.

Four decades later, perhaps realizing how some of the gloomiest moments in *If This Is a Man* might be misread as an effort to blame the victims, Levi returned in *The Drowned and the Saved* to this troublesome theme. One popular gambit in the post-war years to "explain" the atrocity of the Holocaust had been the universalizing argument that what the Germans did only reflected a capacity for violence and evil buried in human nature everywhere. Levi was appalled and offended by this evasion. "I am not an expert on the unconscious and the mind's depths," he wrote,

> but I do know that few people are experts in this sphere and that these few are the most cautious. I do not know, and it does not much interest me to know, whether in my depths there lurks a murderer, but I do know that I was a guiltless victim and I was not a murderer. I know that the murderers existed not only in Germany, and still exist, retired or on active duty, and that to confuse them with their victims is a moral disease or an aesthetic affectation or a sinister sign of complicity; above all, it is a precious service rendered (intentionally or not) to the negators of truth.[18]

As the years passed and he noted an increasing interest in the conduct of the victims and a growing indifference to the behavior of the killers (to say nothing of the will to identify and prosecute them), Levi found himself both vexed and alarmed by the mist of misconceptions into which the outrages that had scarred his life were drifting. Among the many motives driving him to write *The Drowned and the Saved* forty years after the collapse of Auschwitz, this must have been a leading one.

Victims in the camp could be forgiven, as Levi put it, for "drowning one by one in the stormy sea of not-understanding," because the "Lager jargon" was alien to their native vocabulary. But when he discovered that many of his contemporaries, and particularly the Germans themselves, were floating cheerfully in that same sea of incomprehension, he vowed to do something about it. "The further events fade into the past," he conceded in his last volume, "the more the construction of convenient truth grows and is perfected."[19] He launched a campaign against such "truths," and now that he was both a survivor of the camps and a student of their history, he had gained a perspective that allowed him to write with broader authority than had been available to him in *If This Is a Man*, which he finished during the year following his liberation. If in the beginning his role was to bear witness, in the end it included the need to weigh issues like cruelty, responsibility, and judgment. He divided his text between defending his fellow survivors from unjust charges growing out of stereotyped notions of their ordeal, and defining the criminality of the killers and their supporters in a language that leaves the nature of their crimes unmistakable.

First he had to explode the myth, still clung to by some Holocaust commentators, that suffering in Auschwitz was somehow ennobling. "It is naive, absurd, and historically false," he insisted, "to believe that an infernal system such as National Socialism sanctifies its victims: on the contrary, it degrades them, it makes them resemble itself." The shrewd inmate quickly recognized the value of associating with those in power, not in order to mimic their brutality, but so as to gain access to extra rations, for as Levi asserts, without additional sources of food, a starving and weakened prisoner lasted only two or three months in a place like Auschwitz. Some form of privilege—"large or small . . . licit or illicit"—was necessary to stay alive.[20] That is why Levi always argued that the only ones to feel the full horrors of Auschwitz were those who did not return.

Levi dismisses what he charitably calls "a certain hagiographic and rhetorical stylization" which credits survival to a blend of will, resistance, and inner discipline. He replaces this romantic view with a more sober and practical principle: "the harsher the oppression, the more widespread among the oppressed is the willingness to collaborate." But he would reject any effort to identify such camp behavior with the collaboration of free men and women in the Vichy or Quisling regimes in France and Norway. Just as terms like "hunger' and "thirst" were defined differently inside and outside the Lager, so a word like "collaborate," according to Levi, should be stripped of much of the scorn that clings to it in the world beyond the barbed wire:

> Before discussing separately the motives that impelled some prisoners to collaborate to some extent with the Lager authorities, however, it is necessary to declare the imprudence of issuing hasty moral judgement on such human cases. Certainly, the greatest responsibility lies with the system, the very structure of the totalitarian states; the concurrent guilt on the part of individual big and small collaborators (never likable, never transparent!) is always difficult to evaluate.[21]

Levi did not enjoy using a word like "guilt" when raising this problematic topic—and we need scarcely remind ourselves that with rare exceptions he was speaking about the lot of the Jews in all these remarks—because once again the "free" and "imprisoned" definitions did not mesh. In the end, he preferred to speak of "shame" as the primary legacy of the moral swamp into which German coercion had sunk its prey.

When Levi said that the greatest responsibility lay with the system, he set himself the task of explaining what he meant. Even as he used the term, he realized how unsatisfactory it was. On the one hand, the Final Solution was a planned aggression against the Jews of Europe. Mass murder did not erupt spontaneously from the soil of Germany and the countries it occupied. On the other hand, Levi knew that the atrocities he witnessed and endured in Auschwitz did not follow some carefully designed plan issued by the authorities in Berlin. What the Jews suffered during deportation and in the camps was so unpredictable and unsystematic, so dissimilar to other historical episodes of violence, that Levi felt driven to define the special quality of this event. He knew it was a complex challenge:

> Thinking back with the wisdom of hindsight to those years that devastated Europe and, in the end, Germany

> itself, one feels torn between two opinions: Were we witnessing the rational development of an inhuman plan or a manifestation (unique in history and still unsatisfactorily explained) of collective madness? Logic intent on evil or the absence of logic? As so often happens in human affairs, the two alternatives coexisted.[22]

His notion of multiple possibilities could thus be extended to Nazi Germany itself, and the killers it employed.

The idea that Levi wanted to engrave on the minds of his readers was what he called "the practice of useless cruelty." This was the prototypical, primordial German crime during the era of the Third Reich. Even some "use" can be found in the violence of war, brutal as its tactics may be: the defeat of Hitler is a prime example. The goal of useless cruelty, however, is a "desire for the suffering of others" not in order to achieve some essential military or political aim, but simply for its own sake. This was an axiom of Germany's conduct toward its enemies, particularly the Jews, and it left its victims helpless to prepare a useful response. Levi lists a few public examples, some of them well-known: the executions in the Ardeatine Caves outside of Rome, and the destruction of the villages of Oradour in France and Lidice in Czechoslovakia, together with the murder of most of their inhabitants. These are cases, he says, where "the limits of reprisal, already intrinsically inhuman, were enormously surpassed."[23] Victims were so vulnerable for the very reason that they were unable to imagine a system tolerating a practice of useless cruelty that allowed the inhuman to have no limits.

The slow dying from starvation or untreated disease that was the rule in the camps for those not selected for gassing was for Levi a classic instance of the "deliberate creation of pain that was an end in itself." What, he asks, was served by the combination of "gratuitous viciousness" with indifference and negligence that caused so much human misery? If swift and merciless death were the goal, one could perhaps "understand" (without condoning) such behavior. But "the useless cruelty of violated modesty," the public humiliation, especially of women, seemed an assault on dignity without purpose:

> I do not believe that this transformation was ever planned or formulated in so many words at any level of the Nazi hierarchy, in any document, at any "labor meeting." It was a logical consequence of the system: an inhuman regime spreads and extends its inhumanity in all directions, also and especially downward; unless it meets with resistance and exceptionally strong characters, it corrupts its victims and its opponents as well.[24]

This returns us to the ultimate dilemma that even Primo Levi could not solve: a system may be blamed, but cannot be indicted or tried, for the practice of useless cruelty. Only its agents can, but they remain concealed by that very system behind cloaks of anonymity, and in Levi's text, they do not emerge. He does not study the Bogers and Kaduks of Birkenau, the individual torturers and murderers who cheerfully embraced their regime's notion of useless cruelty and devised their own private versions of how if should be applied.

Perhaps we will never comprehend how and why such decisions were made, but every time Primo Levi mentions the subject, he returns to the site of his own internal wound. And because we have no "cure" for that wound, no satisfactory explanation, it continues to fester, in his own imagination and in ours. He tells of two ninety-year-old women in his convoy to Auschwitz, who were dragged from the infirmary and loaded onto his train, simply because they were Jewish. One died en route, the other was gassed on arrival. "Would it not have been simpler," Levi asks,

> more 'economical,' to let them die, or perhaps kill them in their beds, instead of adding their agony to the collective agony of the transport? One is truly led to think that, in the Third Reich, the best choice, the choice imposed from above, was the one that entailed the greatest affliction, the greatest waste, the greatest physical and moral suffering.[25]

But worst of all, and this is implied in everything that Levi wrote about it, is that the crime remains unpunished and unrepented. The ninety-year-old women did not drag themselves from their beds; they were taken by men, who to this day are unknown, uncharged, untried, and possibly, in their *own* feelings guiltless of any misdeeds.

The crimes were monstrous but not, as Levi maintained, the criminals. Camp guards were "obtuse brutes, not subtle demons." The violence that ran in their veins was not a moral disease, but a normal and obvious expression of their roles. "I do not mean to say that they were made of a perverse human substance," Levi concedes, "different from ours (there were also sadists and psychopaths among them, but they were few)." But Levi, for some reason, did not seize the challenge of exploring the nature of his tormentors with the same detailed scrutiny he applied to the idiosyncrasies of his fellow prisoners. Of course, he observed them from a distance and probably did not enjoy speculating about strangers. Even though he calls the Lager his university and admits that it "taught us to look around and measure men,"[26] he chose not to measure with critical appraisal the agents of his misery, their motives or their deeds.

Perhaps one cause is that when Levi wrote about his fellow prisoners, he wrote as a witness. Examining his tormentors would require him to advance to the level of analyst, and his natural modesty, combined with a reluctance to venture into an area where "experts" had already clouded the field, held him back. But I suspect there is a more fundamental reason. "We are neither historians nor philosophers," he wrote in *The Drowned and the Saved*, "but witnesses":

> and anyway, who can say that the history of human events obeys rigorous logic, patterns. One cannot say that each turn followed from a single why: simplifications are proper only for textbooks; the whys can be many, entangled with one another or unknowable, if not actually nonexistent.[27]

"Hier ist kein warum" ("There is no why here") was a lesson learned early and well, but Levi was not eager to hear that it was as valid at the end of the journey as it was at the beginning. Neither Eichmann in Jerusalem nor the accused at

Nuremberg had furnished any insight into how particular individuals had assented to or participated in the crime of mass murder—merely a pastiche of excuses. It was not too difficult to tell the drowned from the saved among the victims of the camps, or to decipher the reasons for the condition of each. Finding a similar distinction among the Germans, on the other hand, was a daunting task, while further refinements were well-nigh impossible.

Levi's despondency on this subject is evident in his last book, *The Drowned and the Saved*, which closes with a chapter called "Letters from Germans," giving us a clue to what was on his mind in the final years of his foreshortened life. He identifies the "new emotion" he felt when he learned that *If This Is a Man* was to be published in Germany. Only then, in 1959, did he realize that "its true recipients, those against whom the book was aimed like a gun were they, the Germans. Now the gun was loaded." Such violent imagery is totally atypical of a man of gentle temperament like Primo Levi; it tells us how pivotal this moment must have been for him. He spoke of cornering his German readers, of settling accounts, not in order to gain revenge, but to provoke a dialogue between them. When he wrote in the mid 1980s of that time in the late 1950s when he still had hoped to acquire some insight into the German mentality of the war years, Levi was in a good position to assess the impact of his work. *If This Is a Man* was about Auschwitz time, what I have called durational time, but Levi's German readers had seen the passage of so much chronological time that the interval had diluted rather than intensified the difference. When *If This Is a Man* appeared in Germany, Levi received some sober and thoughtful letters, some eccentric or exasperating ones too. But in a country of millions, a book read by thousands could not awaken the national self-inquiry he desired. His failure to "understand the Germans"—the useless cruelty of his travail in Auschwitz was but one example of this—remained a "painful void"[28] in his life as a writer and a man. Although he quoted from several of the letters, Levi used the opportunity of this essay to restate his own feelings about the Germans he tried to but could not understand, and he writes with a language of indictment that convinces us he could no longer divide the memory of the victimizers from the memory of the victims. He mentions the SS, of course, but "also those others, those who had believed, who not believing had kept silent, who did not have the frail courage to look into our eyes, to throw us a piece of bread, to whisper a human word." He was not interested in a spirit of reconciliation: "Almost all, but not all, had been deaf, blind, and dumb: a mass of 'invalids' surrounding a core of ferocious beasts. Almost all, though not all, had been cowardly." He cited the "modest courage" of one German technician in Auschwitz who during an air raid insisted on bringing Levi and two comrades into a bunker though it was off limits to Jews. But this only highlights the absence of courage in all the others. Levi alleged that he never hated the Germans, but he leaves no doubt that he still condemns them, and the closing words of *The Drowned and the Saved* invite his readers, especially those who rely on the ideas of others to form their response to the Holocaust, to accept such censure as a legacy that neither time nor pardon can erase:

> Let it be clear that to a greater or lesser degree all were responsible, but it must be just as clear that behind their responsibility stands that great majority of Germans who accepted in the beginning, out of mental laziness, myopic calculation, stupidity, and national pride the 'beautiful words' of Corporal Hitler, followed him as long as luck and lack of scruples favored him, were swept away by his ruin, afflicted by deaths, misery, and remorse, and rehabilitated a few years later as a the result of an unprincipled political game.[29]

These are among the sourest and most disillusioned words Primo Levi ever wrote. They betray a state of mind not usually associated with him, but that may be because he buried beneath his calm demeanor an indignation whose embers had never expired. It is reported that when Primo Levi was wheeled into the operating room for prostate surgery a few months before his death, he rolled up his sleeve and pointed to the number tattooed on his arm, saying "That is my disease."[30]

On the book jacket of the American edition of *The Drowned and the Saved* appears an imprudent statement that reminds us how far we still have to go if we are to grasp the impact of Auschwitz on one of its most outspoken survivors:

> Primo Levi's luminous writings offer a wondrous celebration of life. His universally acclaimed books remain a testament to the indomitability of the human spirit and humanity's capacity to defeat death through meaningful work, morality and art.

Levi would have blanched at such mindless rhetoric, so indifferent to the complex and painful subterranean tenor of much of his work. Although he will long be remembered, he certainly did not defeat death. He left us rather with the lingering question of whether the death he eluded in Auschwitz did not finally defeat him, not as it ultimately conquers us all, but as a unique psychological wound that only graduates of Auschwitz comprehend. Readers of *If This Is a Man* know that it is as much a death story as it is a life story, and I think the same is true, though the tone may be more muted, of everything that Primo Levi ever wrote about his camp ordeal.

Notes

1. Ferdinando Camon, *Conversations with Primo Levi*, trans. John Shepley (Marlboro, VT.: Marlboro Press, 1989), pp. 21–22.
2. See Primo Levi, *Survival in Auschwitz: The Nazi Assault on Humanity*, trans. Stuart Woolf (New York: Collier Books, 1993), p. 92.
3. Primo Levi, "The Gypsy," in *Moments of Reprieve*, trans. Ruth Feldman (New York: Summit Books, 1986), p. 69.
4. Levi, "A Disciple," in *Moments of Reprieve*, p. 52.
5. Levi, "The Gypsy," in *Moments of Reprieve*, p. 67.
6. Primo Levi, *The Reawakening: A Liberated Prisoner's Long March Home through East Europe*, trans. Stuart Woolf (Boston: Little, Brown, 1965), p. 13.
7. Ibid., pp. 12–13.
8. Ibid., p. 222.

9. Primo Levi, *Survival in Auschwitz: The Nazi Assault on Humanity*, trans. Stuart Woolf (New York, Collier Books, 1993), p. 38.
10. Ibid., p. 74.
11. Ibid., p. 39.
12. Ibid., pp. 34, 33.
13. Ibid., p. 157.
14. Ibid., p. 166.
15. Ibid., p. 149.
16. Ibid., p. 150.
17. Ibid., pp. 171–172.
18. Primo Levi, *The Drowned and the Saved*, trans. Raymond Rosenthal (New York: Simon & Schuster, 1988), pp. 48–49.
19. Ibid., pp. 96, 27.
20. Ibid., pp. 40, 41.
21. Ibid., pp. 43–44.
22. Ibid., p. 106.
23. Ibid., p. 107.
24. Ibid., pp. 109, 111, 112.
25. Ibid., p. 120.
26. Ibid., pp. 121, 141.
27. Ibid., p. 150.
28. Ibid., pp. 168, 174.
29. Ibid., pp. 169, 203.
30. See James Atlas, "The Survivor's Suicide," *Vanity Fair* (January 1988), p. 94.

Bibliography of Selected Works by and About Primo Levi

Amsallem, Daniela. “Primo Levi: Un Temoin Dans les Remous de l’Histoire.” *Revue d’Histoire de la Shoah: Le Monde Juif* 162 (1998): 43–95.

Amsallem, Daniela. “Primo Levi ‘juif de retour.’ “ *Les nouveaux cahiers* 114 (automne 1993): 37–46.

Angier, Carole. “Books: Unillusioned Courage.” *New Statesman & Society* (19 October 1990): 32 col. 1–5.

Angier, Carole. “Books: Darkness into Light.” *New Statesman & Society* (23 February 1990): 33 col. 3, 34 col. 1–2.

Angress, Ruth K. “Discussing Holocaust Literature.” *Simon Wiesenthal Center Annual* 2 (1985): 179–92.

Angress, Ruth K. “Primo Levi in English.” *Simon Wiesenthal Center Annual*, New York 3 (1986): 317–330.

Anissimov, Myriam. Translated by Steve Cox. *Primo Levi: Tragedy of an Optomist*. London: Aurum, 1998.

Anissimov, Myriam. “Primo Levi.” *Les nouveaux cahiers*, Paris 114; (1993): 35–36.

Anonymous. “Primo Levi: Questions and Answers at Indiana University.” *Midstream* 32 (4 April 1986): 26–28.

Arato, Franco. “Varietà e documenti Minerva e Venere.” *Belfagor* 48 (1993): 569–584.

Ascoli, Donatella. “Riflessioni su Primo Levi.” *Ha Keillah La Comunita*, Torino 3 (1989): 8.

Atlas, James. "The Survivor's Suicide." *Vanity Fair* 51 (January 1988): 79, 84, 94.

Bassan, Fiorella. "Primo Levi." *Il portavoce*, Roma, maggio-guigno (1987): 12–13.

Biasin, Gian Paolo. "Till My Ghastly Tale is Told: Levi's Moral Discourse from *Se questo è un uomo* to *I sommersi e i salvati*." *Reason and Light. Essays on Primo Levi*. Ed. Susan Tarrow. Ithaca: Cornell University Press, 1990.

Biasin, Gian Paolo. "Food and the Novel." *The Flavors of Modernity*. New Jersey: Princeton University Press, 1993. 128–165.

Bodrato, Aldo. "Nel racconto la verità di Auschwitz." *Humanitas: Rivista bimestrale di Cultura*, 25100 Brescia, Italy (HumB) 44 (1 February 1989): 51–73.

Bons, Eberhard. "Vergangenes erinnern, um Drohendes zu bannen: Judenverfolgung und Partiansanenkampf in Primo Levis Romanen." *Orientierung* 51 (1987): 134–136.

Boone, Susan L. "Unvarnished Truth: the Chemistry of Shame in Primo Levi." *Judaism* 48 (Winter 1999): 72–83.

Borri, Giancarlo. "Le divine impurità: Primo Levi tra scienza e letteraturra." *Rimini Luise* (1992):

Boule, Anne. "Primo Levi, ou l'Ecriture au Service de la Memoire." *Historiens et Geographes* 84 (1994): 75–84.

Bravo, Anna e Jalla, Daniele. "Primo Levi testimone." *Materiali di lavoro*, Rovereto 1–4 (1988): 183–189.

Bravo, Anna. "Primo Levi, un uomo normale di buona memoria." *Passato e Presente*, Firenze 18 (1988): 99–108.

Bura, Claudio. "Primo Levi, La Chiave a stella." *Annali*, Univ. per Stranieri (8 January–June 1987): 111–180.

Bruck, Edith. "Omaggio a Primo Levi." *Il Portavoce*, Roma 3 (1990): 10–11.

Cahnman, Werner J. "If This is a Man." *American Journal of Sociology* LSV: 6 (May 1960): 638–39.

Calcagno, Giorgio. "Primo Levi e i tedeschi: Un carteggio sconosciuto." *La Stampa: Tuttolibri* 13.549 (18 April 1987): 1.

Calvino, Italo. "Le quattro strade di Primo Levi." *La Republic* (June 1981): 18–19.

Camon, Ferdinado, ed. *Autoritratto di Primo Levi*. Padova: Edizioni Nord-Est, 1987.

Camon, Ferdinando. *Conversations with Primo Levi*. Trans. John Shepley. Marlboro, Vermont: Marlboro Press, 1989.

Cannon, JoAnn. "Canon Formation and Reception in Contemporary Italy: The Case of Primo Levi." *Italica*, Madison, Wisconsin, 69. Spring 1 (1992): 30–44.

Caracciolo, Nicola. *Uncertain Refuge: Italy and the Jews During the Holocaust*. Trans. Florette Rechnitz Koffler and Richard Koffler. Chicago: University of Illinois Press, 1995.

Cases, Cesare. "Sodio e potassio: scienza e visione del mondo in Primo Levi" in *Primo Levi as Witness*, ed. Pietro Frassica (Fiesole: Casalini libri: 1990).

Catani, Maurizio. " 'Even if we were to tell it, we would not be believed': A lesson from the work of Primo Levi." *Current Sociology* 43 (Autumn/Winter 1995): 137–160.

Caute, David. "Man a Prisoner." *New Statesman LIX* 1514 (19 March 1960): 410.

Cavaglion, Alberto. "Argon e la cultura ebraica piemontese." *Belfagor: Rassegna di Varia Umanità*, Florence 43.5 (30 September 1988): 541–562.

Cavaglion, Alberto e Aldo Viglione. *Il Presente del passato: giornate internazionali di studio*. A cura di Alberto Cavaglion; interventi e relazioni di A. Viglione et al. *Studi e ricerche storiche*. 156. Milano, Italy: Franco Angeli, 1991:246.

Cavaglion, Alberto. "Sopra una fonte dimenticata di Se questo è uomo", in *Primo Levi: memoria E Invenzionne*, Ed. Giovanna Iola (san salvatore monferrato: 1995).

Ceccatty, Rene de. "Primo Levi: Ne jugez pas." *Nouvelle Revue Francaise*, 75341 Paris, Cedex 07, France (NRF) (October 1988): 68–74.

Cheyette, Bryan. "The Ethical Uncertainty of Primo Levi." *Judaism* 48 (Winter 1999): 57–67."

Cicioni, Mirna. "Bridges of Knowledge: Rereading Primo Levi" (Italian). *Spunti e ricerche: rivista d'italianistica*, University of Melbourne, Parkville, Australia. Volume 3, 1987: 59–94.

Cicioni, Mirna. *Primo Levi-Bridges of Knowledge* (English). Oxford: Berg Publishers, 1995.

Clarke, Bruce. "Aspects of the Daemonic in Primo Levi's Periodic Table." *The Literature of Science: Perspectives on Popular Scientific Writings*. Ed. Murdo-William McCrae. Athens: University of Georgia, 1993: 321.

Collotti, Enzo. "Leggendo il revisionismo in Primo Levi." *Belfagor: Rassegna di Varia-Umanità*, Florence, 44.1, 31 January 1989: 98–102.

Colombo, Arturo. "Primo Levi, a Aqui quella sera." *Nuova Antologia* 122 (July/Sept. 1987): 207–211.

Cravetto, Maria Letizia. *Fidelite a l' apres: A propos du suicide de Primo Levi et de l' interiorite du mal*. Paris: Editions Kime, 2000.

Czarany, Norbert. "Ceui qui apprenait a lire ce siecle." *Les nouveaux cahiersi,* Paris 114 (automne 1993): 50–52.

Deak, Istvan. "The Incomprehensible Holocaust." *The New York Review* (September 1989): 63–72.

Denby, David. "The Poised Art of Primo Levi: The Humanist and the Holocaust." *New Republic* 4 (28 July 1986): 27–33.

Denman, Hugh. "Norwegian and Italian Literature: the Returning Agony." *Times Literary Supplement* (2–8 October 1987): 1081, 1082.

Devolder, Jan. "Primo Levi ecrire et survivre." *Bulletin trimestriel de la Fondation Auschwitz*, Bruxelles 36–37 (1993): 127–139.

Di Antonio, Robert. "Mirror of Memory." *Jerusalem Post* 1539 (1990): 16.

Dini, Massimo and Stefano Jesurum. *Primo Levi. Le opere e i giorni*. Milano: Rizzoli, 1992. 212.

Eberstadt, Fernanda. "Reading Primo Levi." *Commentary* 80 (October 1985): 41, 47.

Eder, Richard. "The Death of Primo Levi." *Los Angeles Times Book Review* (31 May 1987): 11.

Epstein, Adam. "Primo Levi and the Language of Atrocity." *Bulletin of the Society for Italian Studies: A Journal for Teachers of Italian in Higher Education*, Cambridge, England (BSIS). 20 (187): 31–38.

Falkenberg, Betty. "Organic Chemistry." *The New Leader LXVII.* 21 (1984): 16–17.

Feinstein, Wiley. "Primo Levi and Jewish Identity: The Question of Jewish Languages." *Selected papers from Proceedings of the Fifth Annual Conference of American Association of Teachers of Italian.* Ed. Albert N. Mancin and Paolo A. Giordano. Monterey, California: Italiana, Rosary College River Forest, Illinois (1988, 1990): vii. 333.

Ferrero, Ernesto, ed. *Primo Levi: un'antologia della critica.* Torino: Einaudi, 1997.

Ferrero, Ernesto. "Primo Levi scrittore." *Notiziario dell'Istituto Storico della Resistenza in Cuneo e provincia* 32 (1987): 181–188.

Finco, Aldo. "Primo Levi: lo spettro di Auschwitz." *Rivista di Studi Italiani 12.* (2 Dicembre 1994): 54–60.

Finter, H. "Primo Levi as Writer and Witness." *Roman Z Literature* 17.3–4, (1993): 437–450.

Frankel, Ellen. "Primo Levi and the Chemistry of Survival." *Jewish Spectator* 51: 4. (Winter 1986): 41 col. 1–2, 43. col. 2.

Frassica, Pietro, ed. *Primo Levi as Witness: Proceedings of a Symposium Held at Princeton University.* Fiesole: Casalini, 1990.

Frassica, Pietro. "Invarianti dell'evocazione: Se non ora, quando? di Primo Levi." *Prometeo* 3:9 (January/March 1983): 20–32.

Fuhrman, Peter. "Interview with Primo Levi: A Chemist Turned Literary Alchemist." *Christian Science Monitor Book Review* (2 August 1985): 1–2.

Galante Garrone, Alessandro. "Il grido di Primo Levi." *Nuova Antologia*, Firenze (luglio-settembre 1987): 212–227.

Gambetta, Diego. "Primo Levi's Plunge: A Case Against Suicide." *New York Times.* (7 August 1999): A15 & A17.

Garibba, Nicola. "Primo Levi il Testimone." *Karnenu, Roma.* 3 (Aprile, 1988): 1–5.

Garosci, Aldo. "Se questo è un uomo . . ." *La Rassegna mensile di Israel*, Roma 2–3 (1989): 229–232.

Gerrard, Nicci. "A Corridor of Time: Fiction." *London Observer* (10–11, November 1999).

Getzler, Dvorah. "The Key to a Life." *The Jerusalem Post* 1360, 29 November 1986: 17.

Getzler, Dvorah. "Branded in Memory." *The Jerusalem Post* 1360, 29 November 1986: 17.

Giffuni, Catahe. *An English Bibliography of the Writings of Primo Levi*. Westport, CT. Bulletin of Bibliography, 1993. 213–221.

Gilliland, Gail. "Self and Other: Christa Wolf's *Patterns of Childhood* and Primo Levi's *Se questo è un uomo* As Dialogic Texts." *Comparative Literature Studies*, University Park, PA. 29.2 (1992): 183–209.

Gilman, Sander L. "To Quote Primo Levi: 'Redest keyn jiddisch, bist nit kejn jid' ('If you don't speak Yiddish, you're not a Jew')." *Prooftexts: A Journal of Jewish Literary History*, New York, NY. 9.2 (May 1989): 139–60.

Gilman, Sander L. "The Special Language of the Camps and After." *Reason and Light: Essays on Primo Levi*. Ed. Susan Tarrow. Ithaca: Cornell University Center for International Studies, 1990.

Girelli-Carasi, Fabio. "Strategie narrative del macro-testo autobiografico di Primo Levi." *Fifth Annual Conference of American Association of Teachers of Italian*. Ed. Albert N. Mancini, Paolo A. Giordano and Anthony J. Tamburri. Monterey, California: Italiana, Rosary College, River Forest, Illinois, 18–20 November 1988: 4, 333.

Giuntella, Vittorio E. "In Memoria 'In Morte di Primo Levi'." *Quaderni del Centro di studi sulla deportazione e l'internamento*, Roma 12 (1989–1990): 117–119.

Glasberg, Ronald P. "Power in Western Civilization: Structural Parallels Between the Book of Job and Primo Levi's Survival in Auschwitz." *Canadian Review of Comparative Literature* (December 1992): 597–614.

Glasberg, Ronald P. "The Dynamics of Domination: Levi's 'Survival in Auschwitz,' Solzhenitsyn's 'Gulag Archipelago,' and Atwood's 'The Handmaiden's Tale.'" *Canadian Review of Comparative Literature* (December 1994).

Gordon, Robert. "'Per mia fortuna . . .': Irony and Ethics in Primo Levi's Writing." *Modern Language Review* 92 (1997): 337–47.

Gordon, Robert S. C. "Primo Levi's *If This is a Man* and Responses to the Lager in Italy 1945–47." *Judaism* 48 (Winter 1999): 49–57.

Gordon Robert. "The Centaur's Ghastly Tale." *Times Literary Supplement* (9 November 1998): 3–4.

Gordon, Robert S. C. "Reviews." *Modern Language Review* 92 (July 1997): 761–63.

Gordon, Robert. "Primo Levi: Storyteller." *European Judaism*, London 23: 1 (1990): 11–20.

Grassano, Giuseppe. *Primo Levi*. Firenze: La nuova Italia, (1981).

Gunzberg, Lynn M. "Down Among the Dead Men: Levi and Dante in Hell." *Modern Language Studies* 16:1. (Winter 1986): 10–28.

Harrowitz, Nancy. "Representations of the Holocaust: Levi, Bassani and the Commemorative Mode." *Reason and Light*. Ed. Susan Tarrow. Ithaca: Cornell University Western Societies Occasional Paper Series (1990): 26–39.

Hartman, Geoffrey H. *Holocaust Remembrance: The Shapes of Memory*. Oxford: Basil Blackwell, 1994.

Hilberg, Raul. "Books: Primo Levi: Testimony of a Survivor." *Boston Sunday Globe* (27 December 1987): A14 col. 4 p. A16 col. 4–6.

Howe, Irving. "How to Write About the Holocaust." *New York Review of Books* 32. (28 March 1985): 63 col. 1

Howe, Irving. "Primo Levi: An Appreciation." *If Not Now, When?* New York: Summit Books, 1985. 3–16.

Howe, Irving. "The Utter Sadness of the Survivor." *The New York Times Book Review*, 10 January, 1988. 3.

Hughes, H. Stuart. "Two Captives Called Levi." *Prisoner of Hope: The Silver Age of the Italian Jews 1924–1974*. Cambridge, Mass.: Harvard University Press, 1983: 55–85.

Jagendorf, Zvi. "Primo Levi Goes for Soup and Remembers Dante." *Raritan, A Quarterly Review*, New Brunswick, New Jersey 4 12: (Spring 1993): 31–51.

Kakutani, Michiko. "Word and Image: Books of the Times: Primo Levi and the Ghost of Auschwitz." *New York Times* (12 December 1989): C23 col. 1–3.

Kellerman, Stewart. "Shadow of Auschwitz on Primo Levi's Life." *New York Times*. (26 November 1988): 11 col. 1–4.

Klein, Ilona. "Official Science Often Lacks Humility: Humor, Science and Technology in Levi's 'Storie Naturali.'" *Reason and Light: Essays on Primo Levi.* Ed. Susan Tarrow. Western Societies Program Occasional Paper. Ithaca, New York: Center for International Studies, Cornell University, no. 25, 1990.

Klein, Ilona. "Primo Levi: The Drowned and the Saved and the Grey Zone." *Simon Wiesenthal Center Annual* 7 (1990): 77–89.

Klein, Ilona. "Reviews." *Modern Language Notes* 104: (1 January, 1989): 263–265.

Kleiner, Barbara. "Nuchternheit und Konkretion: Der italienische Schriftsteller Primo Levi." *Merkur: Deutsche-Zeitschrift-fur-europaisches-Denken*, 800 Munich 5, Germany (Merkur). 41.8 (1987): 690–694.

Kriegel, Annie. "Ce qu'il faut en penser." *l'Arche*, Paris no. 363 (Juin 1987): 27–28.

Kuhiwcza, Piotr. "Beyond Self: A Lesson from the Concentration Camps." *Canadian Review of Comparative Literature*, Edmonton, no. 19 (3 September 1992): 395–405.

Kurzweil, Edith. "Books: Who Killed Primo Levi?" *Partisan Review* 55.4 (1988): 678–681.

Lang, Ariella. "Reason as Revenge: Primo Levi and Writing the Holocaust." *Symposium* 52 (Winter 1999): 255–269.

Langer, Lawrence. *The Holocaust and the Literary Imagination.* New Haven: Yale University Press, 1975.

Langer, Lawrence, ed. *Art from the Ashes: A Holocaust Anthology.* New York: Oxford University Press, 1995.

Levi, Primo. "Anniversario." *L' Eco dell' educazione ebraica*, Milano 7 (1955): 20, 22.

Levi, Primo. *If This is a Man.* Stuart Woolf, trans. New York: Orion Press, 1959.

Levi, Primo. *Survival in Auschwitz: The Nazi Assault on Humanity.* Stuart Woolf, trans. (originally published as *If This Is A Man.*) New York: Collier Books, 1961.

Levi, Primo. *The Truce: A Survivor's Journey Home from Auschwitz.* Stuart Woolf, trans. London: New England Library, 1966.

Levi, Primo. *Vizio di forma.* Torino: Einaudi, 1971.

Levi, Primo. "Vanadium: A Memoir." *Commentary* 63.3 (March 1977): 65–69.

Levi, Primo. "Iron: A Memoir." *Commentary* 64.2 (August 1977): 45–49.

Levi, Primo. "Our Seal." Ruth Feldman, trans. *Canto* 3.1 (1979): 1–4.

Levi, Primo. "The Hazzan and the Barracks Chief." *Hadassah Magazine* 61.8 (1980): 16, 17, 38.

Levi, Primo. *La riceradella podici.* Turin: Einaudi, 1981.

Levi, Primo. "Lilith in the Lager." *Canto* 3.4 (January 1981: 153–158.

Levi, Primo. "Titanium." George Jochnowitz, trans. *Midstream* (27 June–July 1981): 28, 29.

Levi, Primo. "A Disciple." *Malahat Review* 63 (October 1982): 179–182.

Levi, Primo. "The Juggler." *Fiction* 7.1–2 (1983): 227–231.

Levi, Primo. "Beyond Survival." *Prooftexts: A Journal of Jewish Literary History*, College Park. 4, (1 January 1984): 9–21.

Levi, Primo. *The Periodic Table.* Raymond Rosenthal, trans. New York: Schocken Books, 1984.

Levi, Primo. "Prisoners of Hope." *Prooftexts: A Journal of Jewish Literary History* 4 (1984).

Levi, Primo. "Travels with C." *The Sciences* 24. (September–October 1984): 16–20.

Levi, Primo. "The Story of C." *Harper's* 269.1614 (November 1984): 28, 29.

Levi, Primo. "Itinerario d'uno scrittore ebreo." *La Rasegna mensile di Israel*, Roma nos. 5, 6, 7, 8 (1984): 376–390.

Levi, Primo and Tullio Regge. *Dialogo*. Torino: Einaudi, 1984.

Levi, Primo. *If Not Now, When?* William Weaver, trans. new York: Penguin Books, 1985.

Levi, Primo. "Gypsy." *Fiction* 7, 8.3, 1 (1985): 3.

Levi, Primo. "Two Portraits." *Moment* 10.10 (1985): 45.

Levi, Primo. "Lorenzo's Return." *New York Review of Books* 32.17 (7 November 1985): 3, 4.

Levi, Promo. "I sommersi e i salvati." *Quaderni del Centro studi sulla deportazione e l'internatamento*, Roma, 1986–1990 12, (1986): 137–141.

Levi, Primo. *The Monkey's Wrench.* William Weaver, trans. New York: Summit Books, 1986.

Levi, Primo. *The Reawakening: A Liberated Prisoner's Long March Home through East Europe* (originally published in England as *The Truce.*) Stuart Woolf, trans. New York: MacMillian, 1986.

Levi, Primo. "Small Causes." *Vanity Fair* 49.1 (1986): 78, 79.

Levi, Primo. "Children of the Wind." *Harper's* 272.1630 (March 1986): 32, 33.

Levi, Primo. "Light on the Camps." *The new Republic* (12 February 1986): 28–32.

Levi, Primo. *Moments of Reprieve.* Ruth Feldman, trans. New York: Penguin Books, 1987.

Levi, Primo. "Renzo's First." *Formations* 3.3 (Winter 1987): 1, 4.

Levi, Primo. "This Above All Be Clear." *New York Times Book Review* 1 (20 November 1988): 59–60.

Levi, Primo. *The Drowned and the Saved.* Raymond Rosenthal, trans. new York: Summit Books, 1988.

Levi, Primo. "Shame." *Esquire* 109.1 (January 1988): 99 & 102.

Levi, Primo. "L'accento sulla diaspora. Un'intervista del 1984." *Linea d'ombra* 28 (1988): 16–17.

Levi, Primo. *The Mirror Maker: Stories and Essays.* Raymond Rosenthal, trans. New York: Schocken Books, 1989.

Levi, Primo. *Other Peoples Trades.* Raymond Rosenthal, trans. New York: Summit Books, 1989.

Levi, Primo. "Reflections on Writing." *Partisan Review* 56.1 (Winter 1989): 21–33.

Levi, Primo. "Beetlemania." *Harper's* 278–279. (February 1989): 27–28.

Levi, Primo. "Reflections." *Wilson Quarterly* 13.3 (Summer 1989): 120–127.

Levi, Primo. *The Sixth Day and Other Tales.* Raymond Rosenthal, trans. New York: Simon and Schuster, 1990.

Levi, Primo. "Psychophant." *New Yorker* 65. (12 February 1990): 35, 38.

Levi, Primo. "Man's Friend." *New Yorker* 66. (26 March 1990): 32, 33.

Levi, Primo. "Full Employment." *New Yorker* 66. (23 April 1990): 39, 44.

Levi, Primo. *Shema: Collected Poems of Primo Levi.* Ruth Feldman and Brian Swann, trans. 2nd. ed. London: Faber, 1991.

Levi, Primo and Giorgio Calcagno. *Echi di una voce perduta: incontri, interviste e conversazioni con Primo Levi, Gabriella Poli, Giorgio Calcagno.* Milano, Italy: Mursia, 1992.

Levi, Primo. "Lezioni." *La Terra.* Roma 1. (febbraio 1995): 78–83.

Limentani, Giacoma. "Primo Levi e il rifiuto dell'urlo." *Linea d'ombra*, Milano 23 (1988): 11–13.

Lollini, Massimo. "La storia come 'olocausto': La testimonianza di Primo Levi." *Romance Languages Annual*, West Lafayette, Indiana 2 (1990): 243–49.

Lollini, Massimo. "Il caso Primo Levi e il problema della testimonianza." *Il-piccolo-Hans* 72 (Winter 1991–1992): 193–210.

Lopez, Guido. "Levi's Il Sistema Periodico." European Judaism. London 2 (1975): 46–47.

Lopez, Guido. "Se non lui, chi?" *Shalom* Roma anno XXI, 4 (30 aprile 1987): 22–24.

Losey, Jay. "From Savage Elements: Epiphany in Primo Levi's Holocaust Writings." *Journal of European Studies* 24, part 1.93 (1994): 1–21.

Lowin, Joseph. “Primo Levi’s Unorthodox Judaism.” *Jewish Book Annual*, New York, 45 (1987–1988): 168–181.

Luria, S. E. “Themes Beyond Chemistry.” *Science* 228 (April 5, 1985): 66 col. 3, 67 col. 1.

Macklin, Elizabeth. “An Obiturary for Primo Levi.” *The New Yorker* LXIII. 12 1987: (31–32).

Marcus, James. “Brief Encounters: Elemental magic.” *Village Voice* 30:9 (26 February 1985): 47.

McCord Schenk, Janet. “The Psychaches of Primo Levi and Jerzy Kosinski: Some Preliminary Considerations.” *Journal of Psychology and Judaism*, New York 18.3 (1994): 259–277.

McRae, Murdo-William. “Opposition and Reversal in Primo Levi’s The Periodic Table.” *Publications of the Mississippi Philological Association*, Jackson, MI (POMPA) (1988): 115–124.

Momigliano Levi, Paola ed. *Primo Levi: Testimone e scrittore di storia*. Firenze: Giuntina, 1999.

Motola, Gabriel. “Books: The Secondo Primo.” *American Scholar* 59.1 (Winter 1990): 142–146.

Motola, Gabriel. “Primo Levi: The Auschwitz Experience.” *The Southwest Review* 72 Spring 1987): 258–69.

Motola, Gabriel. “Primo Levi: His Life and Death.” *European Judaism*, London 2 (1987): 42–46.

Motola, Gabriel. “The Varnish-Maker’s Dream.” *Sewanee Review*, Sewanee, TN, 98 (Summer 3 1990): 506–514.

Motola, Gabriel. “Primo Levi: The Language of the Scientist.” *The Literary Review: An International Journal of Contemporary Writing*, Madison, NJ. 34 (2 Winter 1991): 203–10.

Muller-Hill, Benno. *Murderous Science*. Oxford: Oxford University Press, 1988.

Murphy, Bruce. “Jenseits der Menschen: Mourning on the Other Side.” *Pequod: A Journal of Contemporary Literature & Literary Criticism* 36 (1993): 62–72.

Nudelstejer, Sergio. “Primo Levi: el holocausto o el dificil camino de la verdad.” *Coloquio*, Buenos Aires, 23 (1990): 73–78.

Nystedt, Jane. "Realisme et imagination chez Primo Levi." *Modern Sprak*, Goteborg, Sweden (MSpr). 85.2 (1991): 159–64.

Nystedt, Jane. "I critici e l'opera letteraria di Primo Levi: Panorma cronologico, 1947–1990)." *Studia Neophilologica: A Journal of Germanic and Romance Languages and Literature.* Uppsala, Sweden (SN). 64.1 (1992): 101–16.

Nystedt, Jane. "Lunghezza della frase e interpunzione: Mezzi stilistici in Primo Levi." *Studi Italiani di Linguistica Teorica ed Applicata* (SILTA) 21.1–3 (1992): 85–106.

Nystedt, Jane. "Opere di Primo Levi viste al computer osservazioni stilolinguistiche." *Romanica Stockholmiensia.* 14, Stockholm: Almquist & Wiksell, 1993.

Ozick, Cynthia. Reprinted as "Primo Levi's Suicide Note." *Metaphor and Memory.* New York: Knopf, 1989. 34–48.

Ozick, Cynthia. "The Suicide Note." *New Republic*. cxcviii. 12 (March 1988): 32–6.

Pachet, Pierre. "Primo Levi, son dernier livre." *Esprit*, 75003 Paris, France (Esprit). 151 (June 1989): 59–64.

Patruno, Nicholas. "Primo Levi: Science and Conscience." *Italian-Culture*, Pittsburgh, PA. 10 (1992): 159–66.

Patruno, Nicholas. *Understanding Primo Levi.* Columbia: University of South Carolina Press, 1995.

Peterson, Thomas. "The Art Science Conjunction in Primo Levi's Periodic Table." *NNEMLA Italian Studies.* New Brunswick, NJ (MemlaIS), 11–12 (1987–1988): 143–50.

Petrucciani, Mario. "Tra algebra e metafora: La scienza nella cultura letteraria italiana 1945–1975. (p. 273–330).: *Letteratura e scienza nella storia della cultura italiana: Atti del IX congresso dell' Associatizione Internazionale per gli Studi di Lingua e Letteratura Italiana.* Palermo: Manfredi, 1978: xiv, 913.

Poli, Gabriella and Giorgio Calcagno. *Echi di una voce perduta: incontri, interviste e conversazioni con Primo Levi.* Milano: Mursia, 1992.

Quazza, Guido. "Primo Levi letto da uno storicio." *Rivista di Storia Contemporanea*, Torino, 1 (1989): 76–91.

Raczymow, Henry. "Dire Auschwitz." *L'Arche*, Paris 385 (1989): 69.

Reznik, Maurice. "Dans le même Block à Auschwitz." *Les nouveaux cahiers*, Paris 114 (automne 1993): 47–49.

Risk, Mirna. "Italian: Fiction." *World Literature Today* 51.1 (Winter 1977): 75 col. 1–2.

Risk, Mirna. "Razionalità e conscienza etica in Primo Levi." *Italian Studies* 34 (1979): 122–31.

Rosato, Italo. "Primo Levi: sondaggi intertestuali." *Autografo*, Milano 17 (1989): 31–43.

Roscani, Cladio. "Come leggere Se questo è un uomo di Primo Levi." *Come legger*, 22. Milano, Italy: Mursia (1990).

Rosenfeld, Alvin H. "A Double Dying: Reflections on Holocaust Literature." *Holocaust and History.* Indiana University Press, 1980. 37–61.

Rosenfeld, Alvin H. "Elements of a Life." *New York Times Book Review* (23 December 1984): 9 col. 1–3.

Rosenfeld, Alvin H. *Perspectives on the Holocaust: Essays in Honor of Raul Hilberg.* James S. Pacy and Alan P. Wertheimer, eds. Westview Press, 1995.

Rossi-Doria, Anna. "Una lezione etica di Primo Levi." *Confronti*, Roma 4 (1993): 39–40.

Roth, Philip. "A Man Saved By His Skills." *New York Times Book Review.* (October 12 1986): 1, 40, 41.

Roth, Philip. "Primo Levi 1919–87." *The Observer*. (19 April 1987): 23.

Rubin, Merle. "Ideas: On Nature and Humanity: Literary Sampler by Primo Levi, a Modern-Day Renaissance Man: Books." *Christian Science Monitor* (16 August 1990): 14.

Rudolf, Anthony. *At An Uncertain Hour: Primo Levi's War Against Oblivion.* London: The Menard Press, 1990.

Rugoff, Kathy. "Heinrich Boll, Primo Levi, and Saul Friedlander: Portrayals of Self and History." *Connecticut Review* 13: (1 Spring 1991): 41–49.

Rutter, Itala T. "Nature, Reason and Ethics in Primo Levi." *Pennsylvania Foreign Language Conference.* Gregorio C. Martin, ed.

Duquesne University: Department of Modern languages, Duquesne University, 1988: 391.

Santagostino, Giuseppina. "Primo Levi e le facce nascoste del tempo." *Primo Levi: Memoria e invenzione*. Giovanna lola, ed. San Salvatore: Monferrato, 1995.

Schehr, Lawrence R. "Primo Levi's Strenuous Clarity." *Italica*, Madison, Wisconsin 66: (4 Winter 1989): 429–443.

Segre, Claudio G. "Primo Levi: Bearing Witness." *Washington Post Book World* (13 March 1988): 11 col. 1–4.

Segre, Claudio. "Book World: Primo Levi's Curiosity Unleashed." *Washington Post* (27 April 1989): B–6 col. 1–3.

Sherman, Kenneth. "Primo Levi and the Unlistened-to Story." *Brick* 47 (Winter 1993): 63–69.

Signorini, Dr. Franca Molino. "Testimonianza e scrittura." *La rivista di Psicologia Analitica*, 1992.

Signorini, Dr. Franca Molino. "Uomini Fummo . . . Riflessioni su Primo Levi e Jean Améry." *La rassegna mensile di Israel*, Roma 3 (1991): 463–477.

Sizaire, Anne. *Primo Levi: l'humanite apres Auschwitz*. Paris: Desclee de Brouwer, 1998.

Sodi, Risa. "An Interview with Primo Levi." *Partisan Review*, Boston, MA, 54.3 (1987): 355–366.

Sodi, Risa. "Endpapers: Primo Levi: A Last Talk." *Present Tense* 15 (May/June 1988): 40, 45.

Sodi, Risa. "The Memory of Justice: Primo Levi and Auschwitz." *Holocaust and Genocide Studies* 4 (1989): 89–104.

Sodi, Risa B. *A Dante of Our Time: Primo Levi and Auschwitz*. New York: Peter Lang, 1990. 112.

Sodi, Risa. "Primo Levi." *Jewish Profiles*. Murray Polner, ed. The American Jewish Committee, 1991: 168–180.

Stille, Alexander. "Primo Levi: Reconciling the Man and the Writer." *New York Times Book Review* (5 July 1987): 5.

Stille, Alexander. "Primo Levi and the Jews of Piedmont." *Present Tense* 16 (September–October 1989): 1–3.

Stille, Alexander. "Primo Levi: The Naturalist's Eye." *Los Angeles Times Book Review* (14 May 1989): 8.

Stille, Alexander. "What the Holocaust Meant: The Thinking of Primo Levi and Jean Améry." *Dissent* 37 (Summer 1990): 361–6.

Stille, Alexander. "Forward." *At The Mind's Limits.* Jean Améry, ed. New York: Schocken Books, 1990: vii–xvi.

Styron, William. "Why Primo Levi Need Not Have Died." *New York Times* (19 December 1988): A17 col. 1–4.

Tager, Michael. "Primo Levi and the Language of Witness." *Criticism.* 35.2 (1993): 265–288.

Tagliabue, John. "Primo Levi, Holocaust Writer is Dead at 67." *New York Times* (12 April 1987): 42.

Tarrow, Susan, ed. *Reason and Light: Essays on Primo Levi.* Western Societies Program occasional paper; no. 25. Itaca, New York: Cornell University, Center for International Studies, 1990.

Tarrow, Susan. "Remembering Primo Levi: A Conversation with Il Pikolo del Kommando 98." *Forum Italicum* 28.1 (Spring 1994): 101–110.

Tax, Meredeth. "Speak Memory." *Village Voice Literary Supplement* (11 March 1986: March 1986.) Page 11.

Tesio, Giovanni. "Ritratti critici di contemporanei: Primo Levi." *Belfagor* 34.6 (November 1979): 657–76.

Thomson, Ian. "Primo Levi in Conversation with Ian Thomson." *PN Review*, Manchester, England, 14.2 (1987): 15–19.

Thomson, Ian. "Geographical Expressions: Recent Italian Writing." *Encounter* 70.4 (April 1988): 50, col. 2.

Todorov, Tzvetan. "Ten Years Without Primo Levi." *Salmagundi* (Fall/Winter 1997): 3–18.

Toscani, Claudio. *La voce e il testo: colloqui con Bassani, Bernari, Berto, Brignetti, Chiusano, Dessi, Primo Levi, Moretti, Pomilio, Prisco, Silone, Strati, Tombari, Ulivi.* Milano: Istituto propaganda libraria, 1985.

Tranfaglia, Nicola. "Primo Levi, osservatore e storico del presente." *Notiziario dell'Istituto storico della Resistenza in Cuneé e Cuneo provincia.* Cuneo 32 (1987): 173–179.

Traverso, Enzo. "Intellectual à Auschwitz. Notes sur Jean Améry et Primo Levi." *Bulletin Trimestriel de la Foundation Auschwitz*, Bruxelles 36–37 (1993): 97–111.

Valabrega, Paola. "Il segreto del cerchio, la percezione del tempo nell'opera di Primo Levi." *La Rassegna mensile di Israel*, Roma 2–3 (1989): 281–287.

Varchetta, Giuseppe. *Ascoltando Primo Levi: organizzazione, narrazione, etica.* Milano: Guerini, 1991.

Vigevani, Marco. "Primo Levi: le parole, il ricordo, la speranza." *Bollettino della Comunità Israelitica di Milano*, Milano 5 (1984): 1–4.

Vincenti, Fiora. *Invito alla lettura di Primo Levi.* Milan: Mursia, 1984.

Wade, Alan. "What If . . . A Chemist Told Stories." *New Leader* 73. (6–20 August 1990: 21–22.

Waldman, Rhett L. "The Suicide Note." *The Jerusalem Post* 1.448: 16.

Werner, Alfred. "Amid Suffering, the Divine Spark." *Saturday Reviewe* XLIII (2 January 1960): 23.

White, Naomi Rosh. "Primo Levi and the Concept of Shame." *Generation* 2: 46–50.

Wilde-Menozzio, Wallis. "A Piece You've Touched Is a Piece Moved: On Primo Levi." *Tel Aviv Review* 2 (Fall–Winter 1989): 149–165.

Wilson, Jonathan. "Primo Levi's Hybrid Texts." *Judaism* 48 (Winter 1999): 67–72.

Woolf, Judith. *The Memory of the Offence: Primo Levi's If This is a Man.* Market Harborough: University Texts, 1995.

Woolf, Stuart. "Primo Levi's Sense of History." *Journal of Modern Italian Studies* 3 (1998): 273–92.

Zevi, Tullia. "Giobbe di tutti i tempi." *Shalom*, Roma (1991).

Contributors

Gian Paolo Biasin held the position of professor of Italian Literature at the University of California at Berkeley until his death in 1998. He is the author of five books and has been awarded the following literary prizes: the "Orio Vergani" literary prize for his book, *I sapori della modernita* in 1992, and the "Presidential Book Award" from the American Association of Italian Studies for his book, *The Flavors of Modernity* (New Jersey: Princeton University Press, 1993).

Mirna Cicioni has taught Italian at various British and Australian universities. She is currently senior lecturer in Italian at Monash University, Melbourne. She has published on women in post-World War II Italy and on contemporary Italian Jewish writers. Her book, *Primo Levi: Bridges of Knowledge*, was published in 1995.

Brian Cliff is a graduate of the University of Michigan where he wrote his honors thesis on Primo Levi.

Yaffa Eliach is a pioneering scholar in Holocaust Studies, and the creator of the shtetl photo exhibit at the Tower of Life at the United States Holocaust Memorial Museum. Her book, *There Once Was A World: A 900-Year Chronicle of the Shtetl of Eishyshok*, recounts the history of the shtetl. Among her earlier books is the classic *Hasidic Tales of the Holocaust*, which won a Christopher Award.

Dr. Yaffa Eliach is a professor at the Department of Judaic Studies at Brooklyn College.

Stephen C. Feinstein is Emeritus Professor of History at the University of Wisconsin-River Falls and is currently Director of the Center for Holocaust and Genocide Studies at the University of Minnesota, Minneapolis. He is the curator of *Absence / Presence: The Artistic Memory of the Holocaust and Genocide* (1999) and the international touring exhibition *Witness and Legacy: Contemporary Art About the Holocaust.*

Nancy Harrowitz is associate professor of Italian Literature and Holocaust Studies at Boston University. Author of *Anti-Semitism, Misogyny and the Logic of Cultural Difference: Cesare Lombroso and Matilde Serao* (1994), she has edited *Tainted Greatness: Antisemitism and Cultural Heroes* (1994) and co-edited *Jews and Gender: Responses to Otto Weininger* (1995). She is currently completing a study on Primo Levi and science titled, 'Fair is Foul and Foul is Fair': Primo Levi and the Culture of Science.

Roberta Kremer received her Ph.D. in multicultural and museum education from the University of British Columbia in 1992. Her area of specialty is on the educational use of oral testimony, especially within exhibitions. She is presently Executive Director of the Vancouver Holocaust Education Centre.

Lawrence L. Langer is professor of English Emeritus at Simmons College in Boston. His books include *The Holocaust and the Literary Imagination* (1975), *The Age of Atrocity: Death in Modern Literature* (1978), *Versions of Survival: The Holocaust and the Human Spirit* (1982), *Holocaust Testimonies: The Ruins of Memory* (1991), *Admitting the Holocaust: Collected Essays* (1995), *Art from the Ashes: A Holocaust Anthology* (1995), *Landscapes of Jewish Experience: Paintings by*

Samuel Bak (1997), *Preempting the Holocaust* (1998), and *The Game Continues: Chess in the Art of Samuel Bak* (1999).

Nicholas Patruno's full-length study, *Understanding Primo Levi*, was published in 1995. He is also the author of *Language in Giovanni Verga's Early Novels* and numerous articles. Dr. Patruno is currently writing on Italian women's voices on the Holocaust. He is presently professor of Italian at Bryn Mawr College.

Patricia Sayre teaches philosophy at Saint Mary's College, Notre Dame, Indiana. She has a special interest in the work of Ludwig Wittgenstein and has written a variety of essays relating his thoughts to topics in moral psychology.

Franca Molino Signorini is a member of the School of Psychoanalytic Psychotherapy and is a psychoanalyst in private practice in Milan, Italy. She has authored "il Giornale Storico di Psicologia Dinamica L' umo" in *rivolta* (gennaio 1993), "Testimonianza e scrittura" in *La rivista di Psicologia Analitica* (giugno 1993), "Riflessioni sul suicido di Primo Levi e Jean Amery" in *La rassegno Mensile di Israel* (settembre 1992).

Risa Sodi received her Ph.D. in Italian Language and Literature from Yale University in 1995. She is presently preparing for publication a two-volume study on representations of the Holocaust in Italian literature. Dr. Sodi has authored a full-length study of Levi's work titled *A Dante of Our Time: Primo Levi and Auschwitz* (1990), and has published nine articles on Primo Levi. In addition, she writes and lectures on Holocaust film, literature, and philosophy.

Linnea Vacca teaches 20th Century women's literature, mythology, and multicultural literature in the English Department at Saint Mary's College, Notre Dame, Indiana as well as teaching part of each year in Italy. Her recent writing reflects Italian interests.

Index

All works are by Primo Levi unless otherwise indicated by the inclusion of an author's name within parentheses following the title. Page numbers in *italics* denote illustrations.